# STORY
# MATTERS

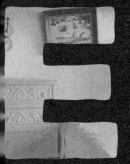

# STORY MATTERS

**TEACHING TEENS TO USE THE TOOLS OF NARRATIVE TO ARGUE AND INFORM**

Liz Prather

Foreword by **KELLY GALLAGHER**

**HEINEMANN**
**PORTSMOUTH, NH**

**Heinemann**

361 Hanover Street

Portsmouth, NH 03801–3912

www.heinemann.com

*Offices and agents throughout the world*

The author and publisher wish to thank those who have generously given permission to reprint borrowed material:

"The Case for Leaving City Rats Alone" by Rebecca Cudmore from *Nautilus* (Issue 038; July 28, 2016). Copyright © 2016 by Rebecca Cudmore. Published by NautilusThink. Reprinted by permission of the author.

Excerpt from "Living Will" in *Incidental Findings* by author and physician, Danielle Ofri. Copyright © 2005 by Danielle Ofri. Published by Beacon Press. Used by permission of the author. www.danielleofri.com.

Cataloging-in-Publication Data is on file at the Library of Congress.

ISBN: 978-0-325-09950-7

**Acquisitions Editor:** Katie Wood Ray
**Production Editor:** Sean Moreau
**Cover and Interior Designer:** Suzanne Heiser
**Typesetter:** Valerie Levy, Drawing Board Studios
**Manufacturing:** Steve Bernier

Printed in the United States of America on acid-free paper

23  22  21  20  19  RWP  1  2  3  4  5

For Kenn Johnson,

a writer first,

and a teacher always

# CONTENTS

**CHAPTER ONE**

# NARRATIVE AS HOME BASE, GROUND ZERO, MOTHER SHIP ........ 1

**CHAPTER TWO**

# IDEAS Finding Stories in Topics and Topics in Stories ........ 28

# FOREWORD

Early in my teaching career, the United States invaded Iraq in Operation Desert Storm, and my students—some of whom had already committed to joining the military after high school—were anxious and eager to understand the first major foreign crisis of their young lives. I sensed an opportunity to engage them, so I made the on-the-fly decision to put our upcoming study of *Hamlet* on the back burner and, instead, I sat at home all weekend excitedly planning a war unit. I pulled together a number of interesting artifacts for them to study, and to anchor this unit, I decided we would read Erich Maria Remarque's classic war novel *All Quiet on the Western Front.*

I arrived fired up to class on Monday morning. By now, my students had heard that Saddam Hussein, ruler of Iraq, had been accused of using poison gas on civilian populations. I decided this was a good entry point; it would be interesting to show them the horror and devastation inflicted by the use of poison gas when it was first used in World War I. I can't remember the exact encyclopedia passage I had dug up from almost thirty years ago for them to study, but it was similar to this current entry found on Wikipedia:

> Chemical weapons ". . . were primarily used to demoralize, injure, and kill entrenched defenders, against whom the indiscriminate and generally very slow-moving or static nature of gas clouds would be most effective. The types of weapons employed ranged from disabling chemicals, such as tear gas, to lethal agents like phosgene, chlorine, and mustard gas. This chemical warfare was a major component of the first global war and first total war of the twentieth century. The killing capacity of gas was limited, with about 90,000 fatalities from a total of 1.3 million casualties caused by gas attacks."

I found this information fascinating. My students didn't. They dutifully asked a few perfunctory questions, feigned minimal interest, and, despite *my* interest, made it clear they were ready to move on. As they walked out the door at the end of the period, I remember being perplexed by their indifference, by their disengagement—I mean, c'mon people! *Soldiers were gassed!*

Flash-forward one year. Same unit. But instead of having students read the encyclopedia entry, I shared a firsthand account from William Pressey, a WWI soldier who had experienced the horror of being gassed. Pressey writes:

> I was awakened by a terrible crash. The roof came down on my chest and legs and I couldn't move anything but my head. I thought, "So, this is it then." I found I could hardly breathe. (Carey 1998, 473)

My students perked up a bit in their seats. I continued reading as Pressey recounts regaining consciousness while others forced a gas mask on him. He recalls choking, suggesting that he resembled a fish with its mouth open gasping for air. Pressey remembers his lungs shutting down and his heart pounding hard, and his last memory before blacking out was glancing at a comrade placed right next to him who had green stuff oozing from the side of his mouth.

I paused, and then asked my students to finish reading the soldier's horrific account. While they read, it became eerily quiet. The good kind of quiet. The kind of quiet that left no doubt students were glued to the text. And when they emerged from their reading, we had a spirited discussion about the ethics of weaponry in war. All these years later, I still remember the heat of that conversation.

This experience early in my teaching career taught me one very valuable lesson: Human beings learn deeply through the power of story. Yes, my students understood that poison gas was used in WWI, but they did not really *understand* it until they read the history from the soldier's point of view. It was his *story* that deepened their understanding and appreciation of history.

Yet, here we sit, many years later, and the reading, writing, and study of story is *still* not getting its proper due in our schools. It has been disrespected by the Common Core and by many states that have developed and adopted their own standards. Curriculum directors, who often see narrative writing as "softer" than argumentative or analytical writing, have devalued it. And some English teachers, who believe their job is to teach the traditional literary analysis paper ad infinitum, have discounted it.

This shortchanging of story has deep and lasting consequences. It deprives our students of developing critical key writing skills, it weakens their agency, and it silences their voices. For these reasons—and others—we need to reestablish the importance of story in our classrooms, and this is where I am hopeful that Liz Prather's excellent new book, *Story Matters*, will serve as a catalyst for a shift in our thinking about the teaching of narrative.

The book's superpower is that it clearly demonstrates how the weaving of narrative elements strengthens all kinds of writing, from arguments to informative and explanatory papers. As Prather points out, "You would be hard pressed to find any text that didn't employ some narrative technique" (3). Narrative is everywhere, and recognizing this is the first step to stop treating it as a separate, stand-alone discourse. In these pages, Prather shows us how to weave narrative into other genres in ways that makes student writing come alive. This book is smart and makes a compelling argument, but beyond that, it is also practical, and I particularly appreciate its numerous exercises and mentor texts I can use in my classroom to enable my students to tap into the power of story.

*Story Matters* also reminds us that strong writing "moves" *are not genre-specific.* A student who develops a strong voice, or a knack for vibrant sensory detail, or who uses dialogue effectively while writing a narrative piece, will use these same skills when later writing an argumentative or an expository essay. This is why I always start my school year with a narrative unit. Yes, I'm seeking the engagement that is generated when students are given an opportunity to tell their stories, but beyond that, I know that if my kids begin the year by learning to write narratives well, they will acquire writing skills that can be applied to *all* writing situations. These skills are foundational and universal; they are not tied to a specific genre.

I also appreciate that this book encourages teachers and students to move away from formulaic and scripted writing. Prather recognizes that students do not learn to write well by practicing "hamburger" paragraphs or by writing five-paragraph essays. Instead of these approaches, she notes students need lots of mentor texts to read, analyze, and emulate so that they develop "an awareness of the possibilities of expository architecture." They also need lots of coaching while they practice, practice, practice.

In other words, learning to write well is hard. There are no shortcuts, and I like how this book embraces this hardness in a way that helps break the unhealthy codependency that young writers often develop with their teachers. Generative writing is not the same thing as compliant writing, and if students make this shift toward generative writing, they need to make the shift toward generating their own decisions. This book is a blueprint on how to make this critical shift: Find texts that expertly weave in narrative elements, have students closely study and emulate them, write alongside your students, model students' thinking, and encourage young writers to make key decisions as they draft and revise. This is the real work of writing teachers.

As I write this foreword, I sit at my desk with only ten days of school remaining, and I am in that state of zombie-like tiredness familiar to teachers during this time of year. Yet, while rereading *Story Matters* this morning, I feel an energy—a buzz of excitement—that comes whenever I read a professional development book that is more than just another "strategies book." *Story Matters* is much more than that. It asks you to reconsider your definition of *genre*, and after you have done so, it will provide you with the tools needed to unleash the potent power of story in your classroom.

They say that a good story should change you. The stories Liz Prather tells in these pages will change my classroom next year. They will change yours, too.

—Kelly Gallagher

# ACKNOWLEDGMENTS

This book is dedicated to Kenn Johnson, a teacher I met in 1996 when we both taught at Montgomery County High School in Mount Sterling, Kentucky. Kenn was the first teacher I had met who was a writer and a teacher. Everything he did in his classroom was filtered through his writer-self: Is this what I do as a writer? Is this authentic? He was the full-time sports editor for our small-town newspaper, *The Mt. Sterling Advocate*, covering every game for every sport, plus writing a weekly column called "Sidelines." He also taught English full time and put out an award-winning student newspaper every month with his journalism students. His program was known statewide, graduating writers and photographers who now work in media all over the United States. One of his students, now the photo editor for the *Minneapolis Star Tribune*, recently said of Kenn, "If you drove up by the high school on any weeknight, the light in the journalism room would always be on. You knew Mr. Johnson was in there working."

Throughout my career, I've used Kenn's columns as mentor texts, and he's been my writing–teaching role model for many years. I am so grateful for his wisdom and his work, and I'm honored to call him my dear friend.

Amanda Wright, my colleague at Lafayette High School, read an early version of this book and lined the manuscript with beautiful questions that helped me connect the dots between theory and practice. I'm thankful for her time and insight. Lafayette High School media specialist Susie Joliffe is a former English teacher, whose assistance in finding mentor texts and hard-to-find resources plus offering to track down random facts for me make her my personal hero. I'm going to miss her indomitable spirit and smiling face next year when she retires.

Many thanks also to Stacy Lyons who commutes down Interstate 64 with me. For two years, she's listened to me break down every teeth-gnashing detail of my efforts to bring this book together. She kept me sane and preached peace and love every mile of the way.

As always, I'm grateful to the students of Room 303. I am honored you have given so much of yourselves to the work we do together. To the class of 2018, Taleah, Michael, David, John, Jenna, Leila, Ruby, Avery, Katrin, and Duncan, I salute your indefatigable life force and the many worlds you spun into existence. To the girls of the class of 2019, McKenna, Autumn, Eliza, Taylor, and Sarah, your leadership, kindness, talent, and grit humble me to the earth.

The problems of writing a book about the highly individualized process of writing is second only to writing a book about the highly individualized process of teaching writing. So many times in this book, I could not see my way, but my editor, Katie Wood Ray, offered her gift of vision, her ear that listens closely, and her kitchen island that could support the weight of a reeling, overwritten chapter. She sought to understand not only what I was saying, but what I was *trying* to say. Katie's questions illuminated this book for me, and I'm so thankful for her guidance.

And finally, immeasurable thanks to my family—John, Cassie, Harper, Hadley, Hudson, Hagan, Harrison—I love you so much. And to my perfect partner, Paul David—you are my everything.

# INTRODUCTION

## MY STORY

Perhaps the fastest growing kind of writing in print and online is narrative non-fiction. It's versatile, engaging, and ubiqutious: newspapers, magazines, journals, e-singles, mixed media, lyrical essays, hypertext, and long- and short-form essays. It's the kind of writing that leads to self-discovery and asks students to join in a larger public conversation.

Narrative nonfiction asks students to take risks and to learn how to com-positionally zig and zag between information, argument, and story. It requires students to see writing as an exercise in problem-solving and to consider their own experience as a starting place for engaging with a subject.

This book is designed for the classroom teacher looking for resources, mentor texts, lessons, and ideas to help students learn how to blend narrative into informative and argumentative texts.

Whenever I read a professional book, the whole time I'm reading it, I'm wondering where the writer's teaching philosophy came from or what the writer's teaching situation is like. So before we launch into the book proper, I feel the need to tell you where I come from.

This is my story.

—

As a kid, all I wanted to do was write. Yet writer wasn't among the approved professions my sensible farming mother was willing to pay tuition for. Becoming a teacher was a much better career decision.

In 1990, I started teaching high school English in a tiny school in rural Kentucky. Kindergarten through twelfth grade were housed in a single two-story building; the senior class had twenty-eight kids. My first year was a nightmare. After one academic year, I left the profession and swore I would never teach again. However, a few years later, I was back at it. This time around I had the support of veteran teachers and a great administrator. I loved it, but the dream of being a writer was still with me.

After thirteen years of teaching, I decided to move to Austin and begin work on an MFA at the University of Texas. During my three years there, I wrote a dozen short stories, two screenplays, a horrific novel that will never see the light of day, and the first five chapters of a memoir. I supported myself financially as a writer and supplemented my income by teaching writing at retreats and professional seminars.

When my mother became ill in 2007, I returned to Kentucky and became the writer-in-residence at Morehead State University, where I taught composition and creative writing and directed the Morehead Writing Project. I enjoyed this professional work, but when an English position opened up at a nearby high school, I jumped at the chance. I missed teaching high school students. During this time, I continued to write fiction and also wrote freelance articles for local and regional magazines.

Later, when a position to teach writing at a high school magnet program in a nearby urban district opened up, I jumped again. Now I teach a group of highly motivated high school writers. I have political and foodie bloggers; music and theatre journalists; screenwriters, sports writers, and songwriters; students who write local reviews of music, movies, and video games; another who writes faith-based devotionals for teens; and another who writes online content for local equine media.

I tell you this so you'll know I am a professional writer and that I work in a unique situation: I teach writing every day in ninety-minute blocks in classes of twenty to twenty-five kids using both a traditional curriculum and a project-based writing framework where students generate writing projects of their own, pitch their ideas, and then publish them for an authentic audience. I wrote about this framework in my first book, *Project-Based Writing: Teaching Writers to Manage Time and Clarify Purpose* (2017).

I want you to know I understand the constraints of a traditional English language arts classroom where I taught for seventeen years, and I understand the limited time you have to devote to any kind of writing, outside of the on-demand response or the five-paragraph essay.

But I also know what it feels like to pretend in front of students that those forms of writing are the only ones they need to master to succeed in college and career and to pretend that those forms of writing are even remotely important or real for any other audience outside academia.

If we're only teaching students how to survive writing in the next academic phase of their life ("You'll need to know this in middle school," "You'll need to know this in high school," "You'll need to know this in college"), then why are we even fretting over the craft of writing at all? Shouldn't we just teach them to download forms and be done with it?

But most of us, I know, are trying to teach students how to communicate in life as well as in college and careers. To be able to think clearly. To actually write to another person. To make writerly decisions for a more authentic audience than just the teacher, such as a prospective employer, a community group, a beloved family member, or the whole world reading your online blog.

I also want you to know that in every department I've ever worked, at every level of education, there have been two distinct camps: those who teach writing by the law and those who practice by lawlessness. The law-thumpers want to make sure students can identify every part of speech and have memorized the five-paragraph essay form before they turn them loose with an idea. They see themselves as the guardians of the language and often feel superior to the lawless.

The lawless, in turn, usually feel sorry for the law-thumpers, seeing them as uptight, rigid moralizers who keep kids in bondage. The lawless prefer to throw some prompts on the board, turn on one of the Bobs (Marley or Dylan), and let the words floooow.

If you've spent any time in any English department anywhere, you might be trying to figure out where I stand in this dichotomy. I will tell you I'm squarely in the middle. I am a relentless sentence reviser and teach my students to hold themselves to standards of clarity and simplicity. But I also refuse to put learning targets on my board, and I think boxing in something as madcap and chaotic as the individual writing process in a one-sentence objective is ludicrous.

Although I often use classic essays, I believe students need to read high-quality, contemporary texts from living writers about current topics they are interested in and relate to. Although I teach grammar and usage, I believe students need to figure out how a sentence works using their own sentences, not someone else's. Although I offer examples of voice and style, I also encourage students to find their own style, which is, as Zadie Smith (2007) says, "a personal necessity, as the only possible expression of a particular human consciousness."

Another large component of my teaching practice and philosophy is that I'm a writer myself. I approach writing as a writer, not as a teacher. I ask myself: is this an activity or exercise or task I would do as a writer? Or is this activity just checking a box for school—getting a grade for the gradebook, looking good for a walk-through, keeping them busy, keeping them in their seat?

I cannot stress enough that you will be more successful at teaching writers if you also write and do so consistently. Writing is a performance art, one that can't be learned by only observing others do it. Before you launch a unit that requires your students to write anything, write that thing first yourself. Before you adopt the lessons and suggestions I make in this book, have a go yourself. Submit a piece to *The English Journal* if you want. Or write your own blog. Or share something you've written with a group of writing teachers at your school or in your district. The lessons you learn about yourself as a writer and as a teacher of writers will be priceless and will improve every single product you ask your students to attempt.

And one more thing before we jump into the book: I'm not as concerned that my students "get it right" as I'm concerned they *practice* getting it right. Getting it right is an ambition that even professional writers fail at. Every time I read an old article I've written, I cringe at half a dozen glaring errors I see on the page. But I keep showing up, practicing this skill, trying to become better.

I want students to *practice* writing every day, making their own decisions, failing and learning from that failure, and continuing to follow, as Smith (2007) says, the "map of disappointments . . . to the land where writers live." That's how students "get it right."

I have a standard for teaching and writing because I am a teacher and a writer. If we teach from the belief that our students are already writers, if we believe they have a significant contribution to the world in the form of their style, their ideas, their communication, they will develop a standard for their own work as well. That standard will be informed by the work I do as a coach and a mentor working alongside them. That standard will be informed by the reading they are exposed to in my class, both self-selected and teacher-selected. And that standard will be shaped by how many opportunities they have to fail and fail successfully to keep on improving.

# NARRATIVE AS HOME BASE, GROUND ZERO, MOTHER SHIP

When I was six years old, I wrote my first short story. At four sentences long, the narrative centered on the epic drama of a rainstorm threatening the day's laundry on the line.

   It went like this: *Mother said the rains are coming. Come here Mary you get the clothespins. Mike you get the clothes off the line. And Liz you help Mary get the clothespins. The End.*

**Figure 1–1**
Liz's Early Story

There are four characters: Mother, my sister Mary, my brother Mike, and me. There's no thematic overture, merely an opening sequence that establishes the problem: the rains are coming. There's no elaborate scene craft. Like all good minimalist works, the story works in subtlety and nuance.

So, why did I write it? Who knows? I don't remember writing it, but there it was, sitting in a box of school work and report cards I found in the attic of my childhood home. Was the story a labor narrative, a cautionary tale, or merely a record of the afternoon laundry as the most dramatic thing happening on Possum Ridge?

Even at that early age, I had a desire perhaps to preserve the truths of my life for future generations. For whatever reason I wrote it, its existence speaks to the larger human activity of storytelling, the urge and need to chronicle our lives.

We are "storytelling animals," says author Jonathan Gottschall (2012) in his book of the same title. "Story is the glue of human social life." In every known human culture, storytelling binds communities with gossip, warning, and instruction. Gottschall writes, "It nourishes our imaginations; it reinforces moral behavior; it gives us safe worlds to practice inside" (177). Early narratives carried important information regarding water and food sources, deadly plants, predators, and natural disasters. Stories help us make sense of our existence. As Natalie Goldberg (1986) says in *Writing Down the Bones*, our stories say, "We were here; we are human beings; this is how we lived. Let it be known, the earth passed before us" (43).

Marketing and media use this venerable form of communication. Our news, especially a dramatically poised event such as the Olympics or the NCAA Final Four, features human stories. Author Christopher Booker (2004) says, "These structured sequences of imagery are, in fact, the most natural way we know to describe everything which happens in our lives" (2). Business writer Carmine Gallo (2016) maintains the key to the success of Starbucks' Howard Schultz, Facebook's Sheryl Sandberg, and Apple cofounder Steve Jobs was their mastery of the corporate narrative. All TED talks dip into the personal story, specifically the sharing of the speaker's own journey. From Shakespeare to Springsteen to the popularity of Dave Isay's *Storycorps* and Brandon Staton's *Humans of New York*, we love stories.

And yet, as one of the oldest and most powerful communication tools at our disposal, narrative is seen as secondary in post-elementary education. Although the Common Core recommends narrative writing in the fourth grade comprise 35 percent of all writing tasks, by the time students ascend to their senior year of high school, narrative writing opportunities have fallen off to 20 percent while argumentative and informative enterprises balloon to 40 percent each. Right now, in Kentucky where I teach, I've heard serious conversations about cutting the narrative standards entirely or using narrative only as a support for argumentative or informational texts. This is certainly on the mind of many teachers in my building. Maybe this is happening in other states as well. The bottom line is, as Tom Newkirk (2014) points out in *Mind Made for Stories*, a conflict exists "between the way we treat narrative in school and the central role it plays in our consciousness" (5).

# THE NECESSITY OF NARRATIVE IN ARGUMENT AND INFORMATION

The narrative finds itself caught in a pedagogical tussle: too vital to be ignored entirely, but too simplistic for any instructional real estate. In 2011, David Coleman, one of the lead developers of the Common Core, voiced this shift to a group of teachers during a professional development event. He asked the audience what they thought the most popular forms of writing in high school were. The audience responded, personal narratives and personal opinion pieces. The problem with that, according to Coleman, was that "as you grow up in this world, you realize that people really don't give a shit about what you feel or what you think" (10).

Coleman's statement, while designed to provoke, was primarily meant to illustrate the notion that narratives are for children, and once students grow up, they should graduate to the rigors of analysis and facts of the real world. Yet I cannot think of one human institution, from art to science to politics to religion to law, that is not predicated on the story of the human experience, ergo what people think and feel.

If narratives—built on the thoughts and feelings of a writer to connect with the thoughts and feelings of a reader—were abandoned in favor of strict analysis, pure information, or classic argumentation, American corporations and politicians would be adrift. They care very deeply about how we feel and think to the tune of billions of dollars spent annually on advertising campaigns that persuade us to think and feel certain ways, regularly using story as a trigger for brand identification. We only have to look at the success of the powerful two-word story in Subaru's latest campaign, "They lived," to understand that narrative is a vital tool in the grown-up world for which Coleman wants American graduates to be prepared. In fact, you would be hard pressed to find any text that didn't employ some narrative technique, including textbooks, news stories, medical journals, travel guides, political speeches, social and historical analysis, and even scientific lab reports.

The problem with casting off narrative as too "creative" for the exacting terrain of adult writing tasks is that writing in the real world doesn't divide itself neatly into categories. Professional writers approach writing tasks with all modes at their disposal. They may dip into any text type if it helps them say what they want to say.

In a recent *New York Times* piece, Richard Oppel and Jugal K. Patel (2019) discuss public defenders all over the United States with excessive caseloads. We are introduced to Jack Talaska, a Louisiana public defender, who's struggling to provide services for the 194 felony cases on his desk; we meet Bob Marro, a public defender from Providence, Rhode Island, with equally mind-boggling numbers. The authors cite studies and statistics. They use analysis, and at the center of the piece is a subtle argument that a standard must be developed "that will help judges and policy makers determine how many cases public defenders can ethically handle before their clients' rights are violated."

How would we characterize this piece of writing? It's nonfiction with narrative anecdotes, characters, and scenes, but there are also facts, and, although not a classic argument, we see certain rhetorical appeals for a commonsense approach to address the public defender caseload problem.

How would we characterize Tom Vanderbilt's (2008) *Traffic* or Margot Lee Shetterly's (2016) *Hidden Figures*? These texts enlighten the reader through stories using data and scientific research surrounding a critical argument (about human behavior in traffic and about racism and sexism in scientific fields) that serves as the beating heart of the work.

Consider Rebecca Skloot's (2011) *The Immortal Life of Heinretta Lacks*, which features a narrative plot about Lacks' life that educates the reader about HeLa cells while delivering an argument about race and medical ethics. Is Skloot's book a narrative? Yes. Is it an argument? Yes. Is it an informational text? Absolutely. As Newkirk (2014) observes:

> Even the arguments we make are often about a version of story, or in the service of story, or in the form of a story. Evidence regularly serves to establish which story, which claim for causality, is most plausible. We critique a story by imagining another story. Informational texts regularly describe processes (evolution, the autoimmune system, photosynthesis, global warning) that take narrative form. (145)

The truth is, effective writing must embrace all of it. A student writer should understand how to use the modes of argument, narration, and information, not as discrete arrangements exclusive of other patterns, but as a smorgasbord of delivery methods used in the service of communication.

Scan the current *New York Times* nonfiction bestseller list to get a contemporary survey of how professional writers use narrative. As I am drafting this chapter, *Killing England*, Bill O'Reilly's story of the American Revolution, sits at number one. Hillary Rodham Clinton's political memoir *What Happened* sits at number two, her narrative argument about the events preceding, during, and following the 2016 election.

The list includes five memoirs, but it also includes several cultural studies wherein narrative is prominently featured, including Geoffrey Ward's *The Vietnam War* and Denise Kiernan's *The Last Castle*, an exploration of the history of the Biltmore House, and several political polemics such as Sharyl Attkisson's *The Smear*, Jonathan Cahn's *The Paradigm*, and Kurt Andersen's *Fantasyland*.

Because narrative is, as Newkirk (2014) says, the "mother of all modes" (6), every writer on the best-seller list employs its tools to make their central argument or deliver critical information to support the aims of their book. Because those writers think and feel. And they know their readers do too.

An intimate knowledge of narrative technique then is essential when reading or writing any subject matter. Understanding history or science, for example, is an exercise in narrative discernment, peeling away the story within a story within a story to find some truth about what it means to be human. Asking students to tell a true story—about the Great Barrier Reef, the battle of Vicksburg, Bosch's *The Garden of Earthly Delights*—requires them to engage the reader using the techniques of narrative, support their argument with research, and showcase their knowledge of the world through information. These are the compositional moves that accomplished writers possess.

Compare the two following entries in Figure 1–2 describing Boston Corbett, the man who killed John Wilkes Booth. Text A is a typical biographical entry I wrote for the purposes of comparison from information I found on Wikipedia. Text B is Ernest B. Furgurson's (2009) essay "The Man Who Shot the Man Who Shot Lincoln." Our eye immediately jumps at Text B that promises the hook-and-roll of a story. Even the first two words "One morning" asks us to lean in and listen to its narrative invitation.

Furgurson's opening paragraph showcases several classic storytelling moves, namely grounding the reader in time and giving the reader a description of a character. Whatever argument Furgurson might make or whatever information he might impart in his essay will be highlighted by this initial narrative image in the mind of the reader.

Corbett was an interesting, eccentric historical character, but Furgurson still must create his story from research, official reports, transcripts, and documents, and figure out how to arrange them for dramatic or rhetorical effect. The essay itself is bound to

| TEXT A | TEXT B |
|---|---|
| Thomas H. ("Boston") Corbett was born in London, England, in 1832. Along with his family, he came to New York in 1839. He eventually became a hatter in Troy. He married but his wife died in childbirth. Later he moved to Boston and continued working as a hatter there. Some have speculated that the use of mercury in the hatters' trade was a causative factor in Corbett's later mental problems. | One morning in September, 1878, a tired traveler, five feet four inches tall, with a wispy beard, arrived at the office of the daily Pittsburgh Leader. His vest and coat were a faded purple, and his previously black pants were gray with age and wear. As he stepped inside, he lifted a once fashionable silk hat to disclose brown hair parted down the middle like a woman's. Despite the mileage that showed in his face and clothes, he was well-kept, and spoke with clarity. |

**Figure 1–2** Text Comparison

fact, but Furgurson spins a tale about this little-known player in American history by pulling the reader forward with the subtextual question embedded in the first sentence: Why *did* Corbett show up at the Pittsburgh Leader one morning in September 1878? This is why narrative is so powerful for any writing task: it pulls us in, sets us up, and drives us forward.

In my classroom, we call this kind of writing narrative nonfiction, and I define it for my students as a piece of nonfiction, such as an informational or argumentative text, that uses a story or a few narrative techniques to engage the reader. This form of nonfiction might also be referred to as creative nonfiction or literary journalism. Of course, most journalism does not tell stories; it reports the news, weather, box scores, and so on. But the kind of journalism that is read and remembered uses a human story at its center.

In this kind of writing, journalists, essayists, writers of long and short forms write literacy narratives, labor narratives, sports narratives, teaching narratives, travel narratives, medical narratives, and so on. Although traditionally associated with memoir and personal essays, narrative nonfiction has more recently been used as a vehicle for classic argumentation, as well as social, political, or cultural criticism. Digital storytelling is also a nonfiction genre that uses the same narrative techniques coupled with video, music, charts, memes, infographics, and embedded Instagram and Twitter posts.

Truman Capote's *In Cold Blood* is an early example of this kind of writing, which made way for nonfiction writers like Tom Wolfe, Joan Didion, Hunter S. Thompson, and Gay Talese to immerse themselves in the stories they reported, using characters, dialogue, setting, and plot to render a nonfiction subject. The subtitle of *Creative Nonfiction*, a literary journal founded and edited by the godfather of the creative nonfiction movement Lee Gutkind, expresses the definition I use most often: narrative nonfiction is "a true story, well told."

I avoid calling this kind of writing creative nonfiction. There's nothing wrong with that moniker, but slap the term *creative* on anything and it seems to automatically lessen how academically serious an administrator or curriculum coach perceives the work to be. (What seems to be at issue is the oft mythologized and highly romantic notion that "creative" writing comes from some pixie-dust landscape deep within our subconscious, accessed only by drugs, alcohol, or writing prompts like "pretend you're a butterfly," and other forms of writing that come to us from a cerebral spreadsheet where statistics, immutable truths, and logically linked claims are high-stepping with flawless military precision. But that's another topic for another time.)

My students and I use the term *narrative nonfiction* because it makes sense for what we are trying to do: using story to engage the reader to deliver information or an argument.

# SOURCES OF NARRATIVE NONFICTION

You can find examples of this kind of writing in almost every U.S. magazine or newspaper in print and online. Narrative nonfiction pops up regularly in *The Washington Post*, *The New York Times*, *Los Angeles Times*, *The Boston Globe*, or *The Atlanta Journal-Constitution*.

Ask your media specialist to purchase The Best American series for your school's media center. The Best American series is published annually and is a collection of the year's best nonfiction essays in science, sports, travel, and nature writing that have been published in a wide range of magazines such as *Pacific Standard*, *Mother Jones*, *The New Yorker*, *The New Republic*, *Nautilus*, *Wired*, *Sports Illustrated*, *Scientific American*, *BuzzFeed News*, *National Geographic*, *Outside*, *Harper's Magazine*, *Psychology Today*, *Natural History*, *Newsweek*, *The Atlantic*, *Audubon*, *Popular Mechanics*, *Orion*, and *Esquire*.

For short pieces that students can read on their cell phones, I find great stuff in curated online publishing platforms like Matter.com, Longform.org, Narratively.com, and Medium.com, with articles on science, technology, culture, health, music, food, and politics. (Also Longform.org has a great podcast where nonfiction writers talk about their process and their projects—#puregold.)

I also look for examples in regional magazines that feature narrative nonfiction. Because I live in the South, I find and use great examples in *Garden & Gun*, *Appalachian Heritage*, *Oxford American*, or *Texas Monthly*.

If your school doesn't have one already, I suggest a subscription to print or digital editions of some of Scholastic's magazines. In every issue of *The New York Times Upfront* and *Science World*, there are at least two pieces of narrative nonfiction. *Junior Scholastic*, for grades 6–8, the *Holocaust Reader*, *Scholastic Art*, and *Scholastic Action* are also great resources for finding narrative nonfiction examples.

The online versions of both *Creative Nonfiction* and *Brevity* sometimes offer great samplings of shorter narrative nonfiction works, but they tend to be heavy with personal narratives and memoir. Lee Gutkind (2005) has also published an anthology called *In Fact: The Best of Creative Nonfiction*, which I have in my classroom library for students looking for models. I also use Judith Kitchen's (2005) *Short Takes: Brief Encounters with Contemporary Nonfiction* as well as *Touchstone Anthology of Contemporary Creative Nonfiction*, edited by Lex Williford and Michael Martone (2007), which features classic nonfiction pieces from the 1970s to the present, including writers such as Jamaica Kincaid, Naomi Shihab Nye, David Sedaris, and Richard Selzer.

My three go-to resources I use for developing prompts, techniques, and minilessons are Brenda Miller and Suzanne Paola's (2012) *Tell It Slant: Creating, Refining and Publishing Creative Nonfiction*, Philip Lopate's (2013) *To Show and To Tell: The Craft of Literary Nonfiction*, and Lee Gutkind's (2012) *You Can't Make This Stuff Up: The Complete Guide to Writing Creative Nonfiction from Memoir to Literary Journalism and Everything in Between.*

# NARRATIVE SKILL AT WORK: AN EXPERT MENTOR TEXT

To help students understand narrative nonfiction, we begin by reading mentor texts that challenge what they think they know about nonfiction, texts such as Becca Cudmore's (2016) "The Case for Leaving City Rats Alone."

Cudmore is a science writer, currently based in Brooklyn, who writes mostly about anthropology and ecology. "The Case for Leaving City Rats Alone" was first published in *Nautilus*, then selected for *The Best American Science and Nature Writing 2017*. I discovered it one day while browsing in my local bookstore. The opening sentence so trapped me, like one of the rats in her essay, that I stood in the aisle until I finished the piece.

The essay clocks in at around 2,000 words. It is a narrative, informational argument. Or an informative, argumentative narrative. Or an argument with informative and narrative flourishes.

Whatever.

It engaged me. It promised purpose plus a story plus information, a case to examine. Is it a classic argument? No. Is it a straight science piece? No. Is it pure narrative? Not by a long shot. It's a blend of all three to accomplish Cudmore's goal in making her case. And the benefactors of all that nuanced mingling were my attention, my time, and, subsequently, my money. I bought the book.

Let's begin the same way, by reading "The Case for Leaving City Rats Alone" and looking at how Cudmore smartly balances her purpose with the narrative devices designed to engage her reader.

Kaylee Byers crouches in a patch of urban blackberries early one morning this June, to check a live trap in one of Vancouver's poorest areas, the V6A postal code. Her first catch of the day is near a large blue dumpster on "Block 5," in front of a 20-some-unit apartment complex above a thrift shop. Across the alley, a building is going up; between the two is an overgrown, paper- and wrapper-strewn lot. In the lot, there are rats.

<< In this opening paragraph, Cudmore uses the kind of world building that novelists use to situate a reader in a fictional moment. Choosing images that resonate both emotionally and intellectually, Cudmore reveals the Dickensian spectacle. Even though she tells us Block 5 of postal code V6A is poor, she doesn't need to. Notice the twenty-one concrete nouns and seventeen visual adjectives that paint this scene? We've already seen (and felt and smelled) V6A for ourselves.

Cudmore positions us in time ("early one morning this June") and place, a specific world that includes urban blackberries, a large blue dumpster, an apartment complex above a thrift shop, an alley, a vacant lot. And, of course, rats.

She opens with Kaylee Byers, a character in action, not passively quoted or cited, but crouching and trapping. This too is a favorite technique of fiction: start with your character doing something, and your reader will keep reading to find out what she's up to.

"Once we caught two in a single trap," she says, peering inside the cage. She finds a new rat there, and makes a note of it on her clipboard; she'll be back for it, to take the animal to her nearby van, which is parked near (according to Google Maps) an "unfussy" traditional Ethiopian restaurant. Once inside the van, the rat will be put under

<< Notice that Cudmore uses present tense, which does a couple of things narratively: it places Cudmore herself in the thick of the action, and it provides an immediacy and intimacy for the reader. We're peeking over Byers' shoulder as she checks the traps, and we're listening to Cudmore's reporting.

Cudmore shares a quote from Byers about trapping two rats in one cage. Quoted experts are often used in argumentative and informative writing to provide evidence, but this dialogue doesn't do that. Byers' snippet tells anesthesia, and will then be photographed, brushed for fleas, tested for disease, fixed with an ear tag, and released back into V6A within 45 minutes.

Byers is a PhD student under veterinary pathologist Chelsea Himsworth, a University of British Columbia School of Population and Public Health assistant professor who has become a local science celebrity thanks to her "Vancouver Rat Project." Himsworth started the project as a way to address health concerns over the city's exploding rat population— exploding anecdotally, that is, as no one has counted it.

Prior to Himsworth's work, in fact, the sum total knowledge of Canada's wild rats could be boiled down to a

us: I'm a regular person, not a science bot, but someone who still finds it remarkable that two rats could find their way into a single cage. It's pure characterization and context.

Then Cudmore deftly jumps forward in time, another narrative trick. Byers will anesthetize, photograph, brush, test, and tag the rat in a white van. Cudmore chooses to add this interesting detail about the van, "which is parked near (according to Google Maps) an 'unfussy' traditional Ethiopian restaurant."

Why does she include this tidbit? The Google Maps reference is a cultural pin drop as we view-find this spot ourselves and shows us the proximity of an eating establishment. That *unfussy* would sell us on a Tuesday night when we wanted a chill spot for a quick meal. By referencing Google Maps and a restaurant review, she's made a connection with the reader who, she's betting, has recently checked out a restaurant and sought directions via Google Maps. V6A is not so distant and remote a land as you, gentle reader, might imagine.

<< In these three paragraphs, Cudmore steps out of narrative time and place to give us backstory and positions us in the argument of her essay. We meet Chelsea Himsworth who heads up the Vancouver Rat Project. We learn a bit more about Byers (she's a PhD student), we learn about a previous rat study in 1984 Richmond and about Himsworth's early efforts. And most importantly for the argument, Cudmore discloses the situation that will direct the rest of the essay: Vancouver has a rat problem. She follows up the problem with the claim her title alludes to: we should leave rats alone instead of treating them like "invaders" that need to be exterminated.

Notice that even though Cudmore has moved out of scene into exposition, she's still using the kind of language that fiction writers love: specific, concrete nouns (rats, minivan, syringes, needles, gloves, DNA, bacteria, sidewalks, single study of 43 rats living in a landfill in nearby Richmond in 1984. So, six years ago, she stocked an old mini van with syringes, needles, and gloves and live-trapped more than 700 of V6A's rats to sample their DNA and learn about the bacteria they carried.

Her research has made her reconsider the age-old labeling of rats as invaders that need to be completely fought back. They may, instead, be just as much a part of our city as sidewalks and lampposts. We would all be better off if, under most circumstances, we simply left them alone.

Rats thrive as a result of people. The great modern disruptions caused by urban development and human movement across the world have ferried them to new ecological niches. "Rats are real disturbance specialists," says biologist Ken Aplin, who has studied the rodents and their diseases for decades. "Very few wild animals have adapted so well to the human environment without active domestication." Rats invade when ecosystems get disrupted. In terms of the bare necessities, "rats need only a place to build a burrow (usually open soil but sometimes within buildings or piles of material), access to fresh drinking water, and around 50 grams of moderately calorie-rich food each day,"

lampposts) and visual verbs (started, boiled down, stocked, live-trapped, reconsider).

<< Did you happen to notice the space between the paragraph that ends "simply left them alone" and the paragraph that begins "Rats thrive"? That gap, achieved by white space and sometimes asterisks, is called a lacuna, and it's a trick writers use to indicate a passage of time or a change in scene, point of view, or perspective. Cudmore uses the lacuna to break from the scene and launch her argument proper, but she doesn't stove up the prose with abstractions, formal language, or nominalizations. She introduces expert testimony from biologist Ken Aplin, mixes in research about the rats, while maintaining the kind of vigorous prose both nonfiction and fiction writers use to keep the reader on the page.

Cudmore introduces the rat as a character with priorities and agendas. Rats are "disturbance specialists." They have been "ferried." They adapt, invade, burrow, and "access resources." Are we talking about rats here or successful CEOs? Cudmore wants us to admire their wily ways in human terms, so she can set up the next paragraph, which debunks the idea that rats are parasites.

according to Matthew Combs, a doctoral student at Fordham University who is studying the genetic history of rats in New York City. In a human-dominated landscape like New York or Vancouver, "It comes down to where rats have found a way to access resources, which often depends on how humans maintain their own environment."

It's not hard to understand why humans often think of the rat lifestyle as a parasitic response to our own. But that's not entirely true. "I have to stop myself sometimes because I want to say that rats have adapted to our cities," says Combs. The reality is that rats were perfectly positioned to take advantage of the disruptions caused by human settlement long before we arrived. They've been on Earth for millions of years, arriving long before modern humans evolved, about 200,000 years ago. Before cities were even a glimmer in our eye, rats were learning to become the ultimate opportunists. "They were likely stealing some other species' food before ours," Combs says. Even in the still-remote mountain habitats of New Guinea, says Aplin, "you tend to find rats living in landslides or along creek systems where natural disturbance is going on." Walk into a lush, primary, intact

<< Cudmore gives us more backstory and props up our antihero, the rat. Christopher Vogler (2007) in *The Writer's Journey* defines *antihero* as not the opposite of the hero, but "a specialized kind of hero, who may be an outlaw or a villain from the point of view of society, but with whom the audience is basically in sympathy" (34). This is Cudmore's critical aim—to make the reader sympathize and understand the plight of the rat, just trying to get a drink and some food before he goes home to the wife and kids.

Listen to the word choice she uses to describe our antihero. Rats are "perfectly positioned to take advantage" of modern humans. They are "the ultimate opportunists" of human destruction. Rats continue to "thrive," "manage," "create," and "live." Again, she might be describing business executives here. Cudmore chooses words that ping on the positive end of the connotation continuum. She clearly understands how the nuanced word choice characterizes the rats and provides emotional depth for her argument.

Cudmore spins a story within a story within an argument. The first story is Byers', standing in vacant lots, trapping rats, and tagging them in her van. Within those present tense moments of trapping and tagging, Cudmore delivers another story of rats and their lives and our misguided attempts to exterminate them. And both stories contextualize the argument Cudmore is making.

forest, "and they're pretty rare." It's not that rats have become parasitic to human cities; it's more correct to say they have become parasitic to the disturbance, waste, construction, and destruction that we humans have long produced.

Which brings into question the constant human quest to disrupt rats and their habitats. As much as rats thrive in disrupted environments, Byers says, they've managed to create very stable colonies within them. Rats live in tight-knit family groups that are confined to single city blocks, and which rarely interact. The Rat Project hypothesized that when a rat is ousted from its family by pest control, its family might flee its single-block territory, spreading diseases that are usually effectively quarantined to that family. In other words, the current pest control approach of killing one rat per concerned homeowner call could be backfiring, and spreading disease rather than preventing it.

The diseases that rats might be spreading aren't just their own. Himsworth likes to say that Vancouver's rats are like sponges. Their garbage-based diets allow them to absorb a diverse collection of bacteria that live throughout their city,

Which is, rats live in "tight-knit family groups" and "stable colonies" and in "single city blocks" when left alone. When attempts are made to eradicate them, they flee these lovely familial arrangements and spread diseases. The descriptive stories of Byer's research and rat life work powerfully in service of Cudmore's argument against extermination.

<< Notice Cudmore's metaphorical chops here. Rats are "sponges" and "mixing bowls." These are symbols of the kitchen, the center of domesticated life. Coincidence? Metaphors make a comparison of two things, and the most effective are quickly grasped by the reader, both visually and cognitively. But the super-duper ones, like what Cudmore wields here, strike a thematic

in human waste and in our homes. "So it's not like the presence of harmful bacteria are characteristic of the rats themselves," she says. They get that bacteria from their environment, and when they move, they take these place-specific pathogens with them.

When "stranger" rats come into contact, Byers says, territorial battles ensue. "They urinate out of fear and they draw blood," she says—perfect for expelling and acquiring even more bacteria. It's during these territorial brawls, Byers and her colleagues believe, that bacteria can converge, mix, and create new diseases. "The rat gut acts as a mixing bowl," says Himsworth, where bacteria that would otherwise never interact can swap genes and form new types of pathogens.

One example is a strain of methicillin-resistant *Staphylococcus aureus*, or MRSA, that Himsworth found in V6A's rats. It included a piece of genetic material from a very closely-related superbug called methicillin-resistant *Staphylococcus pseudintermedius*, or MRSP, which is often only associated with domestic animals like pet dogs. It seems that rats pick up human MRSA from the sewers or the streets, and canine MRSP from our yards, then mix them in their guts. These new human-rat

chord. Once sponges and mixing bowls are in the same sentence with rats, we're thinking about rats in our kitchen and, of course, contamination. And when we are thinking about contamination, it's not hard to leap to diseases and death. Which is where Cudmore wants us to go.

At this choice point, Cudmore singles out a MRSA strain Himsworth found in her rats that could potentially spread a new superbug back to humans when rats "swap genes" during territorial brawls.

If you're anything like me, you've been thinking about the Black Death for about five paragraphs now. I'm sure Cudmore is banking on that. She's said nothing up to this point, but she probably suspects her audience remembers the theory that rats and their fleas spread the bubonic scourge of the Elizabethan age. Cudmore seems to trade on this awareness to create a real tension, the kind of subtextual force that keeps a reader turning the page of a mystery thriller.

bugs could then potentially spread back to people via the rat's droppings and saliva.

In V6A, it's hard not to notice the litter around us. Garbage has bubbled out from under the lids of trashcans and a pile of empty syringes surrounds a parking lot trap. Walking across this landscape of debris, cracked concrete, and weeds, Byers stops at another trap, which is set on what she has named "Block J." She and two student assistants are heading the project's second phase, which involves tracking the real-time movement of rats, using ear tags. Once these trees are mapped, she will begin to euthanize individual rats, and see how their family responds. Part of her PhD work is to understand how human-caused disruptions, pest control in particular, affect how rats move throughout V6A. The hypothesis is that the disruption will send communities scurrying for new ground. With nearly 100 cages to check today, Byers moves hastily to a trap on Block 8. No rat here, but this one did catch a skunk.

A significant finding from the project's original phase, Byers tells me, is that not every rat in V6A carried the same disease. Rat families are generally confined to a single city block,

<< Another lacuna before this paragraph shifts us dramatically back into scene. Back in the V6A postal code and back in present tense. Even though we've been aware of Cudmore's presence close to the action, we see her now in personal pronoun: "it's hard not to notice the litter around us." She again puts the reader in the physical setting of this world—bubbling garbage, trash can lids, empty syringes, debris, concrete, weeds—and we follow Byers as she and two assistants check the traps.

Cudmore also unveils how Himsworth's hypothesis will be tested. In this second phase of the experiment, Byers will kill off individual rats and record how its family reacts. Cudmore hits her thesis again: the disruption of extermination will disperse the rats, sending new pathogens into greater areas.

<< In this paragraph, Cudmore uses indirect dialogue, reporting something Byers says instead of having Byers say it. Fiction writers use indirect dialogue to sum up something that would take too long in dialogue to express. Perhaps Byer's explanation was long and drawn out, overtaxed

and while one block might be wholly infected with a given bacteria, adjacent blocks were often completely disease free. "Disease risk doesn't really relate to the number of rats you're exposed to as much as it does which family you interact with," says Robbin Lindsay, a researcher at Canada's National Microbiology Lab who assisted the Vancouver Rat Project screen for disease. If those family units are scattered, diseases could potentially spread and multiply—something Byers is hoping to figure out through her PhD work.

If that's true, a city's rat policy should include doing the unthinkable: Intentionally leave them where they are. "It might be better to maintain local rat populations that already have some sort of equilibrium with the people who live there," says Alpin. Many of the diseases that we share with rats are already part of a human disease cycle established over centuries, he says. Seen this way, rats are irrepressible—"a force of nature, a fact of our lives." Rather than focusing on killing them, we need to try to keep their populations stable and in place—and that includes managing rat immigrants.

with scientific jargon. This summary reporting by Cudmore keeps Byers as a character and an expert without having to deliver the actual dialogue. Again, Cudmore neatly hammers her central claim—that leaving rat families undisturbed would curb the spread of disease.

<< In fiction, when narrators or characters wander forward or backward in time or in or out of place, readers intuitively bookmark where they are narratively because the writer has established them in that moment. They know where the writer has left them and have no trouble holding (1) when and where the action left off, and (2) when and where the narrator or character are roaming out of time simultaneously.

The vantage point is still positioned in the V6A with litter all around us, even as we weigh the evidence of management versus extermination. That Cudmore is talking outside of narrative time in exposition is not confusing because we've been narratively bound by scene. We are still with her, even as she further develops the rat as an "irrepressible" character.

An established rat society in a neighborhood makes it a much less viable destination for other rats, for example, those entering through ports. Exotic rats can be more of a threat than those adapted to the region because each rat community evolves with its own suite of unique pathogens, which it shares with the other vertebrates in its ecosystem. New rats mean new diseases. The big question now, Aplin says, "What happens when these different pathogens come together? This is something that I'm just starting to think about now," he says. "If the local rat population is suppressed, if you're actively getting rid of it, then you're also actively opening up niches for these foreign rats to enter."

In Vancouver, this is a fact of life. "One important thing we do have right over there," says Byers, motioning with her left hand, "is Canada's largest shipping port." Vancouver sits on Vancouver Harbor, which houses the great Port of Vancouver. In one of Himsworth's earlier studies, she found mites on the ears of rats that live by the port and compared them to rats that take up residence around V6A. Port rats had malformed ears full of a strange breed of mite previously unknown to Canada—"an exotic species that's found

**<<** In this paragraph, Cudmore still doesn't return to the scene, but develops her argument instead: stable rats have stable diseases. Notice Cudmore's job isn't to recite facts, but to tell a compelling story. Part of this story involves the balancing of history, claims, research, scientific studies plus using scene, characters, tension, and point of view. In a syntactically sharp sentence, "New rats mean new diseases," she blends in the expert information from Aplin, who delivers a rhetorical question at the crux of Himsworth's research: what happens when rats mingle their pathogens?

**<<** Now we're back in the dominant scene. In the reader's mind, we've never left. Byers has reemerged. We're standing in the litter again, and this time, we're listening to her, watching as she motions with her hand, taking in the sinister implication of the port's proximity and the specter of foreign rats.

in Asia," Himsworth says, which happens to be where Vancouver gets the majority of its imports. These foreign ear mites were not found on rats from any other block.

"So I think Aplin's theory has a lot of merit," Himsworth says. "It seems that the established rat population at the port acts as a buffer." Himsworth wonders if this is precisely what has kept an otherwise highly contagious mite from spreading throughout V6A.

Disruption, of course, doesn't come from just ports and pest control. It is part and parcel of modern civilization. Vancouver's population is growing steadily (by about 30,000 residents each year), bringing housing development, demolition, and more garbage. Even our love of birds can be a problem. Two years ago, for example, rats invaded a playground and community garden in East Vancouver, a bit outside of V6A. Several media sites reported on the visitors, which were evidently drawn in by birdseed dropped by a single individual. The area soon became known as "Rat Park." The City of Vancouver urged the garden's coordinator to put up signage asking people to avoid feeding the birds and to pick up their overripe vegetables. An exterminator was hired, as well—adding more disruption still.

<< Cudmore swings her narrative camera out for the long shot here, looking at the whole of Vancouver's population, with its roiling swells of demolition and development, then zooming back down to a specific park where rats (described as "visitors") "invaded." This expository excursion moves from large summary sentences into smaller, specific, visual moments, such as "bird seed dropped by a single individual." This is another example of Cudmore's "story within a story" trend, providing the reader with a specific descriptive example of human disruption she cited in the topic sentence. Humans dropped the birdseed that drew the rats, then exterminators scattered the population.

Himsworth hopes the new science will sway Vancouver's existing policy on rats, which, she stresses, is currently "essentially nonexistent." This bothers her a lot. "I know that Vancouver Coastal Health essentially has the standpoint that, 'Well, we don't see the disease in people so we don't worry about it,'" she says of the region's publicly funded healthcare authority. Homeowners with rat infestations can ring 311, Canada's "411," to report an infestation, but that's not a preventative response. "Rats are pests, and we don't spend healthcare dollars to track pests," said media officer Anna Marie D'Angelo of Vancouver Coastal Health. It was a message echoed by Issues Management Communications Coordinator Jag Sandhu of the City of Vancouver: "The City of Vancouver does not track the rat population." To Himsworth, this is shortsighted. "They're not taking the rat disease risk seriously because they haven't seen it in humans yet—but that's not where diseases start." She also believes the issue is, in part, one of social justice. Rats typically affect poor areas, like V6A, that have little political clout.

<< Here's where Cudmore delivers the counterclaim to her argument with two swiftly delivered portraits in dialogue: Himsworth explains the position of Vancouver's Coastal Health, then we hear from media officer Anna Marie D'Angelo and Jag Sandhu with the City of Vancouver. They stand against the research. They say: we will continue to deal with rat infestation as we have in the past because we don't see any cause to change. Narratively, Cudmore is trading on the old trope where the scientist frantically warns the politicians of the coming apocalypse, and the tone-deaf politicians respond with: "We do not track the rat population." This will be replayed on the six-o'clock news when the pandemic hits.

Back inside one of Byers' traps in V6A, needle-like nails are lightly scraping on the metal. "It's a black rat," Byers tells me—the famed carrier of the Black Death. Byers says she isn't concerned about bubonic plague, which, in North America, is mainly carried by prairie dogs. But there were 13 rat-driven bubonic plague outbreaks in seven countries between 2009 and 2013. And there are plenty of new diseases cooking.

<< Here, at the end of the essay, Cudmore reveals the real fear that underscores this entire essay—a deadly pandemic of rat-borne superbug diseases. The classic fictional technique of withholding and revealing serves to build suspense until this paragraph, where she delivers the blow we've been dreading. By withholding any mention of Black Death, which has, as I pointed out earlier, been creeping around in our heads since the beginning of the essay, she creates suspense.

Listen, she says, to the "needle-like nails." All around her feet are empty syringes, needles euthanize the rats in the van, and needles will administer the medicine to fight the new superbugs, so Cudmore chooses "needles" to describe rat talons. (Did she deliberately choose this simile or was it an artful accident? Who knows, but it's there, and it works and it's wonderful.)

Cudmore uses direct dialogue ("It's a black rat," Byers tells me) for effect also, but then uses indirect dialogue to report that Byers isn't concerned. But, of course, we should be. And we are. In her final moments of exposition, Cudmore alludes to the tension-bearing clincher: rat-driven bubonic plague is not dead. And new diseases are "cooking." We are back in the kitchen, once again, with this visual metaphor, back to the unfussy Ethiopian restaurant, back to mixing bowls and sponges, back to the center of where we live, in our safe delusion of a plague-free life.

# NARRATIVE TOOLS AT WORK IN STUDENT WRITING

Cudmore executes some very sophisticated moves here. And they aren't moves in isolation; the narrative contributes to her purpose, supports her claim, and delivers the information we need to make sense of this rat problem. As you can see, the different expository elements of this essay are not sectioned out in clunky points, but blended seamlessly.

Here, for example, are fifteen narrative techniques Cudmore uses to great effect in her argument. She:

- describes the physical surroundings in rich, sensory language
- initiates world building to ground the reader in time and place
- starts with a character in action
- uses direct and indirect dialogue for characterization and as evidence to support her claim
- uses lacunas to move around in time as well as move between narrative, information, and argument
- uses concrete, specific nouns and active verbs for visual and kinesthetic effect
- uses sentence variety to create rhythm and movement in the prose
- creates narrative tension through withholding and revealing information
- uses flashbacks and flash-forwards, time techniques normally found in fiction
- uses dynamic word choices with rich connotative power to characterize subjects
- uses anecdotes or smaller stories within the larger story to provide evidence to support her claim
- uses figurative language, such as extended metaphors and similes, to create verisimilitude and to explain facts
- establishes a clear point of view, which serves as a narrative and expository filter
- uses rhetorical questions to move the reader forward
- uses backstory to both characterize the subject and provide history and research.

It's important to remember that students don't need layer upon layer of digression, subplots, and fancy-smancy braided narratives like Cudmore expertly uses; they only need to understand how one or two narrative spices work to season an otherwise dry and tasteless essay. Students who consume a steady diet of essays like this begin to get a feel for the balance between narrative and exposition. The goal of all this work is for students to write blended text with all expository modes at their disposal.

Taylor had written a speech for her AP English language class about the need to make CPR training required for high school health and PE classes, and she decided to turn the speech into a narrative nonfiction piece to submit as a writing sample with her college application. She had researched the information and was working on outlining her argument, but she didn't have anything narrative to really tie it together and give it the engagement she wanted.

The next Monday, however, Taylor came bounding into my room. She was practically jumping up and down.

"You'll never believe what happened to me," she said.

"You won the lottery?" I said.

"A guy had a heart attack at our gym! Now I have narrative for my CPR essay!"

We high fived. Then I inquired about his health. He lived. And he survived because someone administered CPR.

This is a rare instance where the universe dropped a narrative gift into a writer's lap. Taylor chose to open her essay with this compelling moment to introduce us to the necessity of her argumentative claim. Here's a portion of her draft and some notes about the techniques she uses along the way.

---

I looked over at my boyfriend, Nathan, who sat next to me stretching. I took my headphones out, "Hey can we start abs now?"

"Yeah, hang on."

I scanned the gym looking at all the different types of people working out. The macho weightlifters who do nothing but lift weights. The cardio lovers who just run all the time and drink detox water. The folks who started coming

>> In this opening section, Taylor uses several of the strategies our class had listed on our menu of narrative techniques. She grounds us in time and place. She and her boyfriend Nathan are introduced as characters as well as several others (bodybuilders, cardio junkies, New Year's resolution makers) and the

to the gym as their New Year's resolution but will probably stop after this month. I continued scanning until I saw out of the corner of my eye a man collapse to the ground with a thud. His maroon dri-fit shirt was soaked through with sweat, and his thick curly hair was greying.

I looked around and for a second or two, no one noticed. I froze. I thought about trying to get the attention of one of the workers, but before I acted quick enough two women jumped down from the treadmill next to him and were already surrounding the man on the ground. He was turned on his side facing away from me. He seemed young, like a middle aged man.

"Sir? Sir, can you hear us?" A man who was lifting weights tapped him and shook him to try and wake him. A Y worker rushed over and immediately called 911.

"Should we turn him over on his back?" One of the women from the treadmills asked.

"No, this is the rescue position," the man from earlier said, kneeling down.

"Hey, he's not breathing!"

I stood only about 6 feet from a man who one minute was working out like every other person in the gym this morning, and the next was fighting for his life. They turned him on this back, and I saw a glimpse of his swollen, purple face between the people surrounding him.

victim. She uses dialogue and sensory description. She also uses a lacuna to separate the narrative portion of her essay with the information.

According to the American Heart Association, 90 percent of people who suffer out of hospital cardiac arrests will die waiting for the ambulance to arrive. If someone you know, or a loved one, goes into cardiac arrest, and you're unsure of how to begin CPR, the first thing you will probably do is call 911. After talking to a dispatcher for around 2 minutes, they will send first responders and paramedics. That's two minutes the person has gone without oxygen.

On average the EMTs arrive at the scene 8 minutes after the call. After approximately 9 minutes without oxygen, the brain has begun to develop Cerebral Hypoxia, which is lack of oxygen to the brain. By this time, your loved one has gone without oxygen for 10 minutes. This can cause severe brain damage or even leave the person brain dead.

"We need to do CPR!" One of the Y workers started to do compressions while the woman sitting by his side held his hand and told him everything was going to be okay, if he could even hear her. I looked around at the rest of the people in the gym to see their reactions. Nathan sat next to me, his mouth in a fine line, his eyes wide.

Some stood and watched from a distance, others kept working out as if nothing had happened. As if this man's life wasn't in danger. My attention turned back to the people who had stopped doing compressions, and began hooking him up to a defibrillator.

<< In this section, Taylor weaves in facts she'd researched from the American Heart Association plus she executes a pretty sophisticated narrative move that we had identified in several other mentor texts: she embeds a ticking clock. We know the victim is on the gym floor suffering a heart attack. The EMTs have been called, but how soon will they get there? As time passes—two, four, six, eight minutes—we know his chances of survival become slimmer. This narrative technique heightens the tension of the piece.

<< Again, Taylor moves us back into narrative with the continuation of the opening scene. Not only does she give us a description of the scene, but she makes a small detour into the seemingly nonchalance of the rest of the gym. She writes, "As if this man's life wasn't in danger." She again uses realistic dialogue that puts us right into the moment, and she describes in clear, physical action the electric shock coursing through the man's body. His mouth is

> "Stand back, hands off."
>
> The machine whirred up, and everyone stepped back. The machine sent a shock through him, and his chest raised up and fell back down, violently thrown by the electrical shock. I stood up to try to see better, as they continued CPR. His mouth was now open and foam began spilling out down his chin.

open and "foam" comes out. I love her choice of words here. I can see this so clearly. It's not a medical term or a bit of figurative language, but a clear descriptor of what she saw that is now firmly registered in the mind of the reader.

For the remainder of the text, Taylor goes back and forth from narrative to information, providing statistics, information, and research to support her argument. She doesn't reveal the status of the heart attack victim until the final paragraph, but he survived, "thanks to those who helped save his life by doing CPR." All of the elements of fiction—character, tension, description, dramatic stakes—serve the purpose of her argument.

# HOW TO USE THIS BOOK

The premise of *Story Matters* is that if we teach students how expert nonfiction writers use narrative techniques to engage readers, our students can use these same techniques to make their own writing better. The narrative techniques I offer in this book are not built on mastery, so feel free to move around in the book and explore different moves that make sense for your students. Try out different techniques in isolation or with a variety of combinations—not all of the techniques need to be used in every essay, of course. The writer determines what the essay needs, and what tools of engagement will best deliver the purpose.

The bottom line is that reading and writing nonfiction need not be so dry and dreadful. Stories are the cornerstone of all human communication, and for a student who sets out to write a compelling argument or an interesting informational piece, that foundation can be narrative. A writer's voice can be engaging with word choices that reveal a real personality behind the page. They can feature world building and characters, fully developed, that both engross the reader and support his argument. And they can tell a story, an enchanting or ironic one, a dark or buoyant one, that will make us think and feel and act.

# **IDEAS** Finding Stories in Topics and Topics in Stories

When you read an essay like Becca Cudmore's (2016) "The Case for Leaving City Rats Alone," you can't help but wonder, how did she do it? How did she find her structure? What was the recipe by which she mixed all those ingredients? At what point did she go from a straight argument to peopling the essay with characters, scene, and world building?

What choices did she make as she approached the task? What was she looking for? Did she decide on the narrative in the middle of gathering information? After she made some notes?

Is the argument she makes in the essay the argument she intended to make at the outset? What did she plan ahead? What just happened in the drafting? And how did she choose *those* narrative moments to feature among the dozens or hundreds she must have had at her disposal?

I don't know the answer to any of these questions. If I were to interview Cudmore today, she might not know either.

My husband is a successful journalist who has been writing for forty years. When I recently asked him how he knows how to build a piece of writing, he said, "Nothing I can tell you about writing is uniformly true. Sometimes it depends on what section of the paper my piece will be in, sometimes it depends on how much space I have to unlimber, sometimes I hear a subject tell a story and it shifts my entire approach. There are rules, but there are no rules."

It's impossible to codify how good writing arrives because the process isn't distinct; it's born of simultaneous, recursive, microscopic, sometimes blind decisions. The writer's intention is led by the writer's intuition. The writing, it seems, follows a pattern it has set for itself, the merit of which is based on the writer's range of reading, technical skill, language dexterity, critical thinking, and amount of time spent in practice.

So, we have no idea how Cudmore's brilliant essay came to be, but what is clear is that she was open to the idea of blending text styles or modes. Specifically, she was open to narrative as a means of delivering her argument. And this is where we should start, too: by developing this same openness in our students, by building narrative awareness through reading and annotating high-grade mentor texts, by bringing in story from the expository cold and giving it a seat at the table.

We also know that Cudmore's essay came out of her interest and work in ecosystems and anthropology, and the argument stemmed from her passion for a sensible solution to the rat problem of Vancouver. Writing what you know is not as important as writing what you care about. When we assign generic topics like dealing with the opioid crisis, abolishing the death penalty, or establishing local zoning laws, then ask students to care about those topics enough to write about them, we're asking them to fake an urgency, to work up a head of steam over a topic about which they may have no knowledge, passion, or even a remote connection. The challenge, of course, is leading students to discover stories, ideas, and topics they care enough about to warrant the struggle of writing well. That's what the exercises in this chapter are all about.

# EXERCISES FOR FINDING NARRATIVE CONNECTIONS

## Universal Time Line

Every generation has a singular moment that defines them. For our grandparents, it was Pearl Harbor; for our parents, the day JFK was shot; for my generation, 9/11. Most of my seniors were born in 2001. For them, it will be another moment. All of these very public moments were experienced in a million, small, private ways. At this intersection sits a myriad of writing opportunities. (For a beautiful example of an essay that connects the personal and the public of both Pearl Harbor and 9/11, read David Halberstam's [2004] essay "Who We Are.")

I use an activity called Universal Timeline to illuminate how individual moments are connected to large historical events. The setup is fairly easy. First, draw a horizontal line across the board. On the left end of the line, write the birth year of the oldest person in the room, and on the right end of the line, write the present year. Then hash mark off the timeline into five- or ten-year increments. That's the timeline template.

In groups of four, students then replicate this template on a large piece of butcher paper and begin to brainstorm historical events along the timeline (see Figure 2–1).

"OK, working from your memory, populate the timeline with international or national or local events," I say. Some students have better memories of big events than others, so I circulate the room, making suggestions.

"When was Obama elected the first time?" Holly asks.

"Two thousand eight," I say.

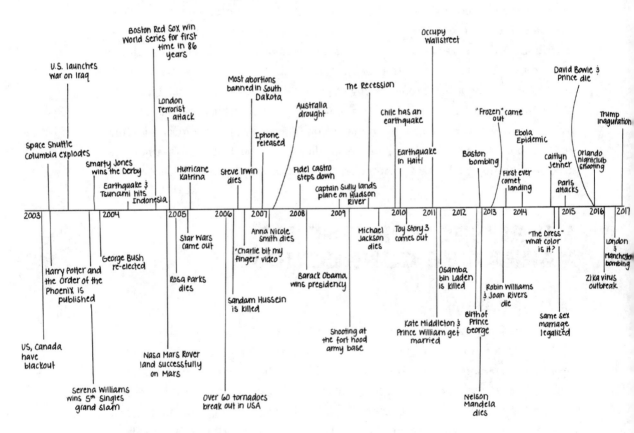

**Figure 2–1** Universal Timeline

"I remember that because we were at my aunt's house having a birthday party for my cousin, and I remember all the adults talking about it," she said.

"Do you remember what they said?"

"Just that it was historic and what a time to be alive," she said. "And we ran out of ice cream."

Holly naturally made a connection to an event that millions of people had experienced by linking this public event to a personal story. How could Holly use this small birthday celebration as an entry point to contemplate the larger celebration of democracy?

Once the groups have met for five minutes or so, we reconvene and do this exercise as a whole group on the board.

Once the timeline is full, I ask students to choose one event and write for five minutes, telling a straight journalistic account of the moment without adding any personal reflections or analytical details. Samantha, a seventh-grader, decided to write about Logan Paul. Here is her objective reporting on the subject:

> On January 5, 2018, famous YouTuber Logan Paul uploaded a video that would make history. In the video, Logan Paul is exploring the suicide forest in Japan with his friends. He finds a dead body and starts to film it while making jokes and acting immature. Paul then started receiving hate and shock from the media and he took the video down and apologized. He hasn't uploaded since and people are still pretty upset about it.

After students jot down an objective rendering of the event, they write for five more minutes, telling their subjective account of the moment, just as they experienced it. Samantha wrote:

> I was sitting on my bed eating an apple and wondering if I should start my homework now or later. Grabbing my phone, I lay back and looked at YouTube. I am curious when I see the thumbnails and titles of so many videos popping up. They all say something about Logan Paul and a forest. I click on one and am immediately updated on the situation. I understand what he did was wrong, but I am shocked that people are taking something like a YouTube video and overreacting to it so much.

After students have written one objective account and one subjective account, I ask them to develop three or four questions or observations around the topic. Showing students how to inquire about their own experience or their memory of a public event is a valuable tool. Samantha wrote:

> Why did Logan Paul go into the forest in the first place? Is anyone on his side? Should Logan Paul continue to make YouTube videos at all?

As Samantha generated questions in the space between the public and the personal, she was on the path to discovering a writing topic that she had a personal connection with. Perhaps she'll want to write an argument about YouTube content. Or an informational piece on Japanese suicide forests or the celebrity spiral of Logan Paul.

It really doesn't matter which topic she settles on. What matters is that Samantha and her classmates see that their own experience can be part of the informational and argumentative reporting of a public and historic event. When we ask students where they were when X happened, we extend an invitation to enter public discourse through the portal of their own story.

This exercise builds a student's narrative awareness and reinforces that even though they're in middle or high school, their own experience gives them access to public conversations. Several of my high school students have used this exercise to produce a solid college admission essay that answers the question: "Choose a significant event and explain its impact on your life."

## Your Life at a Glance

On September 26, 1983, Stanislav Petrov, a lieutenant colonel in the Soviet Air Defense Forces, made a decision that impacted the entire world. In a command center in a forest outside Moscow, his job was to monitor the Soviet nuclear assault warning system. About four hours into his shift, the early warning system sounded an alarm; five intercontinental American missiles were headed toward Moscow.

With his crew looking to him for leadership and the fate of the whole world at his fingertips, Petrov decided it was a false alarm. He was correct; the satellite had mistakenly interpreted sun beams off the clouds as a missile launch (Chan 2017).

I am a Cold War baby, raised during a nuclear arms race that shrouded my adolescence with visions of mushroom clouds. Last year when I read Petrov's obituary in

*The New York Times*, I wondered where I was on this fateful day in 1983. I went to my closet and pulled out a banker's box where I store my high school journals. I found the spiral notebook marked 1983. There's an entry on September twenty-first and another one on October eighth—both of them are about boys, my hair, grades, and being mad at my mom for not letting me drive the car to school that morning. I was sixteen.

Knowing how your story aligns with the larger story of history is to understand history. The story of Stanislav Petrov is an incredible one, but made more so by my personal connection—that 8,000 miles and ten time zones away from Bourbon County, Kentucky, a forty-four-year old Soviet officer made a decision that allowed my innocent reality to continue, unabated by a nuclear disaster.

Our students often don't recognize that history is happening all around them; it's just a regular Tuesday, and they're mad at their mom. But giving them opportunities to make personal connections with historical events creates another invitation for them to connect nonfiction topics with the stories of their lives.

A Writer's Digest book I found at a yard sale, *How to Write the Story of Your Life* by Frank P. Thomas (1984), has a number of great exercises I have adapted to help students see the value of their life stories. In an exercise Thomas calls Your Life at a Glance (120), he suggests would-be memoirists write each year of their life on three-by-five index cards and add brief personal and public information to the cards.

To adapt this idea, I created a table to assist students in collecting personal history aligned with public events (see Figure 2–2).

On this template, students write the years of their life in the far-left column. In the next column, they write down important events from their own life, followed by events that were occurring at the same time globally, nationally, and locally. I also have a column where they can jot down cultural movements that occurred during their lives.

Figure 2–3 is an example of a table from Taylor, an eighth grader.

Notice how Taylor's life events—the year her brother was born, her first trip to Disney, when she saw Hamilton in Chicago—are nestled in a larger context. Taylor was excited to discover that YouTube was invented the year she was born. Is there a possible nonfiction topic here? What's it like to grow up in a world where everyone is a potential star? What's it like for kids who can unbox their toys, make banana bread, put on makeup, or tell knock-knock jokes to millions of people online?

To fill in large public events they don't remember, students may use online sources, and I encourage them to interview their parents, grandparents, and teachers to discover unique local events.

## Your Life At a Glance

NAME_____

| Year | Important Life Events | World Events | National Events | Cultural Events | Local Events |
|------|----------------------|--------------|-----------------|-----------------|--------------|
|      |                      |              |                 |                 |              |
|      |                      |              |                 |                 |              |
|      |                      |              |                 |                 |              |
|      |                      |              |                 |                 |              |
|      |                      |              |                 |                 |              |
|      |                      |              |                 |                 |              |
|      |                      |              |                 |                 |              |
|      |                      |              |                 |                 |              |
|      |                      |              |                 |                 |              |
|      |                      |              |                 |                 |              |
|      |                      |              |                 |                 |              |
|      |                      |              |                 |                 |              |
|      |                      |              |                 |                 |              |
|      |                      |              |                 |                 |              |
|      |                      |              |                 |                 |              |
|      |                      |              |                 |                 |              |
|      |                      |              |                 |                 |              |
|      |                      |              |                 |                 |              |
|      |                      |              |                 |                 |              |
|      |                      |              |                 |                 |              |
|      |                      |              |                 |                 |              |
|      |                      |              |                 |                 |              |
|      |                      |              |                 |                 |              |

**Figure 2–2** Your Life at a Glance Template

| Year | Important Life Events | World Events | National Events | Cultural Events | Local Events |
|------|----------------------|--------------|-----------------|-----------------|--------------|
| 2005 | I was born to a 35-year-old mathematician and a 33-year old engineer. | London hit by suicide bombers. 60th Auschwitz Liberation anniversary. | Creation of YouTube. George W. Bush, President . | Harry Potter and the Goblet of Fire released. Velour jumpsuit/ flared jeans popular. | Bluegrass Community and Technical College established. |
| 2006 | I ate my first solid food: chicken pot pie. | Many killed/ injured in a Mumbai train blast. Nuclear standoff with Iran. | US immigration protests. Democrats control both House & Senate. | The top song was Beyonce's "Irreplaceable." Blu-Ray disks made available. | Flight 5191 crashes at Bluegrass Airport while attempting to take off. |
| 2007 | My brother, Nicholas, was born. | Bulgaria & Romania join the European Union. iPhone announced. | Gunman kills 5 people in Salt Lake City. Chrysler sold. | Reunions between the Police, Genesis, and Led Zeppelin. | |
| 2008 | My family took me to Myrtle Beach for the first time. | Expo 2008 opens in Zargoza, Spain. Summer Olympics in Beijing. | Barack Obama elected President. Phoenix spacecraft lands in Mars polar region. | Actor Paul Newman dies. Marvel's Iron Man released. | |
| 2009 | I attend preschool at South Elkwood Church. | 66 people die in a nightclub fire in Bangkok, Thailand. | NASA's Kepler Mission launches from Cape Canaveral. Water found in moon crater. | Star Trek (2009) released. Food Network Magazine begins publication. | Alltech Arena opens. Lexington Film League is formed. |
| 2010 | I attend kindergarten at Garden Springs Elementary. | 7.1 magnitude earthquake affects Christchurch, New Zealand. | Deepwater Horizon oil drilling platform explodes in the Gulf of Mexico. | Partial-shaved heads are popular. Kesha's "Tik Tok" topped song charts. | Lexington becomes first city outside Europe to host the World Equestrian Games. |
| 2011 | I went on my first trip to Disney World. | Osama bin Laden, leader of a militant group, Al Qaeda, is killed. | U.S. declares an end to the Iraq War. Occupy Wall Street protests begin. | HGTV magazine begins publication. Angry Birds gains popularity. | Jim Gray becomes Mayor of Lexington. |

(continues)

**Figure 2–3** Taylor's Life at a Glance, Eighth Grade

| Year | Important Life Events | World Events | National Events | Cultural Events | Local Events |
|------|----------------------|--------------|-----------------|-----------------|--------------|
| 2012 | Family trip to Charleston, SC. | Encyclopedia Britannica discontinues its print edition. | Shooting occurs in Aurora, Colorado. Sandy Hook Elementary shooting. | JK Rowling launches Pottermore website. | The Town Branch Distillery opens. |
| 2013 | Attended Meadowthorpe's accelerated program. | North Korea conducts its 3rd underground missile test. | Boston Marathon bombing occurs. | Pope Francis is named Time's Person of the Year. | Andy Barr becomes US Representative. Construction on Centre Point begins. |
| 2014 | I started SCAPA. | Malasian Airlines flight 370 loses contact and disappears. | Obama's economic sanctions against Russia go into effect. | Robin Williams dies. Top song was "Happy." | Redevelopment of the Fayette National Bank building. |
| 2015 | School trip to Washington, DC. Saw Wicked. | Russia, Ukraine, Germany, and France end conflict in eastern Ukraine. | Donald Trump launches campaign for US President. | Tom Brady becomes only the 3rd quarterback to win 4 Super Bowls. | Keeneland hosts the Breeder's Cup. |
| 2016 | Began archery lessons. | El Chapo is captured in Mexico. Zika virus outbreak begins. | After dragging a 3-year-old boy who entered his enclosure, Harambe is shot. | App Pokemon Go is released on smartphones. | |
| 2017 | Saw Hamilton in Chicago. | A snap general election is held in the UK in the midst of Brexit. | US withdraws from Paris climate agreement. | Apple becomes the first company to be worth more than 800 billion. | Civil War statues are removed from downtown Lexington. |

Similar to the Universal Timeline, not only do students record important personal life events, but they see how their lives are enmeshed with living history. Middle school students, especially, make connections between their early preschool years and newsworthy events they've heard or read about.

| Year | Important Life Events | World Events | National Events | Cultural Events | Local Events |
|------|----------------------|--------------|-----------------|-----------------|--------------|
| 2003 | I was born to a thirty-year-old weather reporter and thirty-year-old special education teacher. | The Space Shuttle Columbia burned up on re-entry, which killed all astronauts onboard. The Human Genome project was completed. | "French Fries" were renamed "Freedom Fries" due to France's position on Iraq. (Which the Americans did not like.) | Mr. Rogers from "Mr. Roger's Neighborhood" died on February 27th, 2003. | The Bluegrass Ice Storm hit Lexington and Louisville on February 15–16th, with one inch of exposed ice and power outages. |
| 2004 | I visited Double Stink and Bi Water Farm to look for pumpkins for Halloween. | Facebook was created by Mark Zuckerberg. The 2004 Summer Olympics were held in Greece. | George W. Bush was elected president. | The film "Fahrenheit 9/11" is released in American theaters. | Hurricane-Force Derecho strikes southern Indiana and central Kentucky. |
| 2005 | My younger sister Claire was born. I wanted to name her Cracker. | Hurricane Katrina forms into a Category 5 hurricane after starting in the Bahamas. | The Olympic Park Bomber, Eric Rudolph, was sentenced to four consecutive life terms. | K. Sello Duiker, a South African novelist, died. | Tornado outbreak on November 15th, 2005. |
| 2006 | My family rescued a greyhound named Daisy. I started school at Providence Montessori. | Photos from the NASA Mars Global Surveyor hint that there is a presence of liquid water on Mars. | A 6.6 magnitude earthquake hits the state of Hawaii. | The movie Eight Below is released into theaters. | Widespread flash flooding, which left six people dead after six to nine inches of rain fell. |
| 2007 | I took my first trip to the Atlantic Ocean with the entire family and relatives. | Steve Jobs from Apple Inc. announces the release of the first iPhone. | Virginia Tech student Cho Seung Hui kills 30 students, his girlfriend, and neighbor before killing himself on April 16th. | The Spice Girls have a reunion tour starting in Vancouver, Canada. | The Fall Tornado Outbreak of October, 2007, which had 8 tornadoes touch down within hours of each other. |
| 2008 | I performed "Harry the Dirty Dog" at the Lexington Children's Theater. | At the Beijing 2008 Summer Olympics, Usain Bolt sets a record of 9.69 seconds for the 100 meter dash. | The United States government approves of marketing and producing foods from cloned animals. | Britney Spears is the most searched term on Yahoo. (And still is.) | The Unbridled Harmony A Capella group hosts a membership drive. |

(continues)

**Figure 2–4** Anna's Life at a Glance, Ninth Grade

| Year | Important Life Events | World Events | National Events | Cultural Events | Local Events |
|------|----------------------|--------------|-----------------|-----------------|--------------|
| 2009 | I graduated to the lower elementary school of Providence Montessori. | Sri Lankan government defeat the LTTE after 26 years of fighting between the two sides. | Barack Obama is elected as the 44th president of the United States, and also the first African-American president. | Michael Jackson dies at age 50 from intoxication. | The Unbridled Harmony Chorus performs Christmas Tunes at the Meeting House in Shakertown. |
| 2010 | I began second grade in a public school. My family adopts a six-week-old beagle-Boston terrier mutt named Gidget. I meet my current friend Devyn. My family visits Disney World. | The Deepwater Horizon oil rig explodes, dumping 3.19 million barrels of oil into the Gulf of Mexico. | A successful launch of the Dragon capsule into low-Earth orbit by SpaceX. | Justin Bieber becomes famous through a video posted on Youtube in 2008. | Bluegrass Printmakers' Cooperative host a printmaking workshop called "3rd Friday at the BPC." |
| 2011 | I began third grade. I also meet my current friend McKenna. | Osama bin Laden is killed by US special forces in Abbottabad, Pakistan. | Gabrielle Giffords was shot with twelve other people in Tucson. | The Royal Wedding takes place on April 29th between Kate Middleton and Prince William. | The Lexington Art League hosts a Black Friday Art Sale. |
| 2012 | I began fourth grade. My family gets our first set of chickens, who are now very old ladies. | The American Episcopal Church is the first church to approve a gay marriage. | Adam Lanza attacks Sandy Hook Elementary in Connecticut and kills 26 students and staff. | Marvel Studios "Marvel's the Avengers" is released and becomes one of the highest-grossing movies. | Gallery on Main and the Madison County Library partner up to showcase regional artists. |
| 2013 | I began fifth grade. My family adopts another Boston terrier named Evie June. | 3 people were killed and 183 injured in the Boston Marathon Bombings. | President Barack Obama was inaugurated for his second term on January 21st. | Taylor Swift wins her third artist of the year award at the AMA's on November 25th. | Lexington Vintage Dance hosts Waltz Basic, a waltzing class. |
| 2014 | I began sixth grade and started middle school. My family gets our first beehive. | The West Africa Ebola breakout began, which led to the death of 11,310 from Sierra Leone, Liberia, and Guinea, and 28,616 confirmed cases. | Same-sex marriage becomes legal in Oregon and Pennsylvania. | Robin Williams committed suicide by hanging himself. | The Ann Tower Gallery hosted a new exhibit of paintings by Chris Segre-Lewis, called "Tended Earth." |

(continues)

| Year | Important Life Events | World Events | National Events | Cultural Events | Local Events |
|---|---|---|---|---|---|
| 2015 | I began seventh grade. I went to my first World Archery Tournament with the Beaumont Middle School Archery Team. | ISIS struck four different places in Paris, France. | Gun deaths climbed so high that they became as common as traffic deaths in the United States. | The viral video of the white and gold or blue and black dress. | The Carnegie Center for Literacy and Learning held a workshop called "The Art of Iris Paper Folding" on January 31st. |
| 2016 | I began eighth grade. I go on my first multi-state camping trip with my family to Cherry Springs Dark Park and Niagara Falls. We camped on the shore of Lake Ontario. | Michael Phelps and Team USA, winning a total of 46 gold medals. | Donald Trump was elected President of the U.S. after running against Hillary Clinton. | The new Netflix series "Stranger Things" dominated television screens. | The Lexington Children's Theater performed "Frankenstein" on October 29-30th. |
| 2017 | I began ninth grade. During my eighth grade State Science Fair competition I placed third in environmental science out of all the middle school projects in Kentucky. | The Las Vegas Country Concert shooting which killed 58 people and injured over 500. | The Hamilton Musical begins to go on tour, and will be traveling around the country to different cities. | The #metoo movement and accusations against Harvey Weinstein, which led to the downfall of many other powerful male figures. | The Lexington Chamber Orchestra performs "Mediterranean Portraits" on January 28th. |

Sometimes this activity reveals a student's obsessions and interests (see Figure 2–4). Notice that Anna's local events are all centered on natural disasters—thunderstorms, tornados, ice storms. In the first column, she notes she was born to a teacher and a weatherman. Her connection to the metrological events of the past is clear. What nonfiction topics could she extract from this exercise? What topics of interest will pop out at her when she realizes all the many momentous events of history she unwittingly lived through? How will she see her life differently?

# The 100 Topics Project

Everything we experience is connected to larger social, cultural, or political issues, but students often don't see those connections. Asking them to identify their individual curiosities, then connect those to a broader nonfiction issue is the first step in helping them find topics they care about. Topics from their lives hold the personal significance needed to sustain a writing project.

At the beginning of the year, I lead students in numerous low-stakes writing exercises. Part of my goal with these writing jaunts is to build fluency with writing and to get to know my students, but I also want them to build a topic compendium they can dip into for inspiration for future writing assignments. These are just starting points, a mass of writing topics. The connection to writeable purposes, claims, stories, and issues embedded in these topics comes later, but generating topics from their own lives is where we start.

With The 100 Topics Project (see Figure 2–5), even though the goal is to generate a hundred topics, some kids don't get to that number, but if they even generate fifty ideas, that's a great starting place. You can do this as a series of bell ringer–type prompts that last for a couple of weeks or as a lesson that lasts one or two class periods. I like to ask one question a day for the first twenty days of school as an opening invitation to write and think and get to know one another.

| Day | Question | Priming suggestions |
|---|---|---|
| 1 | What are five places you pass every day and you wonder about? You pass them either on your way to school or your way to temple or your way to the community center and you wonder: What goes on in there? Who lives there? What's he building in there? (my apologies to Tom Waits) | Is there a spooky old house, an abandoned church, a bright and shiny building, a lopsided silo, a giant field with llamas, an alley with red flags across it? |
| 2 | What are five things that you use everyday that you couldn't live without? | These can be as simple as your toothbrush or as intricate as your smartphone. Think about the essentials of your life here. |
| 3 | What are five kinds of animals, insects, birds, bugs, or slugs you find endlessly fascinating? | Pesky or friendly, domesticated or wild, in the zoo or in your yard? What animals are you drawn to? What animals are exotic, interesting to you? |
| 4 | What are five kinds of plants, trees, shrubs, weeds, flowers, vegetables that you find amazing, compelling, or mysterious? | This could include the state tree and flower or the tobacco your grandparents raise on their farm. What about the herbs your dad's girlfriend keeps in those pots by the back steps? |
| 5 | When are five times in history you would like to have lived? | Think of the roaring '20s, the Gilded Age, the Iron Age, the '60s, or '70s. Where would you like to land in a time machine? |
| 6 | What five people in history would you like to have met? | In history class, whose story has intrigued you? Joan of Arc? York? Abraham Lincoln? Frederick Douglass? |

Figure 2–5 The 100 Topics Project Template

| Day | Question | Priming suggestions |
| --- | --- | --- |
| 7 | What five historical events would you like to have witnessed? | Think back over the events of human history. What are the events that have always intrigued you, interested you? The Great San Francisco fire? The Alamo? The Battle of Little Big Horn? |
| 8 | What are five things you'd like to do before you die? | Sky dive? Spelunking? Write a book? Ride an elephant? |
| 9 | What five rituals give your life meaning? | What rituals do you participate in weekly or daily that make you happy? Playing chess after school? Tending to the garden with your grandmother? Family meals? Cleaning your room? Snapchatting with friends? |
| 10 | What five food dishes are your most memorable, treasured, and nostalgic? | Because it stimulates our sense of smell and taste (and in the case of bacon or other brittle foods, sound), food can resurrect a body of associations and memories. There's something about hot black coffee and salty country ham that always takes me back to my childhood. |
| 11 | What are five things you'd like to produce, build, or create in your life? | This is a very wide open category. Is there an invention you'd like to make that would solve a problem? Is there something artistic you'd like to create, like a movie, a book, a play? Is there a structure you'd like to build—a tiny house on wheels? A food truck? |
| 12 | Where are five of the most dangerous places you've been to, lived in, or heard about in your town, neighborhood, or community? | There's something about danger that creates automatic significance, largely because there's a built-in tension or conflict between safe and unsafe, a condition that middle and high school students are keyed into even if they can't articulate why. What places have you been told to avoid? |
| 13 | Who are five people you know that have special talents, distinction, or achievements? | I know a girl who holds the Kentucky state muskie record. I know three sets of twins. I know someone who recently sailed across Drake's Passage to spend New Year's Eve in Antarctica. |
| 14 | What are five pieces of music that would be found on the soundtrack of your life? | "Eye of the Tiger"? "Adagio for Strings?" "24K Magic?" |
| 15 | What are five myths or legends that you'd love to know more about? | Mothman, Bigfoot, Loch Ness Monster? |
| 16 | What are five natural or supernatural occurrences that have always fascinated you? | This might include photosynthesis or ghosts that haunt the catwalk above the stage at school. |
| 17 | What are five lessons that you've been taught or that you've taught others? | This might include the lesson of sharing that your mother taught you or this might be when you taught your little sister to tie her own shoes. |

(continues)

(continued)

| Day | Question | Priming suggestions |
|---|---|---|
| 18 | What are five memories that will stay with you for the rest of your life? | These can be small memories, like a special birthday or when you learned to ride your bike or when you got a pet. Or they can be weighty memories like the day you moved out of your house or the day your little sister was born. |
| 19 | If the world blew up this afternoon and explorers from another dimension discovered the remains of our planet, what are five assumptions they would make about how we lived? | Think about how we live, what we value, how we consume, how we feed, how we shelter, and how we clothe ourselves. |
| 20 | Where are five places you'd love to visit? | Backpack across Europe? See the Grand Canyon? Waverly Sanatorium? New York City? |

For each of the twenty questions, students give five answers. Students will then generate a hundred topics from their experiences and memories.

In terms of writing stakes, this activity exists at the lowest, but that's its power. It's just an invitation to begin wondering about things, like the abandoned building you pass on the way to school or the coolest historical time in which to live or bugs you find endlessly fascinating. Because I stretch out this questioning over twenty days, students can concentrate on a single prompt per day, which doesn't overwhelm them. We just generate five answers, then share them around the class. I generate five answers too.

The sharing and discussing is the most important part of this process. Ask questions of students' choices. Get curious. Create the expectation that all topics are worthy, that all topics are significant, that all topics deserve to be examined.

"I wrote praying mantis," Miriam said, sharing one of the five insects she found interesting.

Immediately, three other voices broke out.

"Me too!"

"So did I!"

"I had that too."

"So what's the deal with praying mantises? What's the plural of praying mantis? Mantises? Manti?"

"They have sex for three hours and they kill their mate," Miriam said.

Giggles all around.

| Day | Question | Evelyn's Topics, 8th grade | Devyn's Topics, 9th grade |
|---|---|---|---|
| 1 | What are five places you pass every day and wonder about? | • The office buildings behind the bank on the way to school. The lights are on. <br> • The house that is mostly lavender. The painter never finished. <br> • The private, well-landscaped university <br> • The small fashion shops bordering the street <br> • Willy's house at the end of the street | • Baskin-Robbins coffee and donuts <br> • Giant building on New Circle with round window <br> • Patch of grass <br> • LA Fitness |
| 2 | What are five things you use everyday that you couldn't live without? | • Pencil/journal <br> • All friends/family <br> • Piano <br> • Eyes <br> • Headphones | • Blanket <br> • Laptop <br> • Pillow <br> • Facewash <br> • Nunchucks |
| 3 | What are five kinds of animals, insects, birds, bugs, or slugs you find endlessly fascinating? | • Slugs <br> • Fireflies <br> • Blue heron <br> • Migratory birds <br> • Migratory insects | • Cat <br> • Tiger <br> • Panther <br> • Lion <br> • Zebra |
| 4 | What are five kinds of plants, trees, shrubs, weeds, flowers, vegetables you find amazing, compelling, or mysterious? | • The pear tree in the yard of my old house <br> • Any large cover of vinca ivy <br> • The light purple, white, and baby blue blooms of Blackburn Avenue that scream nostalgia <br> • Catalpa tree <br> • Purple irises | • Celery <br> • Wheat <br> • Apple tree <br> • Stupid yellow weeds <br> • Grass |
| 5 | When are five times in history you would like to have lived? | • Turn of the century <br> • '90s <br> • Great Depression. It would be horrible but interesting. <br> • Women's Rights Movement <br> • Cavemen period | • Washington <br> • Lincoln <br> • Vikings <br> • Greece <br> • Sparta |
| 6 | What five people in history would you like to have met? | • Mozart <br> • Jesus <br> • Thomas Edison <br> • Napoleon <br> • Howard Hughes | • Washington <br> • Lincoln <br> • Sacagawea <br> • Street person from '70s <br> • Leader of Sparta |
| 7 | What five historical events would you like to have witnessed? | • Big Bang <br> • Creation of the first light bulb <br> • Jazz age in the '30s (Swing Era) <br> • My own early childhood, but again <br> • Triangle Fire | • NA exploration <br> • Titanic <br> • Roanoke <br> • Athens-Sparta War(s) <br> • Great Crusade |

(continues)

Figure 2–6 Two Student's Responses to the 100 Topics Project

| Day | Question | Evelyn's Topics, 8th grade | Devyn's Topics, 9th grade |
|---|---|---|---|
| 8 | What are five things you'd like to do before you die? | • Travel all across Europe<br>• Spend a summer meeting the most people possible<br>• Publish anything outside of school<br>• Create a bond, becoming comfortable with performances<br>• Comfort somebody with success | • Bungee jump<br>• Fight<br>• Sky dive<br>• Go down a waterfall<br>• Go on an adventure with a gang |
| 9 | What five rituals give your life meaning? | • Eating breakfast alone<br>• Meeting in a weird, cult-like formation with friends<br>• Writing a very lengthy entry in a journal, or a short poem<br>• Drinking cold water<br>• Waking up too early | • Shower<br>• Reading<br>• Soccer<br>• Dancing<br>• Dinner |
| 10 | What five food dishes are your most memorable, treasured, and nostalgic? | • Floury, rustic bread from Papa Tom's house<br>• Celery<br>• Popsicles<br>• Fast food soft- serve | • Black coffee<br>• Cookie dough<br>• Fruit salad<br>• Protein shake<br>• Applesauce cups |
| 11 | What are five things you'd like to produce, build, or create in your life? | • A novel, connecting with the thought I had as a third grade student<br>• A collection of stories, expressing interesting characters or the lives of many real characters<br>• Any type of small compact hideaway<br>• A song that makes people nostalgic for something they've never heard before | • Book where all sides are loved<br>• Book where reader is known by me<br>• Loft<br>• Gang<br>• Play |
| 12 | Where are five of the most dangerous places you've been to, lived in, or heard about in your town, neighborhood, or community? | • A car operated by a texting driver backing up<br>• The front yard alone<br>• The middle of the street<br>• The end of my grandmother's driveway<br>• Too close to the end of the small overlook on a hiking trail | • Hall outside language hallway<br>• Building with round window<br>• Woods behind house<br>• Digital literacy<br>• Storage closet doors |
| 13 | Who are five people you know that have special talents, distinction, or achievements? | • The one graphic designer at the JK Art Museum<br>• My brother's classmate's friends created an ice cream chain<br>• My father knows everybody under the sun including local musicians<br>• A mentally disabled child who died a few years back | • Mom<br>• Grandmaster Kim<br>• Taylor<br>• Tag<br>• Bobby |
| 14 | What are five pieces of music that might be found on the soundtrack of your life? | • "Bridge Over Troubled Water"<br>• "Arabesque"<br>• "Fish Head"<br>• "Wig"–The B-52's<br>• "Dead Puppies" | • Mission Impossible<br>• Detective Conan<br>• Raining Tacos<br>• Dipping Sauce<br>• Pretender |

(continues)

| Day | Question | Evelyn's Topics, 8th grade | Devyn's Topics, 9th grade |
|-----|----------|----------------------------|---------------------------|
| 15 | What are five myths or legends that you'd love to know more about? | • Flat Earth<br>• UFO's<br>• Illuminati (not the meme, the actual group)<br>• Santa<br>• Not necessarily a myth but . . . religions in general | • Greek Gods<br>• Giant squid<br>• 9/11<br>• Egyptian pyramids<br>• Roanoke |
| 16 | What are five natural or supernatural occurrences that have always fascinated you? | • Sunsets<br>• Sunrises<br>• Movement of the ocean<br>• Heredity adaptation<br>• Time/ creation/ space | • Sinkholes<br>• Radiation<br>• Meetings with God<br>• Making pudding<br>• Lightbulbs on |
| 17 | What are five lessons that you've been taught or that you've taught others? | • Don't judge too early<br>• Silence is a virtue, younglings<br>• Hitting your sibling results in a metaphorical slap<br>• Integrity is important<br>• There is a time and place for joking around | • Don't lie<br>• There's always a reason<br>• There aren't any bad guys<br>• The end doesn't justify the means<br>• Treat others like you |
| 18 | What are five memories that will stay with you for the rest of your life? | • Eating celery sitting on a picnic bench at a preschool<br>• Observing a glistening lake in Washington, DC under the moonlight<br>• Getting into SCAPA<br>• Meeting my piano teacher<br>• Saying something ignorant and possibly offensive in front of a group of friends at a camp | • 1st black belt test<br>• 5th birthday party<br>• Mom crying<br>• 3rd black belt text |
| 19 | If the world blew up this afternoon and explorers from another dimension discovered the remains of our planet, what are five assumptions they would make about how we lived? | • We were wasteful<br>• We were greedy<br>• We were war-like<br>• We were diverse<br>• We were complex in history, but primitive<br>• Alien creatures | • Luxury<br>• Pain<br>• Selfishly<br>• Always stealing<br>• Unmotivated |
| 20 | Where are five places you'd love to visit? | • A small town in Switzerland<br>• The bottom of the ocean<br>• The literal sun<br>• Middle of space or Pluto (minus the vomiting caused by the trip)<br>• 2003, but in my own home | |

"What?" I feigned horror. "Who are you? How do you know this?"

"I watched a National Geographic special on them."

"We had one in our rose bush this morning," another student offered.

Generating these topics is just the first step; unraveling the reason why these topics popped up in my students' minds is where the real idea process starts. What's interesting to one student—Seth chose wolves, sloths, inchworms, penguins, snakes, while Miriam chose cats, mice, parrots, praying mantis, and chickens—is a small-scale representation of their mind, their life, their memories, their stories. They have a connection in some way to these randomly generated topics, some established memory, some built-in interest.

I'm not asking students to write about any of these topics yet. But later in the year, I will ask them to return to this topic list again and again to see if there's something they can harvest, and they're delighted by some of the items they don't even remember writing down.

This exercise can be used with very young students, and I regularly use it with my high school classes. In Figure 2–6 you can see responses from two students, Evelyn and Devyn.

Any topic has the potential to turn into an idea for a writing piece. To prove this point, I sometimes give students Gavin Jenkin's (2016) essay, "The Hidden History of Gas Station Bathrooms, by a Man Who Cleans Them," as an example that any topic, with the right angle, the appropriate gravitas, is worthy of being written about seriously.

## The Power of Questioning

Last Thanksgiving, I went to a family reunion at a nearby 4-H camp, which happened to be the same camp I attended every summer from ages nine to fourteen. After talking to the director of the camp, I discovered there are only four remaining 4-H camps in Kentucky, where there once were eight.

What's up with that? Were the camps closed because of financial problems? Had their summer attendance dropped over the years because of social trends? How are the 4-H camps today different from the 4-H camps of yesteryear?

I didn't launch immediately into research on summer camps, but my writing idea alarm was going off. I was questioning, guessing, remembering, and thinking. As a freelance writer, I'm always looking for story ideas, and the idea that the once-popular camps had declined interested me.

And what would I say about this trend if there was one? Would I pitch it to my editor as a feature or an argument for the renaissance of summer camps? Or a humorous piece about lessons you can learn from spending a week with eight other goofy tweens in an un-air-conditioned cabin haunted by a ghost? Would I blend my personal memories into my essay? Could I even call it an essay? Maybe it's a blog post or an article?

If you teach kids to assume that their lives are significant enough to offer up nonfiction topics at the rate of hundreds a day, students will become actively inquisitive and curious about all the possible topics that surround them. This self-examination process starts with questioning.

All writers are seeking answers to questions. In her book *At Seventy*, May Sarton (1984) said, "I have never written a book that was not born out of a question I needed to answer for myself" (36). Documentary film makers often call this the "controlling question." It's the question that clarifies and focuses the shooting, production, and arrangement of the film.

In *Sherman's March*, filmmaker Ross McElwee's (1985) question at the beginning of his quest was: How had Sherman's military approach during the final months of the Civil War impacted the South today?

But right before McElwee embarked on a road trip to follow Sherman's footsteps throughout the South, his girlfriend dumped him, and the march took on a very different pursuit. As Vincent Canby's 1986 *New York Times* review says, McElwee's controlling question became: Is romantic love possible in an age of supermarkets, fast food, nuclear arms?

In Elizabeth Barrett's (1999) documentary *Stranger with a Camera*, her voice-over explicitly states her controlling questions from the outset of the film: "How is a camera like a gun? Can filmmakers show poverty without shaming the people they portray? What are the responsibilities of any of us who take images of other people and put them to our own uses? What is the difference between how people see their own place and how others represent it?"

Because this activity is about self-examination, I ask students to keep a record of their life for twenty-four hours—to pretend they have a camera crew following them around recording everything. Instead of writing just "work" or "school" or "homework," students write a short description of what they were actually doing as if a camera crew was shooting footage. I also ask students to use third-person pronouns to refer to themselves and write "the subject," as in "the subject made a tuna fish sandwich" (see Figures 2–7 through 2–9).

24 Hours in the Life of _____

| | |
|---|---|
| **5 AM** | |
| **6 AM** | |
| **7 AM** | |
| **8 AM** | |
| **9 AM** | |
| **10 AM** | |
| **11 AM** | |
| **12 PM** | |
| **1 PM** | |
| **2 PM** | |
| **3 PM** | |
| **4 PM** | |
| **5 PM** | |
| **6 PM** | |
| **7 PM** | |
| **8 PM** | |
| **9 PM** | |
| **10 PM** | |
| **11 PM** | |
| **12 AM** | |
| **1 AM** | |
| **2 AM** | |
| **3 AM** | |
| **4 AM** | |
| **5 AM** | |

**Figure 2–7** 24-Hour Log Template

|  |  |
|---|---|
| 1:50 PM | Literary Arts, writing this assignment |
| 12:50 PM | Editing a personal narrative in Language Arts |
| 11:50 AM | Finishing corrections on math test/eating Fruity Pebbles |
| 10:50 AM | Reading/summarizing magazines in Health |
| 9:50 AM | In science class, doing a group activity |
| 8:50 AM | In science class, reviewing science fair |
| 7:50 AM | Reading Ready Player One in the car before school |
| 6:50 AM | Waking up, getting ready for the day |
| 10:50 PM | Asleep, no dreams I can recall |
| 9:50 PM | Laying awake in bed, checking Instagram |
| 8:50 PM | Completing a science paper early |
| 7:50 PM | Showering, choosing clothes |
| 6:50 PM | Awaiting science fair results with friends |
| 5:50 PM | Eating soup and a sandwich at Winchell's with mom |
| 4:50 PM | Leaving an afterschool band rehearsal |
| 3:50 PM | Eating Cheez-Its while walking the halls of the school |
| 2:50 PM | In band class, assembling clarinet and arranging music |
| 1:50 PM | Literary Arts, writing a commentary |

**Figure 2–8** Sydney's 24-Hour Log, Eighth Grade

Sydney also jotted down a few possible ideas for a controlling focus:
- The relevance of mindset
- What the future will look like?
- The importance of stability
- What is a thought?
- Food is made better by family and friends.

| | |
|---|---|
| 7:00 AM | Subject is getting ready for school; eating cinnamon toast, drinking coffee, getting dressed, rushing Mom out the door. |
| 8:00 AM | Subject arrived at school, ran from the cold into the bandroom, talked with friends. |
| 9:00 AM | Subject finished watching documentary in first block, sat in the corner and talked to a friend. |
| 10:00 AM | Subject talked with her classmates, waiting for the 10:02 bell to ring, answered texts and snapchats on her phone. |
| 11:00 AM | Subject worked on writing activity in Spanish, joking around with her table mates, complained about the hot classroom. |
| 12:00 PM | Subject stood in line in percussion class, worked on sight reading music with whole class. |
| 1:00 PM | Subject in the band hallway, practicing scales on her own, her friends sitting with her and talking. |
| 2:00 PM | Subject zoned off in Math class, glancing at her friend across the room and smiling, writing polygon notes. |
| 3:00 PM | Subject on her phone, talking to her best friend in Math class, then packing up her backpack. |
| 4:00 PM | Subject in the car with her brother, talking about her day and listening to PTX music. |
| 5:00 PM | Subject sitting on the couch, watching Netflix, then working on music terms with Quizlet, complaining. |
| 6:00 PM | Subject starting SCAPA homework, typing superfast, drinking her drink from Culver's. |
| 7:00 PM | Subject in car with sister and little cousin, just picked him up from after school program, talking about his dog. |
| 8:00 PM | Subject eating at Waffle House with sister and cousin, Star Wars blanket wrapped around her shoulders, stuffing her face with food. |
| 9:00 PM | Subject showering, Ed Sheeran blasting, with the door open and steam rising. |
| 10:00 PM | Subject watching Dexter, slowly dozing off to sleep. |
| 11:00 PM–7:00 AM | Subject sleeping, cuddling her dog, rolling around in the bed. |

**Figure 2–9** Sarah's 24-Hour Log, Ninth Grade

Once we have the 24-Hour Logs in front of us, I ask students to look at their logs as if they were watching a reality show, with the distance and objectivity of an audience or observer. We look for patterns, significant moments, meaning, and eventually, we pretend to be producers, looking at twenty-four hours of footage for a controlling question or a claim that could be proven or challenged by the reality of this footage.

By framing their life in questions, students discover a multitude of great starting points for informational and argumentative texts. Here, for example, are some controlling questions my freshman class formed when they looked at their 24-Hour Logs:

- How does one's differing forms of entertainment influence their completion of everyday tasks?
- How sleep deprived are high school students?
- Can being antisocial be crippling?
- Are teens not reading books anymore?
- Does a church community benefit a student's overall day?
- Why do we sometimes avoid things that make us happy?
- When does obsessive become too obsessive?
- Is sloth bad?
- How can you balance school with everything else you want to do?
- Are teens too attracted to technology and their phones?
- Can reading and music have a positive effect on procrastination and completion of school work?
- Does high school wear down students?
- How does one balance dreams and reality and what is the price of trying?
- Are teens depressed?
- Does politics have to lack good humor across party lines?
- Can a person have a relationship with God without being religious?
- Can someone be social, yet not?
- How does participating in a sport affect a high schooler's life?
- Can a busy high school student still be content and relaxed?
- Do certain daily activities affect the quality of sleep?
- How does one withstand the mind-numbing grind that is high school?
- Why do some try to replace human interactions with nonliving things?
- Are stereotypes about teenagers accurate?
- Why is fiction such a great escape?

You'll notice there's a disproportionate number of questions dealing with fatigue, expectations, procrastination, technology, introversion, and social anxiety, all topics that weigh heavily on teens today. Could a moment in a 24-Hour Log be a narrative launch for an argument about later school start times for high school students? Could students use a day-in-the-life narrative structure to develop an informational text that answers one of their controlling questions?

## Find Your Story in the Big Questions

For the last few years, Michael Gonchar (2014, 2016, 2017, 2018) of *The New York Times Learning Network* has been compiling great lists of writing prompts for personal and argumentative writing. And in the spring of 2018, he compiled 1,225 writing prompts "on everything from video games and fashion to smartphones and parenting." In addition, these prompts have extra questions for more in-depth consideration as well as a link to *Times* articles about the topic. There's even an index of topics, like "School and Career" or "Science and Health," that helps you cruise around this fabulous resource.

When I pose one of these questions to my students for consideration, their first attempts at answering it are always centered in their own experience. They don't pontificate on longitudinal studies or research conclusions; they tell a personal story that connects them to these broad questions or they tell a story about the topic under consideration. Because story is how humans assimilate information and opinions, it's the natural place to help students see that their story is valid.

For this exercise, I select eighteen to twenty of Gonchar's questions and write them on the board. I invite students to select three, then describe instances or experiences in their lives that, in some way, intersect with the questions. In other words, tell a story that is related to the question. I'm not asking students to answer the question per se, although they might answer it in the course of telling their story.

For example, "Are youth sports too intense?" is one of the questions on the list. To connect with this question, Taylor wrote about a soccer game where she was injured, but after telling her personal story, she summed it up with "Unfortunately, injuries are part of being an athlete."

Responding to the same question, Caden told a story about a fan he witnessed who became violent. "I was watching a typical Estill County home game vs Letcher County, when a verbal altercation broke out between two fans. Words were said and the tension escalated until one of the fans, a twenty-year-old man, punched a door frame on his way out of the gym, breaking his hand." Caden's narrative shades the question in a different way, touching less on the intensity of sports and more on the intensity of sports culture.

This activity asks students to interact narratively with a question that would normally prompt a persuasive or argumentative response. Generating these stories helps students see their experiences as portals into a large controversial issue. Here are some of the questions I use for this activity:

- Does reality TV promote dangerous stereotypes?
- Should stores sell violent video games to minors?
- Will musical training make you more successful?
- Does reading a book stimulate your mind more than listening to one?
- Do we still need libraries?
- Are anonymous social media networks dangerous?
- Are the Web filters at school too restrictive?
- Will social media help or hurt your college and career goals?
- Is online learning as good as face-to-face?
- Is there too much pressure for girls to have "perfect" bodies?
- What rules should apply to transgender athletes when they compete?
- Is prom worth it?
- If teens are such bad drivers, should they be allowed to drive?
- Is your generation more self-centered than others?
- Do shame and blame work to change teen behavior?
- Do teachers assign too much homework?
- Do parents have different standards for their sons than for their daughters?

## Find Your Story in the Big Premises

In Lajos Egri's (2004) classic writing text, *The Art of Dramatic Writing*, he posits that all great plays are fixed on a premise. Egri's definition of "premise" is broad and encompasses the play's goal, theme, root idea, and objective. *Romeo and Juliet*? "Great love defies even death." *Macbeth*? "Ruthless ambition leads to its own destruction" (3).

These moral-of-the-story declarative sentences, Egri argues, serve as a thematic claim. Even the greatest story will fail if it's not securely attached to a clear, well-formed premise. The converse of that is true as well: if the story the premise is designed to uphold is weak, the premise itself will be muddled and unclear.

Egri's argument may be contestable, but I love introducing my students to the idea that plays and movies are arguments, the plot of which serves as a proof of its claim.

Egri's premise theory is a great way to introduce themes, but I also like to show students how to use premises as claims for their own stories. How do large universal themes and premises connect to your own life?

The connections students make when they explore these premises can serve as entry points into nonfiction texts. Recently I asked my class, "Have you had a life experience that proved or disproved the idea that poverty encourages crime?" I gave them time to think, then write, then share. Their answers were as different as their personal histories, which gave them a narrative road into an abstract, arguable premise.

One student wrote about her mother, who was an addict and had recently died of an overdose. Her mom, the student wrote, never broke the law regardless of how much the addiction had robbed her of the basic means to live.

Another student compared his grandmother, who was extremely poor and saw her self-sufficiency as a matter of pride and individual independence, to his uncle, who used his poverty as an excuse to exploit others and break the law.

Students write about an instance in their lives that addresses these claims. With each premise, I pose the question: Have you or someone you know ever had an experience that would prove or disprove this premise? The premises I chose to feature from Egri's book are:

- Intolerance leads to isolation.
- Shiftlessness leads to ruin.
- Faith conquers pride.
- Suffering leads to compassion.
- Intelligence conquers superstition.
- Foolish generosity leads to poverty.
- Bragging leads to humiliation.
- Dishonesty leads to exposure.
- Egotism leads to loss of friends.

This activity produces a lot of rich discussions as we examine and share our stories around each of these broad statements. Asking students to think about an experience that proves or disproves a premise positions them to enlist the narrative in service of the argumentative. Of course, a single experience does not serve as evidence in classic rhetoric, but it can be a means to build credibility and engage the audience.

Stories also become the concrete foundation on which an abstract premise is explored. In this way, students' stories can serve a variety of rhetorical roles, as an introductory hook, as an organizational frame, or as part of a larger evidentiary sampling to support a claim.

## Be an Idea Collector

A magazine I often freelance for calls for story pitches two times a year—in January and July. Even though the call for pitches comes every year at the same time, it always caught me off guard when I was a newbie freelancer. I would stay up half the night wracking my brain for suitable ideas to submit. Eventually, I got wise and started to jot down ideas when they occurred to me throughout the year instead of trying to summon ideas out of the ether on the night the pitches were due.

Professional writers know good ideas are like gifts from the universe, and they also know there will be times when they're on a deadline and the idea reservoir is empty and dry. That's why they keep a list. I talk to my class about how and where professional writers keep track of their ideas. I show them the notes section on my smartphone where I keep a running list of writing ideas that pop up throughout my week. I also show them my Google Drive where I have a document titled "0000" where I type up ideas that occur to me as I teach. And I show them a folder titled "Ideas" on my desktop where I store little paragraphs or sentences or ideas I might use for future articles, blogs, or even books. As I have my own preferences for idea collection, I encourage students to develop their own preferred spot to collect their ideas, which might be on a poster board, index cards, a writing notebook, a Google Doc, or their smartphone.

I encourage students who want to be better writers to also become compulsive chroniclers and recorders. To jot things down, to observe others, to pull ideas out of their lives and write them down on paper. I want them to become idea collectors, specifically collectors of stories related to a topic.

As a fun activity at the beginning of the year, I ask students to keep track of story ideas for one week. I give them a spiral eighty-page notebook and a small pencil. The objective is to fill the notebook with as many writing ideas as they can. They need to jot down one writing idea per page, front side only. The expectation isn't that we will write about all of these, but to train ourselves to see writing opportunities everywhere we look.

Where did they find their ideas? From conversations with friends, from social media, memes, news stories, from their coach's pep talk, from movies, or just something they saw waiting for the bus. Just about anywhere you could imagine, stories emanate.

For Autumn, it was a tweeted video of some high school girls dancing and singing along with a rap song and saying the N-word. She was furious and ready to write.

For Kennedy, it was reading her mother's copy of *Girl, Wash Your Face*, a self-help memoir by Rachel Hollis (2018), which calls out all the lies women tell themselves about being perfect. "What if I wrote a piece debunking all the lies that teens tell themselves about who they have to be?"

Invite students to apply the skills of collection to the virtual world and help them flex a research muscle. This exercise is also one students can do on their cell phone or smart watch. The goal is walking through the world with your idea aperture open and noticing those stories worth writing about.

## Be an Internet Scavenger

I blog regularly on topics that are of interest to high school English teachers, but I also love to read blogs by and about professional writers and poets. Often when I'm looking for ideas for a blog post of my own, I spend some time freestyle researching. I don't have any objective other than to light upon a topic that might be interesting to write about.

Blogs like *Literary Hub* (www.lithub.com), *Poets and Writers* (www.pw.org), *Writer's Digest* (www.writersdigest.com), *Brain Pickings* (www.brainpickings.org), *Mental Floss* (www.mentalfloss.com), *TED* (www.ted.com), *Brain Pump* (www.brainpump.com), or *Highbrow* (www.gohighbrow.com) are all bookmarked on my laptop for easy scavenging. I'm looking for a topic that (a) I'm interested in, (b) has crossover potential into the classroom, and (c) I have something to say about.

I model scavenging the Internet for my students, explaining I sometimes skim and scan online when I'm looking for a topic for a blog post. What am I looking for? Something that grabs my attention or piques my interest that I can add my own story to in order to blog about it.

Although Kentucky Virtual Library (www.kyvl.org) provides a portal for my students to access online databases, such as Britannica, Explora, TOPICsearch, and Scholastic Go, and provides a tutorial on how to use key words to find information they're interested in, I encourage them to start in the wild, unbridled Web, wading in and stomping around. What are they looking for? A topic they're interested in and one that they have something to say something about. It's a bonus if a topic has crossover potential for a content class like science or history.

Of course teaching students how to find credible sources comes later, but right now I'm only interested in teaching them how to scavenge for ideas, stories, and topics that might be of interest to them. I'm also interested in teaching them something about narrative: What are the articles they're most drawn to? Most often it's a post that features stories that introduce, conclude, or accompany the content in some way.

We discuss how to search online, then students spend about thirty minutes in collection mode. They don't have to read in-depth to find interesting stories. The key is learning how to skim and scan the Internet, using:

- headlines
- infographics
- tweets
- websites
- titles
- captions
- sidebars.

This low-stakes activity allows a student to merely collect ideas about a topic without being tied down to finding source material that supports a claim. In other words, it mimics what real research looks like—collecting information on stories, or on a topic, to form an opinion about it. The purpose of the activity is to gather a variety of potential starting points for writing.

# CHARACTERS
## Grounding Nonfiction in Human Stories

As a teacher of writing, you may have experienced this scenario:

Two student essays, both alike in dignity, is where we lay our scene. The first essay starts: "According to the Pew Research Center, there are eight million unauthorized immigrants in the United States civilian workforce, including those who are working and those unemployed, but looking for work." And it drones on from there. The student states his claim, then lists evidence, data, statistics, expert testimony. He provides commentary that shows why his evidence supports his claim. The essay is technically sound.

You make perfunctory remarks in the margins related to tone, documentation, or punctuation, but soon you lay it down. You wander around the house, water the ferns, pick up discarded socks. Then you have a serious talk with yourself. The teacher in you forces the reader in you to sit back down and resume reading. Predictably, he counters with a counterclaim. He concludes with a conclusion. The End.

The next essay starts like this: "One day last spring Oscar woke up to the sound of shouting. He should have heard his mother making breakfast in the kitchen and his three sisters fighting over makeup in their bathroom. He should have heard his father tinkering in the garage with his fishing tackle, but instead he heard shouting."

Boom! You don't get up to water houseplants. Until you find out the source of the shouting, you're held. Story holds you there. The topic—immigration—is the same, but the writer of the second essay engages you through a character. Although the first essay focuses on statistics and evidence, the second essay focuses on Oscar, one of those statistics. One who has a name. And three sisters, and a mom who makes him breakfast, and a dad who fishes for a living. It is Oscar, a character, who will make the second essay's argument and information memorable. It is this human story readers will remember long after the facts fade away. The writer of the second essay clearly has researched the topic and understands the parameters of the argument, but she also recognizes that a character at the center of information or argumentation is critical to the essay's rhetorical success.

In this chapter, we'll explore how students can use the narrative tools of characterization to bring information to life or to make a compelling argument. But first let's consider what's similar and different about creating characters in fiction and in nonfiction.

In fiction, writers *create* their characters—Austen's Elizabeth Bennett, Melville's Captain Ahab, Morrison's Pecola Breedlove—then follow them through conflicts, recording their story. A successful writer creates characters the reader perceives as real, warts and all. We may be horrified or charmed by the choices a character makes, but the effective writer *engineers* details to make us believe.

Nonfiction characters, like Oscar, are introduced to engage the reader. In fiction, characters serve the plot; in nonfiction, characters serve the larger intentions of the work, whatever they may be. And it's the *finding* of characters (not creating them) and the revelation of fascinating details (not engineering them) that separates fictional characters from nonfictional ones. The tools of drawing characters with words, the artistry of bringing them to life, however, is exactly the same.

To understand the interplay of research and writing craft, consider Kentucky historian Charles Bracelen Flood's (2005) *Grant and Sherman: The Friendship That Won the Civil War*. The book is an examination of how Ulysses S. Grant and William Tecumseh Sherman formed a friendship that, Flood argues, ultimately decided the fate of the nation. He delivers his argument in small moments of camaraderie that develop both the character of these men and these men as characters.

Flood starts the prologue with a scene "in the early hours of April 7, 1862, after the terrible first day of the Battle of Shiloh" (3). The North had suffered enormous casualities the day before, with thousands killed and wounded, three thousand captured, and the rest "demoralized and useless as soldiers" (3). Sherman considers retreat:

Sherman found Grant alone, under a tree. Hurt in a fall from a horse on a muddy road a few days before, Grant was leaning on a crutch and held a lantern. He had a lit cigar clenched in his teeth, and rain dripped from the brim of his hat. Looking at the determined expression on Grant's bearded face, Sherman found himself "moved by some wise and sudden instinct" not to mention retreat and used a more tentative approach. "Well, Grant," he said, "we've had a devil's own day of it, haven't we?" "Yes," Grant said quietly in the rainy darkness, and drew on his cigar. "Lick 'em tomorrow though." (3)

This opening scene quietly reveals the mettle of the two characters Flood will follow for the next 400 pages and subtly states the thesis of the whole work: this friendship, built on respect and leadership, won the war. Grant and Sherman's humanity is the flesh and bone that supports the argument.

As a professional writer, Flood knows how to use these narrative techniques to bring the reader into that rainy darkness to smell Grant's cigar and feel the mud underfoot. But how did he know there was rain? Or a cigar? Or mud? Obviously, Flood did his research. The book's bibliography runs at more than 150 sources with 401 notes from journal articles, letters, papers and memoirs of people close to Grant and Sherman, multivolume books, interviews, diaries, and other archived items. The facts are all history; the art is all Flood.

In this chapter, the exercises, insights, and ideas are designed to help student writers use research to find compelling characters, then bring those characters to life with narrative techniques.

# FINDING CHARACTERS IN NONFICTION

## Understanding the Different Work Characters Can Do

Characters assume many positions in nonfiction. They may become the central focus of the work, such as David McCullough's (2003) *Truman*, which argues for a particular interpretation of history, both public and private. Or they may serve as an entry point into an argument, such as David Grann's (2017) *Killers of the Flower Moon*, who uses the story of Mollie Burkhart, a member of the Osage Indian tribe, to educate the reader about racism, oil greed, land rights, and the birth of the FBI.

Characters can also be used as an example of the information under consideration. Journalist Malcom Gladwell, author of *The Tipping Point*, *Blink*, and *Outliers*, is a master of this approach. In the opening chapter of *Outliers* (2008), he explains: "This is a book about outliers, about men and women who do things out of the ordinary. Over the course of the chapters ahead, I'm going to introduce you to one kind of outlier after another: to geniuses, business tycoons, rock stars, and software programmers" (17). As promised, he uses hundreds of characters and dozens of anecdotes, yarns, and stories to support his sociological and psychological arguments regarding the nature of success.

Students must first consider how including a character could support their purpose. For example, eighth-grader Magdalena wanted to write about quinceañeras, a coming-of-age rite that all Mexican-American girls arrive at on their fifteenth birthday. With some brainstorming, she discovered several players or characters she might follow in writing about this subject.

- If she wants to show how the tradition had transformed over time, she might interview her grandmother to research how the quince was celebrated in the 1960s and compare it to a contemporary celebration. By including her grandmother as a character in the text, Magdalena could use her as the point-of-view character as well as an example of how the tradition has transformed.

- If she wants to illuminate the coming-of-age ritual—the opening dance, the main course of meals, the candle lighting, and other ceremonial elements of the day—perhaps she features the woman in her community who sews the quinceañera dresses and plans the parties. With this approach, Magdalena could use this character as a kind of tour guide to inform the reader about all the parts of the ceremony.

- If she wants to write an informative text for the school newspaper, perhaps she focuses on her older sister who participated in the rite of passage two years before. This might be a day-in-the-life treatment where the reader follows the sister's narrative to learn more.

- If she posits herself as a character, the narrative argument might follow her own awareness of the burdensome cost of this tradition versus an investment of that money for her college tuition.

- If her purpose is to inform the reader of the history of the tradition, she might develop—through research—a hypothetical Aztec or Mayan character that she introduces as made up to her reader to reveal the origins of the tradition.

Ultimately, Magdalena's purpose dictates what characters she should use and how she should use them, but she must consider the aims of her writing and consider how an inclusion of a character would serve those aims. This is a powerful lesson. It says: there is no absolute right way to write this essay, but there are techniques that are better than others to convey the ideas I want to deliver.

Over time, students need to develop an ear for what is both effective for conveying their purpose and what is appealing to the reader. To practice this writerly decision-making, teach students to ask questions such as:

- Could this essay be improved by including a character(s)?
- How could the inclusion of character(s) support my intentions for this piece?
- Could I lead or conclude with a character's story?
- Could I use a character(s) to exemplify a point or serve as anecdotal evidence?
- Could I frame the whole essay from a single character's point of view?
- Could I use an ensemble of characters to shed different lights on the many facets of my argument?
- Could I become a character, using my own experience to illuminate a topic?

Questions like these don't suggest any expository rules; they just introduce possibilities. Once students have imagined and considered a few entry points for character, they might sketch out how each possibility would work to deliver their purpose. And then it's up to the writer to determine who and where and how the inclusion of a character or a character's story is beneficial.

## Characters Don't Have to Be Human

All nonfiction topics, from sports to travel to cooking to education, are stuffed with folks, but, of course, characters don't have to be people at all. A thing, an event, or a place can also be a character. The character in a science essay might be electromagnetic radiation or an eastern Colorado wheat field.

Listen to Neil deGrasse Tyson's (2017) description of quarks in his book *Astrophysics for People in a Hurry*:

> Quarks are quirky beasts. Unlike protons, each with an electric charge of +1, and electrons, with a charge of −1, quarks have fractional charges that come in thirds. And you'll never catch a quark all by itself; it will always be clutching other quarks nearby. (24)

Quarks might not walk or talk, but Tyson has given them all the narrative agency of a live character. They are "quirky beasts" who don't like to hang out alone, but codependently "clutch other quarks nearby." The cosmos is a middle school playground apparently.

In Joy Williams' (2003) *The Florida Keys*, a geographical location becomes the character. Williams makes an argument about the eccentricity of the Keys by casting a place as the central character:

> Key West has been compromised by the successful marketing of her as "Paradise." Of course, she was never paradise. She was simply strangely unique and that uniqueness is becoming more and more stylized, increasingly fabricated, maintained by expensive contrivance. Key West is a tourist town—one and a half million people visit each year but still, still she is a town of contrast and contradiction, threat and carelessness and charm.

Look at the work the pronoun *she* does for this piece of writing. Of course, we want to read more about this character who is both threatening and charming. Williams' personal knowledge of the place blended with the history of the town gives the text peculiarity, lightness, and a narrative invitation.

Thinking of characters as something other than human requires a student to leap from the concrete to the abstract, to enter the realm of imagination, as a fiction writer would. To assist them in that leap, we can ask students to look at their topic from the character angle by asking questions like these:

- What are the human properties of this topic (place, natural phenomenon, event, and so on)?
- Is it male, female, gender-neutral, or other?
- When was it born?
- Has it died?
- Is this place, event, or phenomenon tall or short?
- If this place, event, or phenomenon were a person, who might be its mother or father? Its siblings?
- What is its personality?
- Does its personality change as it evolves?
- Does it have a history?
- Does it have a fashion sense?
- Does this place have aspirations or dreams?

When students view a topic through the lens of story, characterhood emerges, and they begin to find the narrative strands to support their argument or bring their information to life. The text that includes characters, whether they be actual humans or personified like quarks or tourist towns, is a text that creates an invitation—and a connection—to the reader.

## Using Research to Bring Characters to Life

More than a dozen books existed about Alexander Hamilton before historian Ron Chernow penned his mammoth biography about the treasury secretary. Lin-Manuel Miranda, who became obsessed with Hamilton as a high school student, wrote a musical masterpiece about the same subject. Whereas Chernow's tome weighs in at more than 800 pages, Miranda penned forty-six tight and complex hip hop songs, sung over a three-hour stage production, to tell the same multifaceted story. Both Chernow and Miranda approached Hamilton differently, but the facts of history, the raw material of narrative, remained the same for both.

All figures of history (or phenomena in science or places in geography and so on) are fair game as characters for anyone who wishes to use them, but they come with real biographies. And a score of great narrative details are there for the student alert and intrepid enough to find them.

The art of writing about real characters of science, history, politics, sports, and so on, then, becomes how a writer appreciates, researches, unravels, and ultimately interprets and illustrates the character for some expository purpose. The more research students do on the lives of their nonfiction characters, the more realistic their portrayal of the characters will be. Students still need to practice the fictional techniques of characterization, but their knowledge of their characters *as* characters will enhance their ability to use those fictional techniques effectively.

Nonfiction research is a scavenger hunt for a narrative detail you might not even know you needed until you stumble upon it. Any small detail—the specific brand of cigar your character smokes, an old weather report on the day of a momentous occasion, a list of popular slang during the time your character lived—might prove to be just the right brushstroke to bring a historical character to life. The second you discover it, you know it will make great copy.

If a student wants to insert a character into a nonfiction text, underscore the necessity of primary and secondary research, not just about the character, but about the whole world that existed around the character. To be able to effectively characterize Harriett Tubman, for example, a student must research and understand the times, the culture, the politics, the society in which she lived. For Tubman to come alive for us, we must know and see the world around her.

Cast a wide net. Gather more information than necessary. Read diaries, letters, newspaper articles, interviews, or court records. Our library has subscriptions for ProQuest and Newspapers.com, both of which offer students access to hundreds of newspapers, even from the 1700s, that will help students get a sense of the real world in which their characters existed. Online oral histories will give you a sense of how a person spoke, what register language they used. Look for autobiographies, memoirs, essays a character may have written. Read these primary documents to get a sense of how the character thought, wrote, lived.

Secondary research is also important for building the world of the character. What was going on in sports, culture, politics during the time a character lived? Research can uncover the pressures or the social context wherein the character acted in a certain way. Investigate the character by reading what others said—biographies, articles, essays— about the person or the subject. Narrative world building in nonfiction brings out the little details of history and allows a student to see how a character fits within that history.

Encourage students to jump into video research. Smithsonian Education has a giant playlist of short videos on YouTube that may help students get a few flavorful details for writing about a character or a time period or a place.

Hands-on, real-world research can't be beat for generating narrative details. Students who are writing arguments or informational pieces with local, state, or regional impact can interview the people at the center of their subject. Visit the site of a mountain that's been cleared for strip mining. Interview those families whose water supply has been fouled by mine runoff. Attend a community rally. In those moments, soak up all the sights and sounds and smells that will later become great narrative details. Eyes and ears open, pen posed to jot down details.

By researching the dialogue, physical description, and actions of a character, students discover more deeply what makes the characters at the center of their nonfiction topics tick. Here is some additional advice as students consider characterization research:

- Ask students to see their characters as real people (even if they're not) with real concerns, full lives, hopes, and dreams. Encourage them to get as curious about these characters as if they were the new kid at school and they were trying to find out everything they could about them.

- Ask students in groups to "introduce" each other to the characters about which they're writing. This is a good way to allow students to develop a familiarity with talking about the person or persons they're writing about as characters. Other students can ask questions about the character. Even if the writer doesn't know the answers to these questions, the inquiry might open a new avenue of thinking for the essay they are writing.

- In the midst of researching a human or nonhuman character, students may keep a mini-biography of their character in their notes, recording life events, major world events that would have occurred while they lived that might have influenced them, or even movies or songs that would have been showing or playing when they lived. This allows students to fully immerse themselves in the world of their character, imagining how the character acted and reacted to life. Much of this biography will not be included in the final draft of the essay, but it provides context and rounds out a student's knowledge of the character.

- Try writing in a diary form from the point of view of the character. This produces fiction, of course, and will never be included in the final draft of a nonfiction piece, but allowing the mind of a student to wonder "What if?" and "What would she think about . . . ?" is a great ploy to truly get in the mind of a character.

## The Writer as Character

Of course, the most readily available character in nonfiction is the writer herself. In all writing, the "I" is somewhere present even if the pronoun is not. The reader understands there is someone pulling the levers and turning the cranks.

In "The Score," an argument against unnecessary C-sections, Atul Gawande (2006) never establishes the "I" because his rhetorical situation (his message, his audience, the site of publication) do not demand it. His argument is more formal, more persuasive without his personal experience being overtly present.

However, in *Being Mortal*, a collection of eight essays about the modern experience of dying, Gawande (2014) is on every page. As a Boston surgeon, a staff writer for *The New Yorker*, and a professor at Harvard Medical School, he establishes credibility with his audience by telling deeply personal stories about his father, his mother-in-law, and his many aging patients who have faced their own mortality with both fear and dignity. The use of first person in this collection is warranted and effective.

If Gawande published research on geriatric medicine in *JAMA: The Journal of the American Medical Association*, his audience would expect the allusion, at least, of scientific objectivity that the exclusion of personal pronouns would represent. Even though his subject may be similar, Gawande's approach would be different.

I urge students to use their own experience in nonfiction because it establishes them as the arbiter of that experience, and it builds credibility with the reader to know the author is not some dispassionate reporter of facts, but a living, breathing human with experiences related to the subject. However, choosing to narrate from a first-person point of view has its advantages and disadvantages, all connected to purpose and audience.

For example, freshman Sarah Grace uses the "I" and her own family experience to build narrative clout within her argument exploring immigration and naturalization entitled "What Makes an American?" She writes, "When people talk about Muslims or Travel Bans, I am very sensitive to it, because for me it is not just a group of people in the world. It is my family. And I may only be a quarter Persian, it is still a part of who I am. Something that will impact me every day for the rest of my life." Although the essay goes on to argue a position, Sarah Grace has shown the reader her argument is not just an academic exercise, but an issue that touches her life and the lives of those she holds dear.

In the introduction of *Best American Essays 2015*, editor Ariel Levy (2015) notes in many nonfiction essays, "there is no 'I'; the writer's presence is never acknowledged in the writing. But we feel him there all the same—his intellect and his empathy" (xviii). Students who learn to ask and answer questions like "When does the insertion of 'I' aid and when does it detract?" grow as writers. Asking when to use first person as a narrative prop and when to withhold it is a powerful lesson for students in writerly decision-making. And determining how to render the writer's intellect and empathy as a presence in the writing without actually using first person is a matter of practice, an exercise in trial and error.

## Leading with a Character

Opening a nonfiction essay with a character positioned in a narrative situation allows the reader to identify with a flesh-and-blood person, a story we can follow throughout the essay. Cudmore does this when she opens her essay with researcher Kaylee Byers crouching in a patch of urban blackberries, checking rat traps.

Even if the character is a nonhuman, such as an island or a dolphin or a loch, leading with the character allows the reader to identify with a story that promises an arc, a series of causes and effects, and a narrative through-line the reader can hold onto.

Consider the lead to Gawande's (2006) "The Score." In a fully developed scene with dialogue, he introduces two characters the reader will follow for the entire essay, anticipating the impact of this pregnancy on their lives

> At 5 a.m. on a cool Boston morning not long ago, Elizabeth Rourke—
> thick black-brown hair, pale Irish skin, and forty-one weeks pregnant—
> reached over and woke her husband, Chris.
>     "I'm having contractions," she said.
>     "Are you sure?" he asked.
>     "I'm sure."
>     She was a week past her due date, and the pain was deep and
> viselike, nothing like the occasional spasms she'd been feeling. It
> seemed to come out of her lower back and wrap around and seize her
> whole abdomen. The first spasm woke her out of a sound sleep. Then
> came a second. And a third.

In the opening paragraph, we meet Elizabeth and her husband, Chris. We know them on a first-name basis. It is the morning of the day they will meet their first child.

Because we see Elizabeth—her hair, her skin, her pain—we feel for her and empathize with her. If Gawande aims to change our minds about the rise in unnecessary C-sections, introducing us to this worried, expectant mother will aid his goal.

As an exercise, I ask students to select one or two characters that exist near or inside their subject and try using them as an introduction to their argument. Sometimes these try-its don't work, but sometimes they lead students in unexpected directions that shape an entire piece.

Caden, a tenth-grader, recently moved to our large urban school from a rural area of Appalachia. He wanted to write an argument that basketball was not just a sport in his hometown, but an obsession. After trying this exercise, he decided to open with the people who are central to this premise—the coach and the players:

> The Bobcats are running suicides in their gym during preseason
> conditioning. #23 Billy Lynch lags behind his teammates. He finishes
> last and is visibly winded.
>     Coach Hardy gets up in his face and cusses him out. The whole
> team has to run another suicide. This time everyone but the all-star
> Luke Rogers is struggling. He keeps a deliberate and swift pace.

> Coach Hardy flies into a sub-psychotic rage, screaming how he's "done everything he can to whip the sons a' bitches into shape." He grabs a basketball and flings it into the empty bleachers. The coach storms out of the gymnasium.

This tense and colorful scene pulls the reader into Caden's text. We are standing on the sidelines feeling sympathy for the players and anger toward the infantile coach. Now that Caden has established us in the world of Kentucky high school basketball, he can also lay the groundwork of his argument regarding the darker side of this moment, the obsession to win at all costs.

## Using Characters as Supporting Evidence

In many nonfiction essays, the writer chooses to have the argument play center stage, but supported by minor characters that act, react, support, or counterbalance the claim. Using characters as narrative evidence that supports either a claim or counterclaim is a writerly flourish students can learn and use.

In "The Art of Saving Relics," Sarah Everts (2017) describes how to conserve objects made of plastic that have started to decompose. In the essay, she uses a cast of female conservation scientists from the National Air and Space Museum, the National Museum of Denmark, and the Tate Museums in England. Through their voices and expertise, Everts documents ways to prevent relic degradation. These characters exist on the page as evidence, but with all the human characteristics of real people.

In "Rediscovering Central Asia," S. Frederick Starr (2009) uses a host of characters—intellectuals, scientists, mathematicians, linguists, poets, pharmacists, political scientists, chemists, and astronomers—to bolster his argument: that by looking backward toward central Asia's glorious "explosion of cultural energy" of the past, international leaders can imagine a better future for the region. Although these characters are not fully developed, fleshed-out, and in-action characters like we've seen in Flood's (2005) *Grant and Sherman*, they serve, like Gladwell's (2005) *Outliers*, as examples that support the argument under consideration.

Using characters in this way can be very helpful for students who are often required to write an informational or argumentative essay on a contemporary topic for their social studies or science classes. Most of these essays are fairly bland affairs with a lot of clunky paraphrasing. But when a student uses characters to illuminate a claim, the narratives lift the argument from bland nonfiction and add depth and flavor.

Elke, for example, wanted to write about immigration, and instead of moving directly into an expository treatment, she spent some time looking at characters. She writes:

> Immigration is a hot-button topic everywhere in the world. Sometimes immigrants are welcomed with open arms and sometimes they're rejected. To me, immigrants are friends and family, legal and illegal, with negative and positive stories. An immigrant is Anneke who is Dutch and came to the U.S. legally as an adult because of love. Roel is Dutch and came to the U.S. legally to follow his mother. Sonia is Chinese, came to the U.S. legally based on merit, and is now a U.S. citizen. Maris, from Costa Rica, came to the U.S. legally because of marriage and later ended the marriage with her destructive behavior. Angelo and Regina are illegal immigrants who are abusive to their daughter. Esperanza came to the U.S. as a child illegally and is successful in school. Does where someone comes from make them different or is everyone the same at the core?

Like Oscar in the earlier essay on immigration, this cast of characters feels real, authentic, and Elke uses them to her rhetorical advantage. First, she uses the real names of her family members: her grandmother Anneke, her father Roel, and her mother Sonia. She gives us tidbits about their lives—"with positive and negative stories"—and their reasons for migration—love, following family, by marriage, by merit, illegally. These characters not only provide a face and a life for the reader, but provide Elke an authentic ethos from which to argue the answer to her controlling question: Does where someone comes from make them different or is everyone the same at the core?

## Using a Character as an Example of Theme

Characters embedded in a piece of nonfiction also might represent the theme of the essay. In a *New York Times* feature, "The Woman Who Might Find Us Another Earth," Chris Jones (2016) writes about the necessity of space exploration, but he also introduces us to Sara Seager, an astrophysicist looking for planets that might sustain life. Between paragraphs dedicated to the scientific search for exoplanets, Jones follows Seager on her morning commute, fretting over a forgotten cell phone, then working in her office.

Even though the essay is focused on space exploration, Seager serves as a thematic symbol of all of us struggling to live on Earth, which is the heart of Jones' purpose. Jones weaves in the story of Seager's first husband's death at forty-seven from cancer, her reeling grief, and meeting her current husband Charles Darrow. Jones symbolically aligns the two searches in Seager's character—a grieving woman searching for love and a dedicated scientist searching for "a small light where there wasn't one before."

My student Alec decided to write about post-traumatic stress disorder in returning veterans, particularly because he didn't think enough was being done to provide the necessary medical and psychological support for them. This topic came directly from his life: his uncle Lars was a veteran of the Vietnam War and his cousin Stuart had joined the Army just two months after graduating high school.

I suggested he include these two characters in his argument. With their inclusion, Alec could build credibility for his argument, but also provide a face and life to the abstract definition of "veteran." By featuring Stuart who hadn't seen combat, and Uncle Lars who suffered from PTSD as a result of combat, Alec could engage the reader with two characters who embody the theme of sacrifice, patriotism, and service.

Alec writes: "Lars was a Recon Marine deployed twice in the Vietnam War. Though he now does well owning a successful law firm, and being grandfather to over 15 kids. His return from Vietnam was tumultuous. He has never talked about his experiences in Vietnam in any great detail, and to this day seems deeply emotionally scarred."

Alec and his whole family are concerned about Stuart's upcoming deployment to Afghanistan because of the mental and physical injuries he could sustain, but also because they understand the toll that combat takes on soldiers. Their worry underscores the theme of sacrifice that Alec hopes to stress in his argument.

Encouraging student writers to look for a character (or characters) that might serve as a symbol for theme is another way to clarify purpose in a living example. If the topic has come directly from their lives, they won't have a problem identifying a suitable character for this purpose. Alec was able to provide a character (Stuart) that exemplified the reasons young men seek military service, but by using Lars as a character, he was also able to symbolize the expensive cost of that service.

## Using a Character as a Subject

The New Yorker, Vanity Fair, Rolling Stone, and Harper's all carry some kind of profile feature that examines the lives of famous folk. These biographical profiles are, by definition, a piece of writing about a real person who becomes a fully developed character in the hands of a skilled writer. These profiles feature musicians, celebrities, athletes, actors, super models, and politicians, real people whose lives and accomplishments become the topic of the essay. Although on the surface these essays appear to be merely character profiles, the writer is also making an argument for something else. And this deeper theme is the reason we read in the first place, the human story—how did they live?

In Hanif Abdurraqib's (2017a) "The Night Prince Walked on Water," the homage doesn't just profile Prince, who had recently died, but makes an argument on the enduring quality of Prince's stardom. In the essay, Abdurraqib pays tribute to Prince's half-time Super Bowl XVI performance in a driving thunderstorm. "When we speak of Prince in Miami, at halftime of Super Bowl XVI, let us first speak of how nothing that fell from the sky appeared to touch him. How his hair stayed as perfect as it was upon his arrival, wrapped tight in a bandanna."

Alluding in the title to the Judeo-Christian story of Jesus walking on the Sea of Galilee, Abdurraqib argues that Prince is God, and therefore, not dead, moving this essay from a eulogistic profile to a much larger claim about the nature of Prince's stardom. "His career was that of endless arrivals and rearrivals, and so it makes sense, upon the news of his death, that he would once again return." (As I write this chapter, I discovered that Prince's estate is planning to release two albums of never-before-heard practice sessions. Two years after his death, just as Abdurraqib prophesied, Prince has returned.)

Professional biographers typically don't have an argument in mind, then choose a character to illuminate it; they have a hunch that a person is interesting or has done interesting things in interesting ways, then research to find their interpretative angle or purpose to tell that subject's life story. It's through the investigation that the profile emerges. So, when students elect to use a real person as the topic of a nonfiction essay, they do so at the intersection of argument, narrative, and information.

When Griffin decided to write about video games, he hadn't narrowed down the scope of his essay until another student suggested he write a profile of his favorite video game designer, Hido Kojima. As he brainstormed and researched the character that would eventually become the subject of his essay, he was struck with a theme that would resonate throughout the piece: "I think Kojima managed to fuse a game and art together almost perfectly."

At thirteen, Kojima lost his father and learned to deal with death early. After he had spent four years studying economics, he decided he wanted to write stories for the video game industry. Most of his friends and family discouraged him, but his mother stayed supportive of his dreams. As Griffin researched and investigated the life of Kojima, not only did facts emerge that helped him understand his subject, but Kojima's personality, a man who in the face of disappointment persisted in creating artful games, emerged.

When I show my students different ways nonfiction writers use characters to endow their nonfiction texts with narrative richness, the profile is one of the easiest forms to try on. Often the subject's life has followed a three-act structure, ripe for narrative plotting. The story arc of a profile, such as the rags-to-riches trope that almost all biopics follow, serves not as a recipe or a demand, but as an invitation for students to try out some of these moves in their own work.

## Following a Peripheral Character

F. Scott Fitzgerald's fictional character Nick Carraway serves as the classic example of a peripheral narrator that tells the story of Jay Gatsby in *The Great Gatsby*. This choice by Fitzgerald to filter Gatsby's story through Carraway's Midwestern lens is a narrative structure that is available to nonfiction writers as well. Using a peripheral character, readers follow the narrative guide to discover information or listen in on an argument.

In the opening paragraph of "The Lost Children of Tuam," a nonfiction essay about the Catholic Church's treatment of unwed Irish mothers and their illegitimate children, Dan Barry (2017) writes, "Behold a child. A slight girl all of 6, she leaves the modest family farm, where the father minds the livestock and the mother keeps a painful secret, and walks out to the main road. Off she goes to primary school, off to the Sisters of Mercy."

The child, we later find out, is Catherine Corless, not a lost child of Tuam, but the woman who, after years of research, uncovers the truth about the "home babies" of St. Mary's Mother and Baby Home. Corless, who lived in the nearby village of Tuam, went to school with many of these children, and their stories haunted her as she grew up. As an adult, she uncovered the truth about their lives. This makes her a perfect peripheral character through which Barry can reveal this horrifying chapter of Irish history.

Barry asks the reader to follow Corless, an amateur historian, in her pursuit of this question: Had Catholic nuns, working in service of the state, buried the bodies of hundreds of children in the septic system?

Many nonfiction writers use a character near the action of the subject to lead the reader along the path of discovery. After showing students this move, I ask them to scour their topics for possible "tour guides" that could serve to deliver the purpose of the essay from an oblique stance. Who might be in a position to tell the story better than the subjects themselves? What kind of tour guide would best reveal your argument? What kind of tour guide would best reveal the information you want to deliver?

When Regan discovered that her neighbor, Miss Betty, a ninety-three-year-old spitfire, was once a driver for various generals during World War II, she knew this was narrative gold. She was interested in writing an essay about the changing roles of women in society. However, after interviewing her neighbor several times, Regan decided not to write about Miss Betty in a straight biographical account of her life, but through a friendship Miss Betty developed with Regan's mom.

Through this arrangement, Regan felt like she could bring out information about the nature of women's roles in society, both from Miss Betty, who had remained unmarried and childless, and her own mother, who had married and had a family, but who was also a successful interior designer. The text went from being a flat, straightforward examination of women's changing roles, to an engaging essay about two women who exemplified Regan's argument.

## Ending with a Character

Another narrative flourish students can experiment with is ending an essay with a character-rich story that also bears witness to the essay's purpose. This is especially effective in speeches, such as Senator Barack Obama's 2008 speech on race delivered in Philadelphia, the text of which was subsequently published in *The New York Times*. At the beginning of the speech, he uses his own story—"the son of a black man from Kenya and white woman from Kansas"—as a means to build credibility and establish the parameters of his argument. But by the end of the speech, he doesn't return to his own story; he offers a different story about a young white campaign worker named Ashley and an older black man who had come to a community meeting. Obama relates that during the meeting, Ashley asked everyone to explain why they had joined the campaign:

> And finally they come to this elderly black man who's been sitting there quietly the entire time. And Ashley asks him why he's there. And he does not bring up a specific issue. He does not say health care or the economy. He does not say education or the war. He does not say that

he was there because of Barack Obama. He simply says to everyone in the room, "I am here because of Ashley."

"I'm here because of Ashley." By itself, that single moment of recognition between that young white girl and that old black man is not enough. It is not enough to give health care to the sick, or jobs to the jobless, or education to our children. But it's where we start.

The narrative moment Senator Obama used to end his speech is instructive, powerful, and persuasive, underscoring his message—that we are stronger when we work together. Ending with a character is a great way to show the reader a human example of the argument or information you've explained in the text.

In her middle school social studies class, Anna was introduced to the Sierra Leone Civil War and the 70,000 adults and children who were killed during the conflict. When she came to our high school and took an AP history class as a sophomore, she was still thinking about those children. She was especially interested in researching the children who had survived the war and many who now worked for UNICEF, specifically Mariatu Kamara, the author of *The Bite of the Mango*. After writing about the bitter civil war for power and diamonds, Anna chooses to end her essay with a poignant, character-driven moment:

Mariatu Kamara looks in the mirror, fixing her hair. She turns down a narrow hallway, out of the bathroom, and positions herself on the far right of the stage. The audience murmurs as they catch sight of her wearing a striped black suit, complete with glasses. Mariatu rubs her amputated arms together nervously.

When I asked Anna how she crafted this scene, she said she had watched a video of Kamara on YouTube, then just described it as narratively as possible. "I tried to paint a picture of what was probably going on in her mind in that moment," said Anna. She takes some creative literary license with the moment Kamara looks in the mirror, but it's that moment when the reader sees the subject—nervous, yet confident, an overcomer who is about to speak on the atrocities she has witnessed. She feels fully human in that moment, and we are engaged and convinced of the authenticity of this essay's information.

# REVEALING CHARACTERS IN NONFICTION

## Crafting Physical Descriptions

First, students must determine *how* a character will be used in their essay. Then, students must figure out how to physically depict that character to engage an audience.

In *The Immortal Life of Henrietta Lacks*, Rebecca Skloot (2010) fastidiously describes Lack's body in great detail as her physical stamina withers. The description serves Skloot's argument, and it deserves a lot of space in the book. However, Christopher Bram (2016), in examining how historian David McCullough manages to handle the hundreds of characters in *The Great Bridge*, says, "McCullough tells us just enough about each to make them distinct" (25).

Whether the writer takes a brief snapshot or draws a detailed portrait of a character, the job of the writer is to reveal them in human form. To illustrate this point in my classroom, I read an excerpt from Doris Kearns Goodwin's (2005) *Team of Rivals*, a book length argument about the unity and diversity within President Lincoln's cabinet. After I read, I ask: Is this excerpt fiction or nonfiction? Most say fiction because Goodwin writes like a novelist.

For example, she spends a good deal of time developing a physical description of Lincoln even though the book is an argument for his political prowess. Here is one of a dozen passages at the beginning of the book:

> [His] shock of black hair, brown furrowed face, and deep-set eyes made him look older than his fifty-one years. He was a familiar figure to almost everyone in Springfield, as was his singular way of walking, which gave the impression that his long, gaunt frame needed oiling. He plodded forward in an awkward manner, hands hanging at his sides or folded behind his back. (6)

In nonfiction, the writer must tweak the old fictional maxim of "show, don't tell" into "show *and* tell," using the show as a means of illustrating the subject and using the tell as a means of explaining him. We are not interested in getting a police report here; we are interested in the essence of the character as it relates to the purpose of our piece.

Telling us Lincoln was six feet, four inches tall is not as expressive as showing us his "long, gaunt frame needed oiling."

The best descriptions, of course, do two or three things at once. They show us the character, but they also reveal in what age or what time they lived. They give us a description of the character and also clue us in to some kind of tension skirting the scene. Or connect us to an abstract theme. Or foreshadow something on the horizon.

In Jon Krakauer's (1996) *Into the Wild*, the nonfiction account of Chris McCandless, who attempted to survive alone in the Alaskan wilderness, the physical descriptions underscore Krakauer's point: that McCandless, who called himself Alex Supertramp, was ill equipped for his off-the-grid aspirations

These are not descriptions just for the sake of showing us the subject, but they tell us Krakauer's claim. "Alex's cheap leather hiking boots were neither waterproof or well insulated. His rifle was only. 22 calibers, a bore too small to rely on if he expected to kill animals like moose and caribou . . . he had no ax, no bug dope, no snowshoes, no compass" (5). Alex's hair color, height, and weight aren't important factors in this description because Krakauer is detailing what McCandless isn't, not what he is, which speaks to Krakauer's thesis of McCandless' ill preparedness.

Many students find a character profile sheet to be a helpful tool in visualizing characters. One such tool is the Main Character Checklist from Edward Allen's (1998) *The Hands-On Fiction Workbook*. The checklist is a profiling tool that asks a writer to consider his character's physical appearance, preferences and tastes, family and personal life, childhood, background, and personality.

From Allen's checklist, I've developed a similar tool for nonfiction characters that students can use to generate an awareness of the character-like qualities of their subjects as they answer all the questions in complete sentences referencing their subject (see Figure 3–1). Even if they might be tempted to write "nonapplicable" for some of the questions, I want them to imagine what the answers might be if their character (a distressed cow in a Nebraska feed lot, an assembly-line worker who just received news of a layoff, a celebratory mother of three who just finished her last round of chemo) filled out the questionnaire.

Somehow this activity—thinking of their character *as* a character—helps students' subjects come to life. From there, they can select the narrative details that support the characterization. Using this profile in any content area is a great activity for students to go beyond the rote characteristics of a cell or an isthmus. The subject matter takes on a living and breathing dimension that students will not soon forget.

## Character's Name

Full name at birth _____

What name does the character currently go by? _____

Who is the character named after? _____

Nickname(s) _____

Reason for the nickname(s) _____

_____

## Physical Attributes

Age _____ Hair color _____ Hairstyle _____ Eyes _____

Glasses or contacts? _____ Skin tone _____

Shape of face _____ Facial hair/makeup _____

Weight _____ Height _____ Body type _____

Special physical characteristics _____

_____

Description of character's general health _____

_____

_____

Specific or potential health problems _____

_____

_____

What is the first thing someone notices about this character? _____

_____

## Preferences/Tastes

Favorite color _____ Favorite food _____

Favorite drinks _____ Favorite music _____

Favorite book _____ Favorite movie _____

Relaxation activity _____

Style of clothing _____

Shoe style _____ Jewelry _____

Lives in a _____

Lives with a _____

**Figure 3–1**–Main Character Profiling Tool

## Childhood

Father's occupation _____ Mother's occupation _____
Father's relationship with the character _____
Mother's relationship with the character _____
Income group _____ Social class _____
Siblings _____
_____
Names and ages of siblings _____
_____
_____
_____
Siblings' relationship with the character _____
_____
_____
Other significant family members living or dead _____
_____
_____
_____
Brief description of the character's childhood _____
_____
_____
_____

## Background and Personality

Religious upbringing _____
Present religious practice _____
Present educational status _____
Present career aspirations _____
What is this character most scared of? _____
What is this character's worst problem? _____
Special gifts or talents _____
Good traits _____
Does the character acknowledge these good traits? _____
Bad traits _____
Does the character admit these bad traits? _____
Character's life philosophy _____
How is this character changing? _____
Attitude toward money _____
Attitude toward politics _____
Attitude toward fame _____

(continues)

(continued)

Attitude toward love _____
Public figure character most admires _____
Character's most valued possession _____
Who are the character's friends? _____
_____
Description _____
Who most influenced this character's life? _____
Description _____
Who does this character trust the most? _____
Who does this character trust the least? _____
What is character's greatest regret? _____
What is character most proud of? _____
What doesn't this character understand? _____
What are the character's prejudices/biases? _____
Does the character admit these prejudices/biases? _____
What would this character write on own gravestone? _____

Adapted from Edward Allen's (1998) *The Hands-on Fiction Workbook,* and from lists used at the University of Central Oklahoma.

This tool can also be used as an organizer for research. If students are writing about Harlem Renaissance artist Selma Burke, using a profiling tool helps them "meet" her as a person. By filling out the profile, a student gets a sense of Burke as a real person, not merely as a writing topic. If a student is writing about a nonhuman character, like the asteroid belt, the profile tool may generate opportunities for personification that help a student see this abstract topic as a character. If students are writing about an event, like the Watergate Scandal, encourage them to focus on one central character in the event, such as Robert Bork, as a narrative entry point and fill out the profile tool to understand that person, and his role in the scandal, in more depth.

## Crafting Dialogue

If a student plans to use characters to endow nonfiction texts with narrative richness, dialogue is an important tool to explore. Not just what characters say, but how they say it. Students who have interviewed subjects will be at an advantage, but students who have used secondary sources to gather information about their topic can find examples of actual dialogue as well.

Again, the guideline for using dialogue in nonfiction is the same as the guideline for using physical description: it needs to do more than one thing. Slapping in dialogue for the sake of dialogue alone does the essay a disservice. Dialogue should show us not only the character, but the claim or information at stake.

In "Living Will," an essay that argues against keeping terminally ill patients alive at an enormous cost, Danielle Ofri (2011) features Mr. Reston, an aging Florida carpenter and Korean War veteran, who is under her care. In a touching bedside moment, Ofri chooses to let the reader hear Reston speak about his wife:

> "She's busy with that volunteer work. She don't have time for me and all my pills," he said sadly. An uneasy silence settled in. I could see moisture accumulating at the edges of his soulful eyes. "We haven't shared a bed in fifteen years," he whispered. His voice was plaintive but resigned. "Why should I live this life? I can't walk, my wife don't speak to me, I can't do nothing. What's the point?" He fixed his mournful gaze upon me. "You tell me." (*Incidental Findings*, Beacon Press, 386. Danielle Ofri, physician and author of *What Patients Say, What Doctors Hear*. www.danielleofri.com).

No paraphrase or summary from Ofri's authorial perch could have rendered her claim better than by letting Reston speak. His unique language patterns, his questions, his attendant grief roll out in this resonant example of pathos and dialogue.

After Taleah interviewed her friend's grandmother who had been closely involved with the civil rights movement, she chose to blend elements of her subject's speech into her essay:

> One day, on her way home from working a shift at a Sears in Chicago, she was riding a city bus that went through Cicero, Illinois. As the bus drove into Cicero, the bus was stopped, and a full-fledged race riot erupted. "They were rocking the bus, people were bloody. It was just terrible. And there was another black man on the bus sitting in front of me, and all I saw were these white men who got on the bus, hit this man in the head and blood just shot up everywhere."

Notice how the authentic language of her subject brings this scene to life and makes history real. By allowing her character to speak, a student writer can accomplish several things: reveal the character and create a human connection to the idea at the heart of the argument. Listening to a real person talk in the dynamic language of experience will also influence any reader, reinforcing a writer's claim.

When looking for good character dialogue, encourage students to listen for examples of conversations, explanations, stories, or details that are unique and dynamic. Also listen for the manner in which a person talks and repetitions, analogies, or stories they tell. Listen for colloquialism or vernacular that will characterize a subject in an authentic, unvarnished way so the reader feels they know the character as a real person.

## Crafting Action

In fiction, characters act on their desires. What they want drives the plot. In an interview with *The Atlantic*, Margot Livesay (2004) said, "I'm always trying to put my characters in a situation where there will be something that they want to find. If the characters want something, then very often the reader wants something as well."

In "The Case for Leaving City Rats Alone," Becca Cudmore (2017) starts with the research assistant in action connected to a desire: she wants to collect evidence in V6A. But the rats are in action too. They want to create stable living environments. And the humans that surround the rats want something too: they want to eradicate rat-borne diseases. These actions set the tension for the substance of the essay.

In *Sister Bernadette's Barking Dog: The Quirky History and Lost Art of Diagramming Sentences*, Kitty Burns Florey (2006) executes three narrative moves at once in a single passage: description, dialogue, and action. This paragraph is a mini-manual on how to use a character to illuminate the main idea in a nonfiction text:

> I can still see her: A tiny nun with a sharp pink nose, confidently drawing a dead-straight horizontal line like a highway across the blackboard, flourishing her chalk in the air at the end of it, her veil flipping out behind her as she turned back to the class. "We begin," she said, "with a straight line." And then, in her firm and saintly script, she put words on the line, a noun and a verb—probably something like *dog barked*.

This physical description—"tiny nun," "sharp pink nose"—shows us the character, but by describing her in action, we see what she's about: drawing, flourishing, and speaking. We see her act and know who she is. She represents the kind of efficient and economical personage that embodies the pursuit—sentence diagramming—that Foley hopes to laud in her book.

When I ask students to think about a character in action, I'm asking them to select details that will develop their argument as they develop their character. The action of their character speaks to the action of the essay itself. Like dialogue and physical description, the actions should be selected to support the argument or the information being delivered.

Once students have researched, investigated, and discovered their characters, ask them to spend some time freewriting about their characters in action. Imagine a day in the life of an air traffic controller, an Atlantic mudskipper, or Mount Fuji. Ask students to craft a small, realistic moment of action between two characters. Based on their research and investigation, students could craft a moment of action that might find its way into their essay as a way to engage the reader.

When my student Amelia, a junior, chose to write an argument that challenged the negative perceptions of roller derby, she elected to put the reader in the intensity of a match by featuring her characters in action:

> Jackie Wilson has her toe stop on the jam line, her wall is solid at the front of the pack. As jammer, it's up to her to score the points her team needs to win. The whistle blows and the jam begins. It's the second quarter of the last qualifying bout of the Roller Derby World Cup in Manchester, UK, and the teams are very evenly matched. The scoreboard shows that it's going to be a close game, the crowd is tense with anticipation and nervous energy.

By choosing action as a narrative tool, Amelia does several things in this paragraph: she introduces a character, shows her in action, and creates a narrative tension that can course through the argument and keep the reader engaged.

# TENSION Propelling Readers Forward in Nonfiction

Stories set traps. The good kind. And there's nothing like losing an entire afternoon on the couch being caught in one. One theory about why we love stories is that we can experience dangerous circumstances—bank heists, infidelities, bullfighting—from a safe distance. In *How The Mind Works*, Steven Pinker (1997) suggests that "fictional narratives supply us with a mental catalogue of the fatal conundrums we might face someday and the outcomes of strategies we could deploy in them" (539). In our daily lives, we avoid conflict, navigating the day to minimize stress, not exacerbate it. But when we're looking for a good book or a binge-worthy Netflix series, we're looking for trouble.

Narrative conflict and the ratcheting tension of a plot create the trouble that keeps us in our seats. Several years ago, an all-caps memo written by screenwriter David Mamet (2010) circulated around the Internet. This memo—written to the writing staff of his CBS show *The Unit*—boils down the essential qualities of narrative tension into three questions Mamet says every scene needs to answer: Who wants what? What happens if they don't get it? Why now? These three questions establish the stakes and set the cause-and-effect course that keeps us watching.

In fiction, writers want readers asking, "What's going to happen next?" The goal is to keep readers *reading*. Nonfiction writers have the same goal, but the challenge is different. When writing nonfiction, we have the whole gamut of narrative techniques at our disposal, but we aren't just telling a story; we also have to deliver information or make an argument—or both. We need some method for creating the tension of a story, while carving out space for the information or claims of our nonfiction.

Luckily, most nonfiction topics have a natural tension. "In most public issues," says social scientist Richard Harwood (as quoted in the American Press Institute 2018), "there's a tension. There's a tension in schools between excellence and opportunity. There's a tension in communities between further growth and protecting the quality of life. Not that they're mutually exclusive. But there's a tension there." For example, in Tom Philpott's (2016) essay, "How Factory Farms Play Chicken with Antibiotics," Philpott pits poultry producers that use antibiotics against poultry producers, like Perdue Farms, that do not. Philpott's use of an X vs Y conflict gives his argument tension that aids engagement. Sometimes the tension in an article or essay is simply between ideas that are ultimately good or bad for the human race. Artificial intelligence: good or bad? Cloning: good or bad?

Students who understand the tension inherent in their topics are in a better position to employ the tools of narrative tension to engage their readers. They ask questions like these, first of mentor texts, and then of their own topics:

- What is at stake with this topic or issue?
- Who has the *most* at stake?
- Where is the tension in this topic or issue?
- Does the tension lie between two interpretations?
- Does the tension lie between the old and the new?
- Does the tension lie between two groups of people?
- Does the tension lie somewhere else?

After a sixteen-year-old student at a neighboring high school was injured by a self-inflicted gunshot wound—*in a classroom at school*—several students wanted to write about how useless metal detectors were. Everyone was talking about how this could have happened and what should be done. When Edward and I had a conference, we explored the tension inherent in the topic.

"When parents and the community hear about school shootings, they think that metal detectors are the answer," he said.

"And administrators feel like they have to please the parents?"

"Yes."

"But you don't think that's the answer?"

"They're useless," he said. "We really need more hall monitors and school counsel-ors." By identifying the tension in his argument between what parents and administrators thought versus the students' reality, Edward was in a better position to introduce a story, a character, or a scene that might exemplify the points he was trying to make.

Interested in the same subject, Sarah Grace saw a different tension. She wanted to pit the perceived threat of school violence against the numbers: Was there really enough of a threat in our school to warrant spending all that money on metal detectors, or was the school violence trend just a lot of hype based on a few high-profile shootings? Sarah Grace could exploit this clear tension to serve her nonfiction aims through a narrative arrangement.

When students examine two sides of an issue, encourage them to think about how to use the inherent tension in any controversial topic as a narrative technique to keep the reader reading. If a student can establish a conflict between Group A and Group B from the beginning of a nonfiction essay, the drama between the two opposing groups naturally serves the engagement.

# TOOLS FOR CREATING TENSION IN INFORMATION AND ARGUMENT

When we think about creating tension in an article or an essay, essentially we are asking, "What can I do to keep the reader with me?" or "How can I keep the reader reading?" After all, if the goal is to inform readers or to change their minds, the writer and the reader must be on the same path together.

Unfortunately, inserting tension into a text is not something students can learn to do with a few simple exercises or by employing a couple of tried-and-true techniques. Even for professional writers, creating tension and building anticipation is incredibly hard. That's because no single essay works exactly like any other essay written before it. Each new piece of writing is a unique problem to solve. And how writers solve these crafty problems is a somewhat mysterious process happening blindly between instinct and the gut. Ask a writer how they create tension in a text, and they may not be able to answer you. Most don't think about creating tension in their texts in a conscious, delib-erate way; keeping the reader reading is just presumed in all they do. Creating tension is writing.

Another challenge is that how a writer decides to create tension in a piece almost always impacts the structure of the writing, at least to some degree. Structure is the subject of the next chapter, but separating tension from structure into chapters—or in my teaching—is problematic because which comes first is a bit of a chicken-and-egg mystery. The decision-making process is dynamic, and it's different every time.

So what's a well-meaning teacher to do? First, I teach my students to recognize tension in mentor texts and see the role it plays in pulling readers forward into and across a work. We study it, we name it, and students begin to understand how much tension matters.

And then they must practice. Once they have researched, gathered information, and found human stories connected to that information, then tension building is really a content decision—a "which way to go" decision students will need to practice many times over to develop expertise.

The tools I detail in the following sections are not meant to be a definitive list of tension-building techniques. Instead, my hope is that by pointing out some common ways nonfiction writers build tension in texts, you will be able to see more of the architecture of tension in the texts you study with your students. Also, learning to recognize the development of tension in nonfiction will give you a repertoire of techniques you can recommend to students when they're in the throes of figuring out, "What can I do to keep the reader turning the page?"

## A Powerful Opening Line

So much depends on a first line. When we peruse a library for something to read, we look at titles and authors, but it's the opening lines that usually determine whether we check a book out or put it back on the shelf. The same is true when we read from a morning news feed or skim a magazine. A headline might grab us, but if the first few lines don't hold onto us, we move on to something else.

In "Getting Started," an essay in the collection *Writers on Writing*, John Irving (2001) advises, "Whenever possible, tell the whole story of the novel in the first sentence" (101), and many writers of fiction seem to do just that. Consider the first sentence of Toni Morrison's (1997) *Paradise* ("They shoot the white girl first") or Colson Whitehead's (2016) *The Underground Railroad* ("The first time Caesar approached Cora about running north, she said no").

Some fiction opens with lines more at home in an argumentative essay. Consider Jane Austen's *Pride and Prejudice* ("It is a truth universally acknowledged, that a single man in possession of a good fortune, must be in want of a wife") or Charles Johnson's historical novel, *Middle Passage* ("Of all the things that drive men to sea, the most common disaster, I've come to learn, is women").

Good nonfiction texts are no different. Whether we're reading a blog post or a long-form essay, nonfiction writers establish stakes powerful enough to make us turn the page. In "Not So Silent Spring," an essay examining noise pollution, Dawn Stover (2009) begins, "A male European blackbird was terrorizing the neighborhood." Why terrorizing? And how terrorizing?

In "Graze Anatomy," an argument for sustainable beef production, Richard Manning (2010) opens with, "Will Winter and Todd Churchill have a plan." Anytime there's a plan in the opening sentence of a novel, that plan is bound to fail or at least be tested. By opening with two characters with a plan, Manning trades on that narrative trope for tension.

In "What's Wrong with Animal Rights?" Vicki Hearne (2004) begins, "Not all happy animals are alike" (324). By trading on a fictional allusion to Dostoevsky's opening line of *Anna Karenina*, Hearne inclines us toward narrative and compels us to ask the question, "Why aren't all happy animals alike?"

And straight from the latest eco-disaster blockbuster, David Wallace-Wells' (2017) essay "The Uninhabitable Earth" opens with "It is, I promise, worse than you think." This sentence is direct and ominous with a subject that begs the question, "*What* is worse than I think?"

In nonfiction, just as in fiction, a powerful opening line compels us to keep reading. As you collect these kinds of openers from different mentor texts, students will begin to see the power good opening sentences wield. Here are a few examples of powerful opening lines my students have used in their writing:

- In an essay about book banning, Autumn opens in a classroom scene. She decided to go with a short declarative portentous opener: "We were silent."
- In an essay about La Cave aux Moines for her French class, Taylor begins with "One step into the cave and the temperature had already dropped ten degrees."
- In an essay about the video game *Fate Grand Order*, Griffin begins with a sassy analytical tack: "What is trash? More importantly, what isn't trash?"
- In an essay about musical snobbery and the definition of punk rock, Kailie starts with this provocative stance: "I have a confession to make: I am a poser."

As they develop ideas for essays and articles, encourage students to keep a running list of possible great first lines. Sometimes the ideas for great openers come at the most unexpected times, like in a conversation with friends about the topic.

## A Character in a Tense Situation

One very common way to create tension in nonfiction is to start with a character in a tense situation, and have the resolution of that situation unfold intermittently across the work. Here's an example from the opening paragraph of Sarah Stillman's (2018) *New Yorker* article, "When Deportation Is a Death Sentence":

> On June 9, 2009, just after 2 a.m., Laura S. left the restaurant where she waitressed, in Pharr, Texas, and drove off in her white Chevy. She was in an unusually hopeful mood. Her twenty-third birthday was nine days away, and she and her nineteen-year-old cousin, Elizabeth, had been discussing party plans at the restaurant. They'd decided to have coolers of beer, a professional d.j., and dancing after Laura put her three sons to bed. Now they were heading home, and giving two of Laura's friends a ride, with a quick detour for hamburgers. Elizabeth said that, as they neared the highway, a cop flashed his lights at them. The officer, Nazario Solis III, claimed that Laura had been driving between lanes and asked to see her license and proof of insurance. Laura had neither. She'd lived in the United States undocumented her whole adult life.

The narrative tension Stillman positions at the beginning of her article comes to a resolution at the end as Laura's incinerated body is found in her hometown in Mexico, a grisly example that supports Stillman's argument: without a legislative solution, dreamers will be deported with often deadly results. The piece moves predictably back-and-forth between Laura's unfolding story and passages that provide information and build the argument. The writer sets a narrative hook at the beginning—sets a plot in motion, essentially—and then pulls the reader along the spine of that plot to the end.

Many students who have found characters connected to their topics will also have found compelling stories about those characters. For a story to anchor an entire piece in this way, however, it needs to be compelling *enough* to pull the reader along, wondering about its resolution.

Rachel's mother, Lisa, was born in Guyana, but immigrated to the United States when she was seventeen. When Rachel began working on an informational essay about immigration and naturalization, she knew her mother's story would help reveal the anxiety and frustration inherent in the process, as well as showcase the legal and technical difficulties of immigration. She decided to open her essay with a scene from her mother's childhood showing her anxious anticipation of the prospect of going to America:

"And it snows a lot there." The first girl scooted forward in her seat, eyes wide. "Apparently the snow can get up to 20 feet high."

Lisa raised her eyebrows, as she rubbed her sore knees. The nuns had made her kneel on bottle caps in the pews as a punishment for being late. "20 feet? Are you sure? That seems like a lot."

"It's true! One of my friends went once and said there was a blizzard and they couldn't even drive."

"Well, just as long as it's not as hot as it is here, I would love to go to America." Lisa began to imagine being in the United States, a place everyone talked about but that she'd only seen in pictures.

"Well, my mama told me it was super hard to go there, so I doubt any of us will ever get to see it in real life," her classmate said morosely.

"You don't know that," Lisa whispered under her breath as the teacher scolded them for talking.

The scene sets Lisa's story in motion and is a powerful opening for an essay detailing the hardships of immigration. It leaves the reader wanting to know: Will she make it? What happens next?

Here's some advice to help students consider whether they have a story strong enough to create tension across a piece:

- Ask students to look through their notes to see if there are any stories with enough detail to unfold over time, a story that has a beginning, middle, and end. Kernels and tidbits don't work that well; the writer needs to know enough to stretch a story out. If students find a story with potential but it doesn't have enough detail, encourage them to research and fill in the narrative holes.
- To evaluate the pull of a story, you might have students tell them to each other in partnerships or small groups. Encourage them to tell their stories in segments, stopping at critical moments to gauge the interest the story is

generating. Encourage listeners to ask questions that will help the writer know where the narrative is pulling them.

• If a student decides he wants to create tension by spreading a story across a piece of writing, he might try drafting the complete story on its own first, with as much narrative verve as he can muster, and then decide how to break it up across the work to create maximum tension.

## The Forward Motion of a Question

Another common, time-tested way to create tension in a nonfiction text is to set a question—or two or three or eight—as a hook at the beginning of the essay. Once a question is posed, the desire for an answer can create the necessary forward motion to move the reader to the end. And, of course, questions can also be strategically placed across an essay to create new tension along the way.

Jared Diamond (1997) won the Pulitzer Prize for nonfiction with his book *Guns, Germs, and Steel* and uses questions throughout the book as an invitation to the reader. "This book attempts to provide a short history of everybody for the last 13,000 years. The question motivating this book is: Why did history unfold differently on different continents?" (9).

In each chapter, Diamond poses a few central questions that puts himself and the reader on the same page, investigating, interpreting, thinking. In Chapter 6, for example, he examines the evolution of humans from hunter-gatherers to farmers: "Why did people adopt food production at all? Why did they do so around 8,500 BC in the Fertile Crescent? Why did they wait until 8,500 BC instead of becoming farmers around 18,500 or 28,500 BC?" (100).

Perhaps building tension with a question is so common because questions are often what lead writers to topics in the first place. The writer trusts that the questions they have will be compelling for the reader as well. My student, Holly, was drawn to write an essay about the growing trend of people living in tiny houses because she was initially baffled by why her dad had decided to build one.

She wrote in her writing notebook about the germ of this writing idea: "I have no idea why my dad decided to do this. He bought an unfinished tiny house from his 79-year-old friend and took it upon himself to finish it. There is one issue here—my dad has absolutely no experience building houses. Why would he want to do this in our backyard?"

Holly's experience had left her with lots of questions, and she used them to frame the essay, delivering them artfully in quick succession in her lead much like Diamond did: Why did my dad want to build a tiny house? Is it OK to take risks like this? What does it take to build a tiny house? How much will it cost? How long will it take for an average person to build a tiny house? Can a normal, inexperienced builder get the job done just as well?

By following her dad's story, she not only explores the tiny house trend, but is able to weave in information about construction, the environment, and the downturn in the economy that led many to divest themselves of possessions and build tinier homes.

Even if students don't end up using questions to create tension in their essays and articles, the process of *asking* questions about their topics is a good one. Thinking about the questions a topic suggests can help students realize what is at stake in an issue in ways they might not otherwise consider, and this is bound to make their writing stronger. As an exercise, you might invite students to pose questions about their topics as if they were preparing to interview themselves. "As you look at all this material, what are the questions that it raises?" If you plan to use this exercise a lot, you might even have students listen to a Terry Gross interview on *Fresh Air* to better imagine how to ask compelling questions of a person and a topic.

## Things Are Not as They Seem

Crime fiction writer Jim Thompson once said, "There are thirty-two ways to write a story, and I've used every one, but there is only one plot: things are not as they seem" (Polito 1996, xi). So, Mary and John get married, they're happy, always fulfill each other's needs, and balance their checkbook, but . . . wait, something is amiss. That's the point where the reader perks up and the story starts to get good. Is there any hope for Mary and John?

This same technique can be used to create tension in nonfiction, of course, as Paula Span (2019) does in a *New York Times* article about cognitive rehabilitation for dementia patients, "Dementia May Never Improve, but Many Patients Still Can Learn." Span's "things are not as they seem" arrives quickly, in the second sentence of the article:

> He was a retired factory worker, living with his wife outside a small town in Wales, in the United Kingdom. Once outgoing and sociable, engaged in local activities including a community choir, he'd been jolted by a diagnosis of early dementia. A few months later, at 70, he wouldn't leave the house alone, fearful that if he needed help, he couldn't manage

to use a cellphone to call his wife. He avoided household chores he'd previously undertaken, such as doing laundry. When his frustrated wife tried to show him how to use the washer, he couldn't remember her instructions.

The single word *once* does so much work in these opening sentences, cueing the reader that something has gone awry, and we find out immediately what it is, a dementia diagnosis. What we don't know, of course, is whether there is any hope that the retired factory worker might go back to living his sociable, engaged life. Spann goes on to detail how therapists devise individual strategies to help dementia patients deal with their everyday struggles. It's an informative piece, complete with facts and research citations and quotes from experts, and at the end it returns to the retired factory worker and shows how the program helped him regain some of the independence he had lost.

Generally, writers build the tension of "things are not as they seem" in one of two ways. They either contrast how something (or someone or someplace) used to be one way, but now it's different, as Span does, or they contrast how something (or someone or someplace) *seems* or *appears* to be one way, but can be seen or understood a whole *other* way. In a *New York Times* op-ed titled "Theodore Roosevelt Cared Deeply About the Sick. Who Knew?" Patricia O'Toole (2019) takes the second approach. In the second paragraph, she describes America's response to Roosevelt's death:

> Americans found it hard to believe that Roosevelt was dead, much less that he had died in bed. For as long as they could remember, he had lived at full tilt. He was the frontiersman who faced down a grizzly, the Rough Rider who fought the Spanish-American War, the presidential candidate who made a speech with a fresh bullet wound in his chest.

The op-ed goes on to show how this image of Roosevelt as a man who openly embraced strength—both personal and political—was in such contrast to his "exceptional sensitivity to the needs of the sick and others in the grip of circumstances beyond their control." It's a powerful juxtaposition of strength and vulnerability, and the piece circles back around to it as it closes, satisfying the tension as it reconciles the two sides of the man.

The rhetorical tension found between "then and now" or "you think this, but it's really like this" is actually fairly common in the topics students choose. Amelia, for example, wanted to write about roller derby because she felt the sport suffered from a negative, antiquated perception. She wrote: "When many people think of roller derby, the image that comes to mind is one of tattooed women in fishnets and heavy makeup elbowing each other in the face while a rowdy crowd of drunk men cheers them on. While this might have been an accurate representation of derby in the '80s, it does not reflect the sport as it is today."

Lots of topics have this sort of tension embedded in them; the key is to help students—through conferring and conversation—to see it when it's there and capitalize on its narrative potential if it serves their aims.

## The Clock Is Ticking

In fiction, the ticking clock is a technique that creates tension by setting up a disaster the protagonist attempts to avoid by accomplishing a goal. It's a "Flash, I love you, but we only have fourteen hours to save the Earth" tension that seeks to dismantle the bomb or slice an asteroid in half or drive a speeding bus through rush hour traffic.

All stories, even those that lack a commercially driven race-against-time plot device, have ticking clocks, and stories embedded in arguments and information are no different. Consider two articles highlighted in Chapter 3. In Atul Gawande's (2016) "The Score," the dramatic action starts on the morning of Elizabeth O'Rourke's delivery and ends when the baby is delivered. In Dan Barry's (2017) "The Lost Children of Tuam," the dramatic action starts when Catherine Corliss launches her investigation, and even as Barry roams backward and forward in time, there is a sense that the pressure of the clock is on Catherine to redeem herself from a childhood slight.

Sometimes the clock is more literally ticking. In *Astrophysics for People in a Hurry* (2017), Neil deGrasse Tyson introduces an actual clock. The creation of the universe is the end result of the dramatic action that starts with the big bang. In the first chapter, "The Greatest Story Ever Told," Tyson writes:

> In the beginning, nearly fourteen billion years ago, all the space and all the matter and all the energy of the known universe was contained in a volume less than one-trillionth the size of the period at the end of this sentence. (13)

After grounding us in time and place and the starting point of his action, he generates suspense and forward motion by interrupting the narrative to announce, "A trillionth of a second has passed since the beginning." After a few more astro details of the Earth's development, he drops in, "By now—one second of time has passed." And so on. Readers are drawn through the first chapter by Tyson's embedded narrative timepiece that ticks off the seconds of planetary existence.

The ticking clock works best with topics that have some element of action. A race, for example, is the perfect vehicle for this narrative technique. I suggested this technique to Walker, who opens his piece "Can Alice McArthur win the Poppy Mountain Motor Race?" at the beginning of the race. Throughout the narrative, Walker weaves in information about his grandmother and the female empowerment movement of the 1970s:

> Alice got into her car, gripping the wheel of her 1962 Chevrolet Corvette. The car was brand new, a trade in from her 1959 model. She was wearing her pedal pushers and wingtip glasses accented by a cheetah print jacket that was wrapped around her. This was her final run of the day, and she was still five seconds and twenty-three milliseconds short of the Fastest Time of the Day.
>
> Alice was racing in an event called autocross where the racers are competing against each other on a timed course.
>
> Alice felt queasy. Was that morning sickness or nerves? She sat quietly in the lot, waiting for the event coordinator to tell her the race is going to start soon. She heard tapping on the glass. It was the racing coordinator telling her to roll her window down.
>
> "It's time to go, lady," the event coordinator said in between puffs of his cigar.

In this excerpt, the ticking clock is a literal clock: Alice is racing against time. She wants to achieve the fastest time of the day and she's still five seconds off. The race itself serves to build narrative tension. Will Alice beat the clock?

Ticking clocks don't have to be actual clocks. When a character receives news that he's been diagnosed with cancer, the remaining time alive can serve as the narrative ticking clock. When a coach receives word he's going to be fired and tonight is his last game, that final event adds tension. What will he do?

Familiar with action-filled dramas they watch on TV and in movies, students may be excited to add a ticking clock to their nonfiction. But for this device to really work, the passing of time should be relevant to the topic in some way so that the clock's presence doesn't just seem gimmicky.

An easy way to help students understand the ticking clock technique is to look at several examples of mentor texts and talk about how the passing of time is critical to the meaning of the work. Ask of these texts, "Why does the exact timing of this *matter?*", and then nudge students to ask this same question of their own writing if they are considering the ticking clock as a way to create tension.

## Across Place and Time

A mother picking up her toddler from a Tulsa daycare notices steam escaping from a fissure in the sidewalk. A San Joaquin Valley farmer drives over one of his carrot fields. Everything is dying. A New York City police officer investigates an accident in a subway tunnel and discovers a shimmering ooze of hot lava bubbling from a newly formed sink hole.

A half dozen scenes of innocent citizens blithely going about their day while catastrophe looms in the background is a classic disaster movie opener. It's a trope that creates tension by showing the same thing happening in different places to regular folks. It's always a regular day just before the meteor strikes.

This kind of informational or argumentative "montage" can be used in nonfiction by asking the reader to pay attention to the same thing happening to different people across place and time. The tension lies in the connection as the reader wonders: Why is this happening in all these places? How are all these connected?

A recent article from *The New York Times* Science and Climate section creates this kind of tension in its lead. Hiroko Tabuchi's (2019) "A Trump County Confronts the Administration Amid a Rash of Child Cancers" begins with this powerful paragraph:

> The children fell ill, one by one, with cancers that few families in this suburban Indianapolis community had ever heard of. An avid swimmer struck down by glioblastoma, which grew a tumor in her brain. Four children with Ewing's sarcoma, a rare bone cancer. Fifteen children with acute lymphocytic leukemia, including three cases diagnosed in the past year.

Again, the tension exists in the connection *between* the places, people, and events. When students' research has led them to find a lot of characters or stories or even interesting facts exemplifying the same basic idea, then this kind of tension can work well.

In Chapter 3 you saw how my student Elke decided to follow several characters in her essay on immigration instead of just one, but it's worth returning to her lead again to see it anew and notice the tension she creates between her characters when she chooses to introduce her reader to them all at once:

> An immigrant is Anneke who is Dutch and came to the U.S. legally as an adult because of love. Roel is Dutch and came to the U.S. legally to follow his mother. Sonia is Chinese, came to the U.S. legally based on merit, and is now a U.S. citizen. Maris, from Costa Rica, came to the U.S. legally because of marriage and later ended the marriage with her destructive behavior. Angelo and Regina are illegal immigrants who are abusive to their daughter. Esperanza came to the U.S. as a child illegally and is successful in school.

In just a few sentences, by showing us everything from love to abusive behavior to success in school, Elke manages to capture a really significant idea: the immigration experience is not just one story—it is as diverse as all human experience.

## The Mystery of Foreshadowing

In fiction, writers often use foreshadowing to create suspense, especially in mysteries. They reveal information that hints at something, but they withhold the information that would explain what that something is. Foreshadowing is the fictional equivalent of leaving bread crumbs along the path of a narrative, a path the reader follows to solve the mystery of the plot.

Writers of nonfiction can use foreshadowing to great effect too. In *The New Yorker*, staff writer Elizabeth Kolbert (2009) published a riveting essay titled "The Sixth Extinction" that she would later publish as a book-length environmental cautionary tale. The opening paragraph employs a feast of sophisticated narrative techniques, including a deftly-executed bit of foreshadowing:

> The town of El Valle de Antón, in central Panama, sits in the middle of a volcanic crater formed about a million years ago. The crater is almost four miles across, but when the weather is clear you can see the jagged hills that surround the town, like the walls of a ruined tower.

El Valle has one main street, a police station, and an open-air market that offers, in addition to the usual hats and embroidery, what must be the world's largest selection of golden-frog figurines. There are golden frogs sitting on leaves and—more difficult to understand—golden frogs holding cell phones. There are golden frogs wearing frilly skirts, and golden frogs striking dance poses, and ashtrays featuring golden frogs smoking cigarettes through a holder, after the fashion of F.D.R. The golden frog, which is bright yellow with dark-brown splotches, is endemic to the area around El Valle. It is considered a lucky symbol in Panama—its image is often printed on lottery tickets—though it could just as easily serve as an emblem of disaster.

With the last sentence of this opening paragraph, Kolbert drops the ominous hint that the frogs that were once lucky are now calamitous. But *why?* the reader wonders. We learn in the next few paragraphs that the frogs around El Valle have been disappearing at alarming rates, and disappearance is always a suspenseful trope in fiction—the missing spouse, the missing jewels, the missing code. Kolbert, of course, knows what is killing the frogs, but she strings the reader along, withholding the key to the mystery. As she builds her argument, she drops more little bread crumbs along the way that hint at the frogs' demise: "Whatever was killing [the] frogs continued to move, like a wave, east across Panama."

Learning to hint at something without revealing it is the key to students using foreshadowing effectively, and the more examples they see of it in mentor texts, the more they'll understand how to employ it for their own purposes. For example, after my class studied Amy Barth's (2017) "The Fight over Fracking," Alec had a new vision for how to write his essay about the disappearance of general aviation airports and the impact of this on local economies. He noticed that not only does Barth humanize her topic with characters, she uses foreshadowing to great effect in her opening paragraph:

In 2005, Linda and David Headley purchased their dream home, a 115-acre ranch with hills, trees, and grassy farmland in Fayette County, Pennsylvania. A creek runs through their property, and a freshwater spring supplied them with water. It seemed like the perfect place to raise kids. But suddenly, in 2007, bulldozers began appearing on the Headleys' property.

In his original lead, Alec had basically stated the problem he was writing about in his essay right out of the gate:

> From 1976 to 1979, over 67,000 general aviation aircraft were manufactured and sold. Thirty years later, from 2006 to 2009, just over 11,000 were manufactured and sold . . . an 83.5% decrease. It's not just these years that experienced this. This is the result of a continuing downward trend in the industry that should be considered worrisome, by economists and pilots alike.

There's nothing wrong with this lead, but there's not a lot of tension in it. Taking his cues from Barth, Alec revised his essay to start with a character impacted by his topic, and he employed a bit of foreshadowing of his own to set his essay in motion:

> On June 2nd 1973, Jake Morton started work as a mechanic with a small company based in Jack Northrop Field in Hawthorne, California. Business was excellent. By 1978, he was making over $70K a year as manager. The shop serviced over 1,000 general aviation aircraft a year. He loved his job. The general aviation industry was booming—as a result, more and more aircraft needed work done. Overhead costs, such as liability insurance were very low. Everything was nearly perfect. Yet, by 1987, his company, his job, and so many other jobs like it, ceased to exist.

## Standing in the Shoes of a Character

By now it should be clear that when writers create tension in a piece of nonfiction, they most often tap into characters and stories connected to their topics. If the writer himself is a character, he usually writes with a first-person I, or if he's writing about someone else, as Alec did about Jake in the example above, he employs a third-person *he* or *she*. But there is a third way to write a character into a work of nonfiction, and it actually holds a lot of potential for creating an engaging tension that propels a reader forward.

In *A Story of Us*, a ten-volume history of the United States, Joy Hakim (2005) uses the second-person *you* off and on to lure the reader into the conflicts of history and the characters at the heart of those conflicts. With this stance, she asks readers to imagine themselves in the shoes of historical figures:

Imagine you're an Indian boy, not quite one year old. Your mother is carrying you to the fields. You are strapped to a board on her back. You've just left your home which is part of a 200-room apartment house built on a natural stone shelf on the side of a steep mountain. Don't look down; the canyon floor is 700 feet below.

Across a work, Hakim moves in and out of second person, mixing it with illustrations, artifacts, quotes, and primary source material. Each time she returns to second person, she positions the reader as a participant in the history she's writing about, and it's the powerful immediacy of that stance that creates tension and leaves the reader waiting to be a part of it all again.

In my experience, students love writing in second person for its novelty, and you can help them learn to use it more effectively by experimenting with it in writing exercises. Ask them to highlight points in their arguments or information where a reader might be moved by standing in the shoes of a character, imagining themselves immediately involved in the topic at hand. Then invite them to try writing passages to create that second-person intimacy.

# STRUCTURE Weaving Narrative, Argumentation, and Information into Seamless, Purposeful Writing

Writing is often compared to a puzzle. When I'm talking to students about discovering the shape of ideas, I often use this association. Certainly, the comparison has its merits. Both writing and puzzling depend on seeing detail and figuring out placement for that detail. "Where does this piece go in relation to that one?" both the writer and the puzzler ask. Ultimately, though, the metaphor fails because puzzles come in a box with a color picture. Like an old grist mill at the base of a mountain range with a crystal clear stream running by it.

With writing, there is no box, no precut pieces, and only the foggiest of pictures. You're cutting the pieces to make them fit a picture you're not even able to visualize yet. You might work for two weeks on something that looks like two knees propped up under a duvet before you recognize it's a mountain range. Once you have the mountains, then, is that really a grist mill or a solar windmill those hippies in the valley put up?

When I work a puzzle, I first search for all the straight edges that form the frame. But in writing, when you get the frame figured out, you realize some of the interior pieces are too big to fit inside. Do you expand the frame or trim up the pieces? Some are too small. Do you shrink the frame or expand the pieces? And when you think you're finished and you step back and look at your picture, there's often a gaping fissure running smack down the center.

My point: writing is hard.

And structure—how to marry the various expository parts together harmoniously and aesthetically—is one of the most challenging components of all. Student writers have the same struggle as professional writers with the perennial question: How does it all fit together?

In "The Essay in Dark Times," Jonathan Franzen (2018) cites several lessons on structure he learned from Henry Finder, his editor at *The New Yorker*: "One was *Every essay, even a think piece, tells a story.* The other was *There are only two ways to organize material: 'Like goes with like' and 'This followed that.'*"

When I read Finder's advice, I felt a hundred lesson plans disintegrate in my mental filing cabinet. What if structure really boiled down to that? Tell a story, put like with like, make sure this follows that. It sounds so easy. Until you go to do it.

John McPhee (2013), arguably one of the greatest essayists of the twentieth century, describes how he once fought for two weeks the "fear and panic" of having no idea how to begin a *New Yorker* essay. The topic was the Pine Barrens of southern New Jersey, and here's how McPhee describes this struggle from early in his career:

> I had done all the research I was going to do—had interviewed woodlanders, fire watchers, forest rangers, botanists, cranberry growers, blueberry pickers, keepers of a general store. I had read all the books I was going to read, and scientific papers, and a doctoral dissertation. I had assembled enough material to fill a silo, and now I had no idea what to do with it. The piece would ultimately consist of some five thousand sentences, but for those two weeks I couldn't write even one. If I was blocked by fear, I was also stymied by inexperience. I had never tried to put so many different components—characters, description, dialogue, narrative, set pieces, humor, history, science, and so forth—into a single package.

This is what we ask students to do. Read all the books. Interview all the sources. Assemble the components into a single package. McPhee was a professional writer, yet he says putting it all together drove him to "near tears in a catatonic swivet." I had to look up *swivet* (a state of extreme agitation) but now can think of no better phrase ever written to describe both the paralysis and anxiety of the predrafting state.

Knowing the challenge that even experienced writers face when it comes to structure, we might wonder if we should offer our students—who may be inexperienced writers—more support, more forms. I don't think so. When we sail in with hamburgers, keyholes, and hourglasses, we cut students out of all the decisions, the measuring and cutting, that makes writing meaningful. You might be thinking, "But my students don't know where to start and I'm just helping them avoid frustration." My answer is: *no one* knows where to start, and writing *is* frustration. There are no shortcuts. Students simply need to practice this decision-making over and over to get a feel for the complimentary zigzag moves writers make to structure a text.

However, just because shaping a text is a challenge doesn't mean we can't teach students things about structure that will help them get better at managing it. I've found there are two main ways to do this. The first is to study mentor texts. When students ask themselves, "How will I best deliver this idea to the reader?" it helps for them to have familiarity with a dozen or so shapes they've seen other writers use to do the same. Examining mentor texts gives student writers an awareness of the possibilities of expository architecture. The second way to help students grow is to give them time and support as they practice, practice, practice. The exercises and information in this chapter will help you with both.

# EXAMINING STRUCTURE IN MENTOR TEXTS

In English classes, we spend a lot of time determining *what* writers say, but unfortunately, much less time examining *how* they say it. When students read texts with an eye toward how the essay is built, they begin to see the importance of how arrangement contributes to the meaning. How does like link up with like? Why does this follow that?

Reading to exhume an essay's internal structure takes some practice. The goal of this kind of work is to help students analyze how professional writers put their ideas together and then absorb some of those professional techniques. Consider this a menu of options for mentor text study you might explore off and on across a year as students write different essays. Build student understandings over time as they gain confidence to try some of these structures. There is certainly no need to do them all before students try their hands at drafting their own nonfiction.

## Questioning

As they read, it's important for students to get in the habit of asking not what, what, what, but why and how. Why did the author make these choices and not those? How did the author settle on this framework and not another? I want students to see every piece of writing as an artifact of someone's decision-making.

To start this process, I hand students a copy of an essay and some highlighters, and I instruct them to get in there and root around. Dismember the sections, look for patterns and arrangements, figure out how the composition was composed. It's a very open-ended activity, but I do offer students some questions to guide them:

- Are there facts? Why does the writer use these facts?
- Is there a story? Why does the writer use this story?
- Are there connections between the facts and the story? How does the writer arrange that connection?
- Why does this section follow that section? How does the writer take the reader along?
- How does the writer use transitions to create cohesion? Why those transitions?
- How does the writer blend information and argument? Why does the writer use those techniques?
- How does the writer begin and end the essay? Why does this beginning or ending work or not work?
- How does the writer move between information and narrative? Why do you think they choose to move when they do?
- How does the writer carry the reader with them?

There are no definite answers to any of these questions. I often tell my students if we had the author sitting right here next to us, they might not know the answer to any of these questions either. But they are important questions to ask. They remind students that all writing is a series of choices, and those choices determine the effectiveness of the work.

We typically do this activity together first with a short essay—under 2,000 words—that has a clear structural frame. Michelle Nijhuis' (2012) *Scientific American* essay "Which Species Will Live?" is a good informational text for this purpose. Its thirty-two paragraphs are divided nicely into four subheaded sections. Or if it's argument we need to study, I might pull something like George F. Will's (2001) opinion piece, "Reality Television: Oxymoron," which holds all of Will's snarky delights in thirteen tight paragraphs divided into two short sections.

When selecting mentor texts for these activities, choose ones that have a clear arrangement, aided perhaps by subheadings, numbers, or clear sections. This external signposting will help students see the internal structure. Instead of seeing an essay as an impenetrable box, students start to see the units that make up the whole.

## Listing

To help students begin to see how a text is structured, I sometimes ask them to simply list all the different techniques they see the writer use to structure the essay. I encourage them to list techniques even if they might not know the correct terms for them. The key is not labeling correctly, but noticing how the writer is piecing together the different elements to create an effective whole. For example, when my students analyzed Barbara Hagerty's (2017) "When Your Child Is a Psychopath" by listing its elements, here are a few things they noted:

- She starts with a story about a little kid and her parents.
- She gives professional opinions or facts then follows it up with an anecdote.
- She shifts tone from personal to more clinical.
- She uses foreshadowing like in a fictional story.
- Her transitions are jarring but they work because she's trying to shock us.
- She uses single word sentences like "Silence." to emphasize the moment.
- She asks questions and then answers them several paragraphs later.
- She always moves in and out of a story with a bridge that reads like medical information.

After my students read Hagerty's essay and made their lists, I asked them to determine what percentage of the essay was devoted to narrative. They reported anywhere from 50 to 80 percent. Why the discrepancy? Each student had a different definition of narrative; some thought the anecdotes should count as fact, since she was using them as an example, and others thought the anecdotes should be counted as story within the story. Again, the point here is not precision; the point is to help students begin to sense the movement between the different kinds of elements in a text.

Just asking students if the author made the right decisions in structuring the essay is a vista opener for many students who think authors always make the right decisions. If the essay was written and published, the author must have gotten it right, they think, but by asking them if they would have made different choices about the arrangement, it allows them to entertain how different choices would have created a different kind of essay.

## Mapping

Although questioning helps students consider the decisions a writer has made and listing creates an inventory of sorts, mapping helps students begin to picture how the different elements in a text are working together as a framework. For this exercise, I first model mapping with the entire class on the board, using two simple essays, like "Hidden Forest" by Alessandra Potenza (2019) and "Fossil Hunter" by Mara Grunbaum (2019). Both of these texts are about science topics—Mount Lico and fossils—and they are both grounded with a character who is searching for something: Julian Bayless, an ecologist who spots a hidden forest from satellite images of Mozambique, and Zeray Alemseged, a paleoanthropologist who is searching for bones from the dawn of humanity.

The model maps we create follow the two characters' searches, with detours for information on species development, land formation, DNA, and the fossil record. It's easy to see in a visual way how the authors have woven or blended their narrative tension when you chart it graphically (see Figure 5–1).

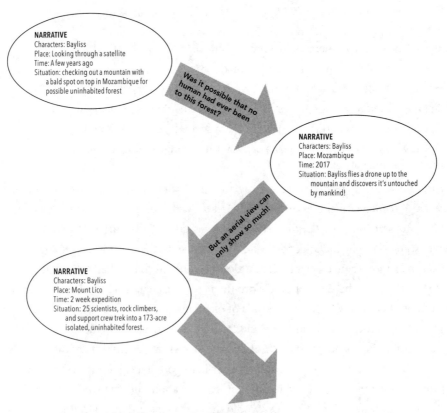

**Figure 5–1** An Example of Mapping a Structure

**INFORMATION**
There are few places like Mount Lico left on the Earth. Building cities, constructing roads, and farming have altered 75% of the Earth.

*But . . .*

**INFORMATION**
In 2015, Bayliss found Mount Lico. He also found different species of bats, snakes, chameleons, butterflies, and plants . . .

*Since then . . .*

**INFORMATION**
Over 1000 years ago, Mount Lico was formed. Hereditary information passed on to create separate species.

**INFORMATION**
Mount Lico is an unusual land formation called an "Inselberg," caused by
1. Granite Underground
2. Slow Erosion
3. Remaining Mountain

**NARRATIVE**
Characters: Bayliss and team of employers
Place: Mount Lico
Time: 45 minutes up the mountain
Situation: The team makes a 40-story climb up the mountain. They encounter big trees and eerie silence.

*During the next few weeks . . .*

**NARRATIVE**
Characters: Bayliss, biologist Ana Merida, and team
Place: Mount Lico
Time: a few weeks
Situation: They discover 200 plants, frogs, fish, mice, shrews, and butterflies.

*Surprise! Human pots were found!*

**INFORMATION**
"Most Lico provides a glimpse of what nature would look like without people's interference."

After we do this as a class, I invite students—usually working in pairs or small groups—to create a visual map of the structure they perceive in a longer, more complex essay. Recently, my students created maps of Virginia Hughes' (2013) "23 and You," an informational essay about the ethics of DNA. Hughes arranges "23 and You" around the central narrative of Cheryl Whittle, a middle-aged Virginian in search of her father's identity. As we are pushed forward by Cheryl's story, we learn about the history of genetic testing, the science of DNA, and the explosion of online sites like Ancestry.com and 23 and Me, but Hughes never lingers too long in either information or argument before she grounds us again in Cheryl's engaging narrative.

When my students drew maps of "23 and You," each group chose a different way to represent its structure (paths, Venn diagrams, charts). One group of students, for example, charted Hughes' movements by counting the number of paragraphs she devotes to narrative, information, and argument. She often blends all three into the same paragraph, but they were able to clearly map out the narrative sections and show how the chunks were predominately dedicated to one of the three text types. Amelia and Kennedy illustrated how Hughes' weaving of information and narrative actually mimics the design of a double helix (see Figure 5–2).

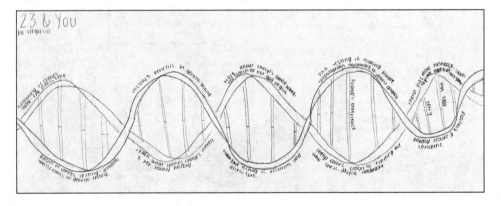

**Figure 5–2** Amelia and Kennedy's Map of "23 and You"

Mapping is challenging and may frustrate students, especially at first, but that's not a bad thing. Structure is sometimes inscrutable, even though you know it's there. In the foreword of *Making Shapely Fiction*, Jerome Stern (1991) quotes Henry James who said there wasn't "a passage of description that is not in its intention narrative, a passage of dialogue that is not in its nature descriptive, a touch of truth of any sort that does not partake of the nature of incident" (xiii). In other words, it's hard to label any slice of text as a singular text type if the writer has blended all three expertly. Asking students to map discrete structural parts of an essay, however, is a great first step in showing them how essays don't follow a distinct, prescribed form.

## Naming

When my students and I analyze an essay for structure, and especially when we map the structure, we often use visual metaphors to name the different options we see. We're not alone in this habit. Stern (1991) delineates fictional shapes such as "the onion," "the iceberg," "the journey," "a day in the life," and "a snapshot." In *Creative Nonfiction*, Tim Bascom (2013) uses metaphors such as "a narrative with a lift," "a whorl of reflection," "a view finder," and "dipping into the well" to describe common shapes in nonfiction.

The names my students and I give these structural options are not unique or original, but they aren't universally recognized among writers as "form" either. They are simply a way of visualizing how a specific structure arranges the different expository elements of an essay. Here are a few examples:

- *Circle*. Framing an essay as a full circle, where the reader ends up where they started in the essay, but are changed, having experienced a narrative or argument that has created a deeper or more significant experience for them, is a classic storytelling frame.
- *Nesting Dolls*. A story within a story. Think of an argument nested inside information nested inside a narrative.
- *Braid*. A framework where three strands—narration-information-argument— are woven over and over into a tight, aesthetically pleasing conclusion.
- *Pearl Necklace*. The argument or information serves as the thread that runs through and the narrative scenes are distinct pearls along that thread that sweeten or compliment the shape of the text.
- *Back-and-Forth*. A classic compare-and-contrast frame, the writer moves back and forth between two positions, two points in time or place, or two expository modes.

The key in this work with students is to let the names for different structural patterns evolve from what students see. Start with the mentor texts, in other words, and let them show you the patterns and suggest the visual metaphors that capture them. And it's fine to use your own language to name them. For example, some of my students like to refer to arguments that begin and end in narrative as "bookends": the story creates a bookend for the argument in the center of the text. Your only goal is for students to have language to talk about structure and think about structure as they make decisions in their own drafts.

# Leading

In Chapter 4, you saw how much work the lead of an essay does to create tension and make the reader want to keep reading. The lead also often determines the framing of the whole piece as it sets everything in motion, so it's an important structural consideration. Studying the opening sequences of mentor texts can help students build a repertoire of ways to get started.

For this exercise, I put students in small groups and give each group an anthology of quality nonfiction essays. You could also do this as a whole class with the same book projected for everyone to see. I ask students to study the table of contents first just to get a sense of the range of writing in the anthology. This gets them thinking about titles in different ways too. Then, I ask them to read just the opening paragraph(s) of different essays and make a list of the different ways writers lead readers into a piece. From this, we create a rich menu of lead possibilities students can refer to when they move to their own drafts. I sometimes encourage them to try on several different introductory possibilities when they begin making decisions about how they will structure their writing.

The tables of contents in The Best American series—Essays, Science and Nature Writing, Travel Writing, Sports Writing—offer a buffet of structural options. For example, of the twenty-four essays in *The Best American Science and Nature Writing 2017* (Folger 2017), ten begin in the middle of a narrative scene, six begin with descriptive exposition, four with a personal observation using the pronoun *I*, three with a simple declarative sentence from third person, one addressing the reader as *you*, and one with dialogue spoken by a character.

This exercise again confirms that there's no right way or wrong way to start an essay. I tell students: think of the material you have researched, think of your point, think of your reader. Now what's the best way to get their attention, state your claim, and create some tension to keep them reading?

# Transitioning

In an undergraduate writing class, my teacher Wendell Berry once said to me during a conference, "These two sentences wouldn't shake hands if they met each other on the street." In other words, why did I put these two sentences together when they have no logical connection?

Learning how to transition between sentences, paragraphs, and sections is an exercise in logic. What is my point in paragraph one? Then what is my next point, and how do they connect and naturally lead to each other? What do I want my audience to know here? What about here? Have I given them enough information to keep them going along this path I've constructed? This part, the *logic* part of transitioning, can only be learned through practice and experience. But the *technique* of transitioning is something you can study in mentor texts.

Once students have listed the elements in an essay or made a map, ask them to go back and look very specifically at *how* the writer moves from one idea or element or kind of text to the next. What words do they use? As a reader, how do you know you've shifted from one segment to another? For example, dissecting an essay like Hughes' (2013) "23 and You" is a lesson plan in effective transitions. Despite its length, the reader is never confused in that essay, even though it zigzags all over the place: forward and backward in time, here's some research, there's some history, now we're back to story, oh, look, we're talking about ethical dilemmas now. But never in the course of reading the essay does the reader feel whiplashed or confused.

A study of transitions will help students see the kinds of words that do important work: words based in time, such as *first, second, then, before, afterward, while,* and *immediately,* and words that show contrast, comparison, emphasis, or clarity, such as *however, in addition, for example,* or *most importantly.*

Another kind of movement you will almost certainly find in mentor texts are word or image "bridges" that carry the reader from one paragraph to the next. For example, Sarah Stewart (2014) uses a bridge from paragraph ten to paragraph eleven in her essay, "O-Rings." The last sentence of paragraph ten reads, "The O-rings, the flexing gaskets that acted to seal the fuel inside the canisters, turned brittle and cracked in the extreme cold." Then the first sentence of paragraph eleven begins, "As a space scientist, I know something about O-rings," creating a word bridge—and an idea bridge as well—that also reflects the title of the essay.

Headings, especially in feature articles, are another kind of transition that mark the movement through a piece, as are lacunas. A lacuna is created either with white space or a symbol like asterisks placed between paragraphs, and it moves the reader forward without the need for transitional phrases or clauses or headings.

The goal of focusing on transitions in mentor texts is to help students build a repertoire of moves they know and can use to help readers keep up. In the initial drafting stages, encourage students to be explicit about their transitions, especially when rendering the narrative components of their texts. They may end up taking them out as word bridges sometimes seem clunky and unnecessary in final drafts, but including them in a first draft helps students keep a check on how the ideas and elements flow together.

## Assembling

William S. Burroughs famously used a method of composition he dubbed "the cut up method" to bypass the critic in his writer's brain and summon the coincidences of chance in his fictional creations. Burroughs took texts, written by himself or others, and cut them up. He then put the text back together randomly. There was a lot more to this experimental form of writing, which was also used by musicians like David Bowie and Kurt Cobain, but I have found the cut-up method is also a great way to help students understand the infrastructure of essays.

For this activity, I look for a short essay—under 1,000 words—that has a clear structural organization. Two recent favorites I used were Ed Yong's (2017) "Tiny Jumping Spiders Can See the Moon" in *The Atlantic* and Jennifer Rich's (2018) op-ed in *The Washington Post*, "A Second Grader Once Pointed a Gun at Me," which argues against teachers being armed with guns. I copy the essay, then I cut it up, either in chunks or paragraph by paragraph. I laminate the pieces and put them in a plastic baggie.

On the day of the activity, students pair up, and I hand them each a baggie. They dump the pieces of the essay onto a desk and try to reassemble it using the structural clues embedded in it. Because the paragraphs are not in logical or sequential order, students have to read differently, searching for patterns, transitions, juxtapositions of images, language. This forces them to recognize the essay's underwiring and look at how many choices the author must have made in cobbling it all together.

Once students have reassembled the paragraphs, I ask them to reflect on the process with questions like these:

- How is this essay built?
- What were some signposts that helped you reassemble the essay?
- What are two or three decisions the author must have made in the arrangement of this essay?
- What are two or three decisions you might have made differently?
- Are there different patterns (other than the one the author chose) that might also work effectively?

This activity and reflection help students see the clues in a text that connect like with like and show how this leads to that. And it shows them there's almost always more than one logical path the structure of a text might follow. Students can also use the activity to consider different structural possibilities in their own drafts. They can ask, "What are the 'pieces' of my draft? Could my 'pieces' go in another order that might work better?"

I also often share my own process of assembling with my students. When I work on a blog post and I feel like something is not working as efficiently as it might, I print the whole thing out, consider it in sections, and try to visualize a tighter, smarter arrangement. I'm simultaneously working with both the "chunks" and the whole post to see if the choices I've made create an efficient vehicle for my ideas.

Sometimes I structure a post two or three different ways and bring them in to show my students. Which do they like best? Why?

## Considering What's Not There

It may seem counterintuitive, but another way to help students understand structural decision-making is to have them consider all the material a writer chose not to include in an essay. When they think about how to organize all their notes and ideas and information, students need to know that deciding what to leave out is just as important as deciding what to include.

In his essay "The Art of Omission," John McPhee (2015) quotes Hemingway who describes his "Theory of Omission," from his 1932 nonfiction book *Death in the Afternoon*:

> If a writer of prose knows enough about what he is writing about he may omit things that he knows and the reader, if the writer is writing truly enough, will have a feeling of those things as strongly as though the writer had stated them. The dignity of movement of an iceberg is due to only one-eighth of it being above water.

In a 1966 interview with George Plimpton, Truman Capote endorses this theory, while reflecting on his nonfiction masterpiece, *In Cold Blood*:

> I suppose if I used just 20 percent of all the material I put together over those years of interviewing, I'd still have a book two thousand pages long! I'd say 80 percent of the research I did I have never used.

I sometimes like to challenge students to infer and identify all the material an author *didn't* use in a nonfiction text. It's like finding textual evidence for details that didn't make it into the final draft, but that the author must have known. Inferring what a writer left out is a great exercise to illuminate the power of writerly choice.

As we read, I ask students:

- What details made it into the final cut, and what was left out?
- Why do you think it was left out?
- What facts, what information, what narrative must have been known by the author but doesn't appear on the page?

My students tried this with Tom Philpott's (2016) essay "How Factory Farms Play Chicken with Antibiotics," about the use of antibiotics in the poultry industry. In its original form, published in *Mother Jones*, the essay is accompanied by ten pictures, four bold-faced blurbs, three infographics, and one video clip. There are fifty-four paragraphs and around 4,700 words.

Philpott's main character, Bruce Stewart-Brown, Perdue's vice president for food safety, serves as the narrator's guide for the whole essay. As the first-person narrator, Philpott starts us in scene: "The massive metal double doors open and I'm hit with a whoosh of warm air. Inside the hatchery, enormous racks are stacked floor to ceiling with brown eggs."

As students read the essay, I asked them to keep a running list of ideas, information, facts, figures, studies, research, and so on that the writer must have known but has clearly left out. As they collected textual evidence, they made guesses about why the author omitted certain material. They noticed Philpott omitted the USDA guidelines for poultry production, much of the history of poultry farming, and the relationship Philpott has with Stewart-Brown. We talked about why.

"He doesn't need it," Edward said. "He's paring it down to the essentials."

"The essentials of what? The story?" I ask.

"He doesn't need it for the story he's telling," he said. "He's only putting in stuff for his reasons."

"His reasons?"

"No, about organic chickens," he concluded. "How they're better for us."

Studying a mentor text to think about what's *not there* certainly reframes our typical work with texts, but it's one of the best ways to lead students to the important conclusion Edward discovered: everything in a text should support the author's purpose.

# PRACTICE, PRACTICE, PRACTICE

Learning to see structure in mentor texts is an important first step, but for students to become proficient at organizing a nonfiction essay, they must practice structuring their own ideas. Encourage students to consider the models of structure they've seen in mentor texts, not as rigid forms, but as a menu of choices that could be used as a starting place for improvisation. This can help them find their way when the catatonic swivet sets in.

What students mostly need to support their practice is time, so it's important not to crowd their time with too much teaching. Focus instead on offering students tools that will help them tackle the challenge of structure in different writing situations. And the beauty of good tools, of course, is that once students know how to use them, they get better at using them with practice. You can focus all your energy on how students are using them and the decisions students are making as writers. Here are three "power tools" you can offer students as they gain experience drafting.

## Know Your Through-Line

Students are knee deep in structuring their essays. Paragraphs and research details and story threads all swirling around in their heads. When they don't know how to proceed, it is helpful to have a tether of purpose—a through-line—to ground their structural decision-making.

In Hollywood, they call it a "logline," a single sentence that distills the entire movie down to its most essential dramatic points. In memoirs, memoirists refer to it as "the spine," the emotional line on which all scenes, summaries, and reflections must hang. In the classic *The Art of Dramatic Writing*, Lajos Egri (2004) posits the through-line as a premise that can be summed up in a single sentence. "Always go back to the premise. If a scene doesn't support the premise, cut it" (3).

In *Ted Talks: The Official TED Guide to Public Speaking*, Chris Anderson (2016) compares the through-line to a path the speaker and listener walk together. "It ensures that there are no impossible leaps, and that by the end of the talk, the speaker and the audience have arrived together at a satisfying destination" (33). The through-line is not your topic: it's the point you want to make.

To help students find their through-line, I ask them to sum up their expository goals in a single sentence that serves as a kind of grounding mechanism or litmus test for every detail in the essay. What is their point? What do they hope their reader knows or feels or thinks when they're finished reading the essay? The through-line forces both the TED speaker and the student writer to think about the absolutely essential thing they want their reader or listener to know. Even though these sentences rarely make it into their actual drafts, jotting down a through-line and having it in front of them helps students make crucial decisions when they're trying to decide what to put in and what to leave out.

Caden, who wrote about the danger of competitive sports in eastern Kentucky, was able to distill his claim into a simple thesis statement that never appears in the essay, but controls the whole text. He wrote: "Competition in high school sports may have a negative impact on communities because of the unrealistic pressures placed on student athletes."

When students question themselves "Should I zig or should I zag?", they learn to go back to their through-line and ask, "How does this help me make my point?" If an element doesn't support the point, it becomes part of that 80 percent that never sees the light of the page.

## Try Different Arrangements

To help students experiment with different ways of structuring nonfiction, I teach them a process I learned from John McPhee. The first step in the process is to get all your ideas in front of you. McPhee (2013) says, "The approach to structure in factual writing is like returning from a grocery store with materials you intend to cook for dinner. You set them out on the kitchen counter, and what's there is what you deal with, and all you deal with."

McPhee describes a process where he writes all the different material he has to work with—facts, anecdotes, quotes, characters, and so on—on three-by-five cards, and codes them with words representing a component of the story. He then lays the cards out on a sheet of plywood—or sets them out on the proverbial kitchen table—and plays with their arrangement.

I have my students replicate this process. After they collect their research, interviews, history, science, characters, and stories related to their topics, I ask them to write down each component on an index card (some prefer to use sticky notes) and assign the card a code word. The code words might be something simple like *Story* or *Research* or *Interview*. They might have eighteen research cards, eight interview cards, and twenty story cards. Or five story cards, fifteen research cards, and no interview cards. It's up to the student to determine what material they have to work with.

Then I ask students to spend some time moving these cards around into different permutations. Think of this as nonfiction storyboarding. The objective is to keep moving the elements around, as if you were making a collage, until something clicks, asking questions like these:

- Where is the best place to start this essay?
- Where's the best place to end it?
- What's the order of the information or the argument that comes in between?

I ask students to produce three different possible outlines from the different arrangements of the cards. One outline might show the essay leading with argument and embedding anecdotal, character-driven stories throughout, then ending with argument. Another outline may start in scene, weave information and argument throughout, and end back at the first scene, wrapping up the essay in a satisfactory, yet surprising way.

When Sarah wanted to write about how abstinence-only programs have zero impact on teen pregnancy, she did the research and interviewed counselors, teachers, students, plus she had a whole raft of notes on the history of abstinence-only programs, as well as cultural studies she wanted to reference. She boiled it all down to eight different components:

Student A (five cards)

Student B (three cards)

Teacher A (six cards)

Counselor A (two cards)

My Thoughts (eleven cards)

Study 1 (one card)

Study 2 (three cards)

Study 3 (four cards).

For example, Student A had five cards representing five different moments related to her life as a teen mom: her childhood, then adolescence, prepregnancy in high school, postpregnancy in high school, and one that Sarah noted as "thoughts," which were some quotes from an interview with the student. Of course, Sarah still has to connect the cards with conventional transitions and make her arrangement logical, but this process helps her visualize and move the elements around before committing anything to the page.

This nonfiction storyboarding occurs before any writing has taken place, when students only have the big ideas or big chunks to play around with. Like collaging, the pieces remain fluid until they are glued down in a final draft where students have crafted them into text and written in the connective tissue between them. The process helps students see the positives and negatives of different arrangements, and it's a tool for thinking about organization that they can apply to any piece of writing.

## Play Around with Time

This last tool supports students who will be using a single story (or possibly more than one) to anchor a piece of nonfiction as it unfolds across the text. In fiction, you can plot linearly through time or nonlinearly, but in nonfiction, the narrative plot must also share the page with information and argumentation. So it's trickier. Creating a vantage point from which the essay is written requires the writer to understand that there are two *nows*: the now of the narrative and the implied now of the argument or information.

Grounding the reader in time and place from the beginning of the essay allows the writer to move around freely in time and the reader will follow. In *Storycraft* (2011), Jack Hart writes that "no law says that you have to tell the story in precise chronological order. You can jump around the arc in any number of ways, using flashbacks and flashforwards" (35). Students can play around with time to add richness to their nonfiction, but they first need to have the actual chronology of events clear in their minds. If they choose to arrange—for the purposes of drama and causality— the events in different order, they still must know the real history of the events from beginning to end before they plot.

For example, if we return to Virginia Hughes' (2013) article on DNA testing "23 and You," we'll notice the actual chronology of Cheryl Whittle's story, which unfolds across the piece (see Figure 5–3).

| Year | Event # | Chronological Event |
|------|---------|---------------------|
| 1941 | 1 | Vivian Tipton, 16 (Cheryl's mother), marries Richard Thompson, 18. |
| 1949 | 2 | Richard dies. |
| 1950 | 3 | Vivian meets Joe Wilmoth. |
| 1951 | 4 | Vivian and Joe marry. |
| 1951 | 5 | Cheryl is born on Christmas Eve. |
| 1966 | 6 | Cheryl, 14, is pregnant and marries Dickie, 21. |
| 1980 | 7 | Vivian, 55, is diagnosed with breast cancer. |

**Figure 5–3** Cheryl Whittle's Chronology

| | | |
|---|---|---|
| 1983 | 8 | Vivian dies. |
| 1989 | 9 | Joe Wilmoth dies. |
| 2008 | 10 | Cheryl thinks a DNA test will give her clues about her daughter's death. |
| 2009 | 11 | Cheryl buys a 23 and Me DNA test. |
| 2010 | 12 | Cheryl buys a Family Tree DNA test. |
| 2012 | 13 | Cheryl buys an Ancestry.com DNA test. |
| 2013 | 14 | Cheryl meets Effie Jane, a woman who might be her sister. |

Notice the first chronological point in Cheryl's story occurs before she is born when her mother marries Richard Thompson, but it's not the first point we're given in the narrative. In Figure 5–4, examine how Hughes rearranges the chronology in her essay for maximum dramatic effect.

| Year | Event # | Dramatic Reveal of Events to the Reader |
|---|---|---|
| 2013 | 14 | Cheryl meets Effie Jane, a woman who might be her sister. |
| 2008 | 10 | Cheryl thinks a DNA test will give her clues about her daughter's death. |
| 1966 | 6 | Cheryl, 14, is pregnant and marries Dickie, 21. |
| 1989 | 9 | Joe Wilmoth dies. |
| 2009 | 11 | Cheryl buys a 23 & Me DNA test. |
| 1941 | 1 | Vivian Tipton, 16 (Cheryl's mother), marries Richard Thompson, 18. |
| 1949 | 2 | Richard dies. |
| 1950 | 3 | Vivian meets Joe Wilmoth. |
| 1951 | 4 | Vivian and Joe marry. |
| 1951 | 5 | Cheryl is born on Christmas Eve. |
| 1980 | 7 | Vivian, 55, is diagnosed with breast cancer. |
| 1983 | 8 | Vivian dies. |
| 2010 | 12 | Cheryl buys a Family Tree DNA test. |
| 2012 | 13 | Cheryl buys an Ancestry.com DNA test. |

**Figure 5–4** Virginia Hughes' Dramatic Structure

Hughes starts with a scene where Cheryl meets Effie Jane, who she suspects might be her sister, which is nearly fifty-plus years in the future from the first dot in the actual chronology of the story. The purpose of Hughes' choice is to hook us with the future revelation of Effie Jane's DNA test. Starting in the 1940s with Vivian's marriage to Richard doesn't pack the same narrative wallop. The marriage is a fact of the story, but not the inciting incident the essay needs.

When students choose to weave a narrative across their text, I teach them to first write out the chronology of events as they actually occurred. This chronology will serve as a roadmap if they choose to rearrange the chronology in the essay for purposes of drama and engagement. For example, when Walker wanted to write about Alice, his race-car-driving grandmother, he knew his grandmother's story began in 1938 when she was born in Idaho to her parents, Chester and Jane Rogers. In 1942, Chester abandoned the family. In 1945, Jane met a nice man named Bobby, and in 1947, Alice and her new family moved to California. This is the actual chronology of Alice's story, but it's not where Walker wants to start his essay.

Instead he starts in 1962. Alice is twenty-four, pregnant with her first child, and sitting at the starting line of the Poppy Mountain Motor Race. Does she win the race? We won't know until the end of the essay. That's the power of dramatic narrative arrangement.

Asking students to sketch out the narrative chronology they plan to weave into their nonfiction texts allows them to more readily manipulate those events for maximum narrative effect. In any given chronology, 80 percent of the events won't make it into the text. But the moments that illuminate the essay's purpose will deliver the narrative flavor and power readers seek.

# DETAILS
## Showing and Telling in Nonfiction

Explicit, clear details are the lifeblood of fiction. They convince us of a fictional world and are delivered precisely, economically. In the *Art of Fiction*, John Gardner (1983) calls them "proofs," evidences that establish a reality (124). It's the accumulated energy of details that creates the emotional and intellectual experience of reading. Details, it might be argued, are the reason seeing a movie based on a book you've read is so disappointing. You've already seen the story in your mind. Nothing else can compare.

In nonfiction, details deliver the same sensory invitation as in fiction, but they do an even larger job, connecting us concretely to the abstract argument or idea on the page. A detail is not just a detail, but an interpretation of the world. Details may seem like afterthoughts, flourishes attached to final drafts, but they're some of the most important tools at the writer's disposal. Details in nonfiction texts support the argument and reveal information in a sensory way that straight argumentation or declaration cannot.

As we listen to someone regale us with a story of a wild night on the town or some heroic good deed, the story's details authenticate the speaker's claims. If the night was truly wild, if the deed truly heroic, we listen for details as proof or call BS if the details don't add up. In this way, details press the rhetorical nerve of ethos. In fiction, one erroneous detail can break the spell of fictional magic. In nonfiction, when a detail doesn't wear the descriptive skin of reality, the writer's

In his book *Art of Description*, poet Mark Doty (2010) writes, "What descriptions—or good ones, anyway—actually describe then is consciousness, the mind playing over the world of matter, finding there a glass various and lustrous enough to reflect back the complexities of the self that's doing the looking" (33). When a student selects details to describe a summer camp, that selection says as much about her subjective experience of the camp as it does about the camp itself. Twenty salient details of the camp are at her disposal, but the eight she chooses capture not only the camp, but her interpretation of her experience at the camp. If she had a horrible time, the details she selects will be haunting—the dark cabins, the gruel-like food, the sadistic camp counselors. If she loved the camp, the details will be buoyant—the sunny meadows, the shimmering lake, walking down to Vespers with her best friend. The selection of details then reflects the describer and the described.

# THE POWER OF THE PARTICULAR DETAIL

Although students have almost certainly experienced the power of details as readers, they're not always adept at wielding that power in writing. During my teaching career, I've had dozens of students say some version of, "I want to keep it vague so that anyone can relate to it." But it's the concrete detail, not the vague abstraction, that cultivates relatability. We write "More details!" in the margins of their essays, and they patch on adjectives to their nouns that are no better for their colorful burdens. Can you see a frog any more clearly when I drop *big* and *green* in front of it? How big? Whopping? Towering? What kind of green? The emerald moss of a Kentucky spring or the dusty lime of a tobacco worm?

The detail that carries the most power is one that creates a sharp, unambiguous image in the reader's mind. Arthur Power (1949) cites in his memoir, *From the Old Waterford House*, a letter from James Joyce who writes, "For myself, I always write about Dublin, because if I can get to the heart of Dublin I can get to the heart of all the cities of the world. In the particular is contained the universal" (65). Getting to the heart of Dublin, or a high school basketball practice, or a roller derby game, then, is what we want students to do well. And to do that effectively, they must embrace the particular. Janet Burroway (2007) offers a three-point test for fictional details that serves just as well for writers of nonfiction. Details must be:

- concrete ("something that can be seen, heard, smelled, tasted, or touched")
- specific (they must feature "a degree of focus" and exactness)
- significant (the detail must "suggest an abstraction, generalization, or judgment") (25–26).

M.R. O'Conner's (2017) "The Strange and Gruesome Story of the Greenland Shark" does all three. In this science essay, O'Conner attempts to unravel why the Greenland shark lives so long. The first paragraph captures a picture of its subject:

> Lumpish, with stunted pectoral fins that they use for ponderously slow swimming in cold and dark Arctic waters, they have blunt snouts and gaping mouths that give them an unfortunate, dull-witted appearance. Many live with worm-like parasites that dangle repulsively from their corneas. They belong, appropriately enough, to the family *Squalidae*, and appear as willing to gorge on fresh halibut as on rotting polar bear carcasses.

The language O'Conner uses—*lumpish, stunted, ponderously slow, blunt*—physically describes the shark, but also hints that its lumbering, unhurried physiology may contribute, scientist believe, to its longevity. We get a sense of O'Conner's interpretative style as he explains that their "gaping mouths" make them look "unfortunate" and "dull-witted." O'Conner may have delighted in selecting these details for a nonscientific audience, imagining us recoiling from the image of parasites dangling "repulsively from their corneas." Well played, O'Conner. Those details took me right into the cold Arctic waters. I'm grossed out and intrigued.

In Gay Talese's (1996) opening sentence of his *Esquire* profile of Muhammed Ali titled "Ali in Havana," he describes the chaotic world of Havana that Ali, in retirement and suffering from the effects of Parkinson's, will soon visit. Grounding the reader in Havana first creates an impression that allows us to see Ali later in the essay even more clearly:

> It was a warm, breezy, palm-flapping winter evening in Havana, and the leading restaurants are crowded with tourists from Europe, Asia, and South America being serenaded by guitarists relentlessly singing *"Guan-tan-a-mera . . . guajira . . . Guan-tan-a-mera"*; and at the Café

Cantante there are clamorous salsa dancers, mambo kings, grunting, bare-chested male performers lifting tables with their teeth, and turbaned women swathed in hip-hugging skirts, blowing whistles while gyrating their glistening bodies into an erotic frenzy.

This single, long sentence shimmers with energy. It boasts twenty concrete nouns and twelve adjectives, and it uses the language of action—*flapping, singing, grunting, lifting, blowing, gyrating*—to create an atmosphere of the "erotic frenzy" on which he ends.

The details are sensual, concrete, and specific to the setting. Although the essay eventually focuses on moments in buses and hotel lobbies as a slow and shuffling Ali greets fans and reporters, this square one description gives the reader a long shot in vivid color, mirroring the former frenzy and flurry of The Greatest.

Talese's and O'Conner's styles are very different, but they serve to show the power of the particular—concrete, specific, significant details that pull a reader into a text. This is the writer's first job—to see his subject distinctly enough to describe it without sentimentality or prejudice. The next job, the main job, really, is to then *select* the details that support the purpose.

# THE POWER OF THE PURPOSEFUL DETAIL

To understand the power of selecting details that support the writer's purpose, let's consider a student example. During his senior year, John wanted to write about his sports hero, Boston Red Sox's David Ortiz. In a Google Sheet he used to track his sources, he lodged dozens of articles about Ortiz. He had tons of information to sift through.

During one of our conferences, I asked John about his purpose.

"I'm just going to write about his life," he said.

"OK, but what specifically about his life?"

John shrugged. "I guess, all of it."

At this point, I knew John was struggling to find an entry point into the warehouse of research he had amassed. As we discussed in the previous chapter, he needed a through-line he could lay down next to every bit of information, every interview, every detail, and ask: "Does this support the picture of Ortiz I want my audience to have?"

"What's the one thing your readers should know about him? What makes him memorable?"

"Well, he's a three-time World Series Champion."

"That's good. That's a starting place. How did he get there? What made him so great?"

"He came from nothing. He was really poor."

"Good. That's a big part of his story also." I thought for a moment. "Do you remember that article you read on Nick Saban?"

During his research on Ortiz, I had hyperlinked several articles and long-form essays to John's Google Sheet including a Warren St. John (2013) GQ piece on Alabama's coach Nick Saban. The essay was an analysis of Saban's coaching life, but its insight softened Saban as a man known for his stony composure and commitment to winning.

"Do you remember the big takeaway, the point the author was trying to make?" I asked.

"Yeah, Saban was never satisfied. He never relaxed and enjoyed anything," John said. "Which is why people think he's a maniac."

"Exactly. That was the writer's big message. He's telling us about Saban's life, his coaching career, but he's showing us something else: the human side of a man who seems like a robot."

Throughout the conference, I pressed John to think of a thematic premise that would serve as a through-line for all the research he had amassed. What was the big idea—in one sentence—he wanted to present to the reader? As we talked, John kept circling the point of Ortiz's childhood poverty. It struck John as the thing that made Ortiz really great. He wasn't typical. He had to overcome incredible odds.

John returned to class the next day with some freewriting about Ortiz. In that brainstorm, he wrote the sentences that would eventually become the opening lines of his essay: "For some people, baseball is a game or a lifestyle or a good time, but for him, it was a way out."

Once John decided to tell the story of Ortiz through a rags-to-riches narrative structure, he knew he needed a detail that would illustrate the great player's humble beginnings. In an interview with Ortiz he found online, John discovered a detail—a broomstick bat and a baby doll's head—that was concrete, specific, and significant enough to represent Ortiz's poverty. Here's the excerpt where John brings this detail to life:

As a kid, Ortiz didn't have a baseball or a bat. His solution? For the bat, use a broomstick. For the ball, use his sister's old doll. Take off the head, shave off the hair.

"It made for a perfect baseball," he later said. "You know how I got the idea? I read that Pedro did it. I stole that trick from him."

Because his makeshift ball wasn't completely round, it would dip and curve in the air.

"Listen, bro: If you can hit a baby doll head with a broomstick, you can hit an inside cutter," David Ortiz said. "You don't need a batting cage in the Dominican. You just have to love the game. And you need to be able to fight off your sister when she comes looking for her baby doll."

This incredible detail goes to the very essence of John's through-line: that Ortiz was great, not in spite of being poor, but likely because of it. Because he had to use primitive equipment, he learned to succeed in the worst circumstances, which fortified his skill and trained his eye to hit those inside cutters.

The great thing about this detail is its visual, auditory, and tactile properties. We've all cuddled baby dolls, we've all swept with a broom. Most likely the reader knows what the surface of a broom handle or a baby doll's head looks and feels like.

Because we know these items, we can imagine what the sound might be—a dull, hollow thwack of a handle to the plastic—as little David Ortiz sends the baby doll's head sailing. This detail works. The items are familiar, easily grasped both intellectually and emotionally and connected to John's premise.

As John's story illustrates, selecting details requires a student to first know the picture they're trying to paint before selecting the colors and shapes the reader will see. Is this a somber picture or a vibrant one? Should I choose muted colors and dulled shapes or vibrant colors and crisp straight edges? Student writers don't need detail upon detail. In fact, too many can be a barrier. The key is to think about how details will work in concert with the purpose, the theme, and all the other expository elements.

# TEACHING STUDENTS TO SELECT DETAILS

## Examining Details in Mentor Texts

Teaching students to notice the different jobs details do in a text—to narrate, to inform, or to lead the reader to conclusions—makes them aware of the power of details and develops their detail-writing abilities. When we examine the details in a mentor text, I like to use history or science texts so rife with colorful details they challenge students' preconceived notions of boring nonfiction. For example, Nicola Twilley's (2016) "The Billion Year Wave," a nonfiction text about the discovery of gravitational waves, is written in engaging, accessible language. Powerful details are a main ingredient of her style.

"So how does she use details?" I asked.

"She compares the cosmos to things we know," Regan said.

"Like what?"

Regan consulted her annotated copy of the essay. "Like when she talks about black holes that orbit each other, they're like children running in circles on a trampoline. They create waves that go to the edge."

"So she uses a simile as a kind of detail. Does she use details in other ways?"

Our conversation generated a half dozen ways Twilley uses details—to compare and contrast, to inform, to explore, to characterize, to explain, to classify—and all of the details are connected to her purpose: to explain how scientists are tracing gravitational waves from the beginning of the universe.

Even in a short text, writers make hundreds of choices, and their selections can serve as a master class for students poised to look closely. Encourage students to ask questions about why a writer might have chosen one detail over another. Twilley chose "water at a roiling boil" to reveal a detail about the nature of space and time a billion years ago. Why not water tumbling down a waterfall? Perhaps she needed a detail that showed time and space bubbling violently, swirling and expanding. The goal of conversations like this is not to come up with the right answer, but to help students think about selecting details as a process of decision making.

In "The Invisible Catastrophe," Nathaniel Rich's (2016) essay on methane gas leaks in southern California, he explains why he chooses specific details: "In order to translate findings to a public lacking a basic understanding of atmospheric chemistry, climatologists must resort to metaphor and allegory" (155).

He describes the Aliso Canyon gas field near Los Angeles as a "kind of a gas treasury" and later as "an overinflated balloon." The 115 wells in the canyon he describes as "long straws dipping into a vast subterranean sea of methane."

"So why are these metaphorical details effective?" I ask.

"Balloons and straws, everybody knows what they look like," says Kailie.

"Is there another detail that might have packed the same wallop?" I say. Asking students to consider other details Rich might have chosen reinforces the idea that professional writers have to tinker with details and their effectiveness. "Maybe an overinflated tire? Would that have been just as good?"

A tire is shaped like a donut, my students surmised, not like a balloon, which best describes a canyon space bulging with gas. In the last paragraph, Rich uses a list of details to both characterize the community most affected by the Aliso Canyon leak but also to underscore future effects of methane gas use:

> It's not like next year will be warmer because of the car trips that Porter Ranch residents make to their temporary rental homes, or the gas they use to cook dinner, or the energy required to heat their swimming pools. Next year won't be warmer because of the 200,000 airplanes passing through Van Nuys Airport. Next year won't even be warmer, necessarily, because of the roughly 140 billion cubic meters of natural gas that oil companies flare into the atmosphere. But next year will be warmer.

Why does Rich use these details—car trips, dinners, swimming pools, airplanes—to conclude an essay on methane leaks? He wants to direct the reader's attention to the daily life of the Porter Ranch residents, the average, workaday details that show the impact this invisible catastrophe will have on every family.

As you study mentor texts with your students, be sure to first identify the details throughout the text, and then connect them to the purpose at the center of it. Encourage your students to ask questions and consider alternatives as they learn to see the value of the intentionally chosen detail.

## Details of Character

In *Good Prose*, Tracy Kidder (2013) says readers aren't looking for characters to be merely described, but for their "essence" to be revealed in prose. "A character has a wart. You could describe it in detail, but the reader would probably see it more clearly if you described not the wart but how the character covers it when he's nervous" (31).

It's immaterial that a character has a wart unless that detail tells us something about the character that connects us with another element of the text—his insecurity or his anxiety. Do those details carry some weight with the argument or the information?

In Alice Walker's (1967) essay "The Civil Rights Movement: What Good Was It?" her description of her mother is central to her argument. Her mother, a maid, identified with the wealthy white characters in the soap operas she watched on her days off.

All these men and women were white and lived in houses with servants, long staircases that they floated down, patios where liquor was served four times a day to "relax" them. But my mother, with her swollen feet eased out of her shoes, her heavy body relaxed in our only comfortable chair, watched each movement of the smartly coiffed women, heard each word, pounced upon each innuendo and inflection, and for the duration of these "stories" she saw herself as one of them. She placed herself in every scene she saw, with her braided hair turned blonde, her two hundred pounds compressed into a sleek size seven dress, her rough dark skin smooth and white.

This exacting and unflinchingly rendered description shows us Walker's mother and exemplifies the central premise of her argument: "Like everyone else, in her daydreams at least, she thought she was free."

Character details are not the height, weight, and build you find in a police report. They are potent details that reveal the character or the event in an interpreted fashion, interpreted by the writer for the reader. A few clear details put the character, the reader, and the writer all on the same page.

In Taylor's argument for CPR that I shared in Chapter 1, she uses small details of the characters—women on the treadmill, bodybuilders, and the Y workers. She and her boyfriend Nathan are also characters. When selecting details for character, students should look at the role the character is going to play. Are they minor characters like the women on the treadmill or the bodybuilders at the squat rack? If so, use clear, concise details to merely identify them. But for the man having the heart attack, Taylor must not only characterize him as a person, she also establishes his struggle. We must see him through the details she chooses. If she wants him to serve as an example of someone who might have died if bystanders hadn't administered CPR, we must recognize and relate to him. Details do that work.

As they consider details of character, teach students to ask:

- Does this character serve as an example or merely as a narrative device to engage the reader?
- How does the character show up in the text, fully developed or merely as an anecdotal example?
- Does the central character change during the course of the text or remain the same? Do my details convey this?

## Details of Action

Just like character details, action details can direct the reader's eye and mind toward the central argument or information. If we return again to "How Factory Farms Play Chicken with Antibiotics," we see in the opening paragraph that Tom Philpott (2016) describes the action on the inside of a chicken hatchery, and at the same time, brings us to the subject under consideration. The reader walks into the hatchery through "massive metal double doors" where a "whoosh of warm air" hits our faces. We hear chirping and see "thousands of adorable yellow chicks" who are dropped on conveyor belts, "plopped" and "gently shaken" until they are "clean and fluffy," then "stacked into trucks for delivery to nearby farms, where they'll be raised as America's favorite meat."

This paragraph swells with action details, smacking us at the end with a one-syllable word that renders, literally, those fluffy chicks into wet slabs of meat. (My student's annotations: "this makes me sad," "gross, I'm a vegan now," "laying on the guilt . . . ouch," "#punchy," "nooooooo!!!!," and "from cute to gross in one paragraph.")

Philpott's description of the action in the hatchery serves his argument well. He shows us the process of chicken production as a way to put the reader in the middle of that jostling, chirping hatchery. From there, he can diverge into history, research, statistics, backstory, policy, or wherever because he's captured our attention with the details of action.

Alec wanted to explore the claim that the Korean War was the "forgotten war," often overshadowed by the more widely covered Vietnam War. To engage the reader in his informative text, Alec moved back and forth between information about the war, which he wrote in past tense, and action-packed scenes written in present tense as if they are happening as you read:

> The Marine lays out frozen branches and places his sleeping bag atop them. He looks toward this coming assault, and to the assured good night's rest. Of course, there can really be no such thing in war.
>
> Suddenly dancing, blistering lights tear through the dark sky. Illumination flares. Then there is an eerie quiet, a knowing and dreadful stillness. Every man gets to his feet, and readies his weapon. Then, as if emerging from the ground, hundreds and hundreds of silhouettes approach. Screaming. Charging. Firing.
>
> Rifles become clubs, fists become bloodied, bodies—rigid and still.

When selecting details of action, ask students to consider their purpose with questions like these:

- Will these details provide the reader with an intimate experience of the information I'm explaining or the argument I'm making?
- Will action details make the information or argument clearer, more personal for the reader?
- Instead of stating facts, could I use a small scene that shows these facts through active detail?

## Details of Place

In "Brooklyn the Unknowable," Phillip Lopate (2010) opens with alliteration, rhetorical cheekiness, and literary allusion: "I sing of Brooklyn, the fruited plain, cradle of literary genius and standup comedy, awash in history, relics from Indian mounds, Dutch farms, Revolutionary War battle, breweries and baseball" (115). In addition to this list of showing details, Lopate also uses the details of comparison: "Manhattan is the tower, Brooklyn the garden; Manhattan is Faustian will, Brooklyn, domestic life. Manhattan preens, disseminates opinion; Brooklyn is Uncle Vanya schlepping in the background to support his flamboyant relative" (115). Lopate's carefully selected details do so much more than just describe a place; they lead the reader toward his central argument.

Returning to Rich's (2016) "The Invisible Catastrophe," we find ourselves situated in Porter Ranch, California, with concrete, specific details:

> Beyond the Ralphs grocery store and the Walmart rose a neighborhood of jumbo beige homes with orange clay-tiled roofs and three-car garages. The lawns were tidily landscaped with hedges of lavender, succulents, cactuses, and kumquat trees. The neighborhood was a model of early-1980s California suburban design; until October it was best known for being the location where Steven Spielberg shot E.T.

During the course of the essay, as Rich describes the Aliso Canyon gas leak, we get a different picture, "the meandering streets were desolate, apart from the occasional unmarked white van." The American suburbia described in the lead contrasts sharply with the abandoned neighborhood after the leak. Rich's goal is not merely to describe the place, but to lead us to this realization: what was once movie-set perfection is now derelict.

When my student Sarah went to Budapest over Christmas break with her boy-friend's family, she was struck by the political similarities between Hungary and America. She told me, "Prime Minister Viktor Orban uses the same language President Trump does when he's talking about refugees on their southern border." Sarah wanted to write a comparative piece on the two leaders, using her own experience in Budapest as a starting point. In the opening paragraph, she beautifully situates us in the capital city:

> It's January in Budapest, and it's snowing. The buildings are intricate, carved with the soft ebb and flow of a woman's body. At night especially, when streets are decked out in Christmas lights and the Chain Bridge stretches over the Danube in a white glow, the city is lovely. There is a lot of wind—cold, unforgiving. It hits me hard across the cheek as I step off a tram in the heart of the city.

Notice all of Sarah's details are centered in the picturesque locale of Budapest. She personi-fies the city—curvy, lovely, but also cold and unforgiving. But the strength of her descrip-tion is in the particularity of her descriptions. It's not just any bridge or any river, but the Chain Bridge and the Danube. We see the details, carefully curated by Sarah's experience, and are engaged by this vista to hear what she has to say.

As with details that describe characters and action, encourage students to select details of place to bring the reader's eye toward the central argument or information. Remind them:

- The more specific and physical the detail, the more clearly the place will appear in the mind of the reader.
- Swap out common nouns for proper nouns. If we're in a grocery store, what kind? An urban Whole Foods or Mrs. Terry's rural Jot-Em-Down store? Sometimes it's OK to just use the word *grocery*, but there are world building benefits from the proper noun.
- Always ask: "What am I seeking to illustrate in the mind of the reader? How will this detail put them in this place while also interpreting the place in a certain way?"

## Details of Time

Time details are the markers a writer needs to help situate the reader in history. Specific dates, references to centuries, years, epochs, ages, and so on, or just simple temporal words like *once, now, someday,* and *long ago* keep the reader grounded in the chronology of the argument or information, especially when the writer needs to move about in time to make her case.

For example, in the essay "Trouble in Paradise," Diana Preston (2018) writes about the colonization of Australia. In the lead paragraph, Preston starts in the past, then moves further into the past to deliver a little backstory, and then flings the reader forward in the future, all within a single sentence. The reader is never confused because Preston's time details allow her to move around easily:

> On 4 January 1688, buccaneers aboard a worm-riddled English ship, the Cygnet, sailing south from the Spice Islands of Southeast Asia (now Maluku in Indonesia), spied a finger of land projecting into a sparkling blue sea. Avoiding tidepools and tidal races, they anchored in a wide bay now called King Sound, north-east of Broome in Western Australia, to rest themselves and to career and repair their ship. They had become the first Britons to reach the mainland of New Holland, as it was then known—it would be another 116 years till British naval explorer Matthew Flinders, who led the first circumnavigation of the island continent, renamed it "Australia."

If you break down Preston's first three sentences, you can see how the details of time keep us grounded in the chronology:

- In the first sentence, Preston establishes us on a ship in 1688, but gives us some footing in the present with a parenthetical "now Maluku in Indonesia."
- In the second sentence, the sailors are still anchored in 1688, in a wide bay, which Preston tells us is *now* "called King Sound," a detail that secures the reader both firmly in the past and the present.
- And in the third sentence, she uses the past perfect tense, "they *had become* the first Britons" to show an event that happened in the past before another event, "it would be another 116 years till," which was also completed in the past.

Throughout the essay, Preston continues to use then/now details to bring us to the subject under consideration: what was once known as New Holland is now Australia. These time details aid her purpose, to unpack and examine the colonization of Australia. Understanding how to work in narrative time is critical to Preston's opening paragraph, which gives us information from both the past and the present.

When Autumn wanted to write an argument about the use of racial slurs in popular rap music, she used the details of time to succinctly track its use through centuries of time:

> From there, it's important to think about the history of the word. The first derogatory usage of the word was recorded in 1775 towards Africans being shipped to the Americas as slaves. The word flourished in usage through 1865 when slavery was ended in the United States, and well into the 20th century, as we can see in famous works of literature such as *All the King's Men* by Robert Penn Warren, published in 1946 and *To Kill a Mockingbird* by Harper Lee, published in 1960. Ninety-nine years after slavery was ended, the Civil Rights act was passed in 1964 and banned all acts of segregation. But the use of the word persisted.

In this paragraph, Autumn's goal is to show the persistence of a racist term from its inception to present day. Her use of actual dates is appropriate, given that she's attempting to cover 250 years in a single paragraph. The dates are meant to show, not the history of the word as her topic sentence would suggest, but its persistence through time.

Using dates as time stamps in an essay helps the reader move through the text, but I also encourage students to use details of time that deliver descriptive qualities instead of actual months, days, and years. For example, in "The Strange and Gruesome Story of the Greenland Shark," O'Conner (2017) describes the inability of scientists to accurately judge the ages of Greenland sharks. Using actual dates is one way to deliver that information, but O'Conner writes, "There may be Greenland sharks alive today that were born before Christopher Columbus." Columbus's life (1451–1506) is a descriptive time stamp that gives us a sense of how old these sharks might be from a comparative point of view. This kind of time detail draws on a familiar chronology to illuminate an unfamiliar one.

Both argument and information exist in time, and students will need practice to learn how to use that element in their nonfiction. To build that awareness, you might study time details specifically in a few mentor texts, and then encourage students to ask questions like these of their own drafts:

- How important is time to the case I am making or to my purpose?
- What details of time do I need to help the reader understand my information or my argument?

- Do I need to move around in time in this piece? If so, how can I make that movement clear?

## Details as Examples

So far in this chapter, we've seen writers describe concrete and specific characters or places with concrete and specific details—a Greenland shark, a street in Havana, a southern California neighborhood, a man having a heart attack, Budapest. But what if a writer needs to describe something that is unseen, untouchable, unsmellable? How do you describe something abstract or conceptual—like love or loneliness or grief—with specific and concrete details?

When my students read Eula Biss' (2007) lyrical essay "The Pain Scale," they were overwhelmed by the details as the essay swirls and bends and circles back on a half dozen topics—Dante's "Inferno," mathematics, her father, Jesus, the Beaufort, Kelvin and Celsius scales. The essay, built along the structure of an actual Wong-Baker Pain scale, wrestles with the inadequacy of a scale to measure something so indefinable as pain. In an attempt to describe "the worst pain imaginable," Biss writes, "Stabbed in the eye with a spoon? Whipped with nettles? Buried under an avalanche of sharp rocks? Impaled with hundreds of nails? Dragged over gravel behind a fast truck? Skinned alive?"

Biss' details—posed as questions as well as descriptive possibilities for what a 10 on the pain scale means—connect us with her purpose: the struggle to classify pain. Essentially, the details are also metaphorical; they're examples of something *like* what she's trying to describe, though not the thing itself. This kind of metaphorical detail list is common when writers grapple to describe the indescribable. It's almost like writers layer in examples knowing that one of them is bound to pierce the reader's understanding. "Yes, that," the reader thinks.

In his lyrical essay "Joyous Voladoras," Brian Doyle (2004) attempts to capture both the sorrow and the delight of the human experience, and like Biss, he draws on metaphor and simile to do his descriptive work. First, he compares a hummingbird's heart to "a pencil eraser," then later to "an infant's fingernail." A whale's heart is "as big as a room," or "bigger than your car." By comparing the hearts of a tiny hummingbird and a gigantic whale, Doyle makes his point: all hearts, both large and small, both animal and human, are vibrant beating engines that feel both pain and joy. And the pain is unavoidable, Doyle argues.

The pain of living is part of the joy of living, and though a person can try to "brick up" their heart and pretend not to feel, Doyle reminds us of things that can bring down the seemingly impenetrable heart in an instant:

> A woman's second glance, a child's apple breath, the shatter of glass in the road, the words *I have something to tell you*, a cat with a broken spine dragging itself into the forest to die, the brush of your mother's papery ancient hand in the thicket of your hair, the memory of your father's voice early in the morning echoing from the kitchen where he is making pancakes for his children. (72)

These are not details that one could research or even observe. These are not details of place, or character, or time. They are the details of Doyle's rich imagination, his experience, his lyrical style. But they do their job, by making something abstract—like the churning heartache of living—concrete in the details of a glance, a breath, a glass, a broken spine, a voice, the smell of pancakes.

The power of the particular charges this final paragraph with poetic energy. The seven examples of heartbreaking human experience Doyle assembles are accessible, explicit, and precise. Through these distilled particulars, Doyle delivers the universal sentiment at the center of his text.

When student writers find themselves needing to describe the indescribable, encourage them to think metaphorically and use their notebooks to generate examples of things that are like what they're trying to describe. They can ask: "How is X like Y? How are the qualities of X represented also in Y?" If they generate a big, robust list of possibilities, they might find the one example they think is perfect on its own, or they might layer in multiple examples that capture different nuances of meaning, as Biss and Doyle did in these examples.

## Details of Information

Not all nonfiction writing need be luminously descriptive, but writing in the language of pictures registers information more swiftly and more soundly than writing that lacks figurative qualities.

Returning one more time to "The Invisible Catastrophe," we see that Rich (2017) uses comparative details to describe the scope of the Alios Canyon gas leak. He says the leak produced "the same amount of global warming as 1,735,404 cars," or the same amount as "the entire country of Lebanon." He writes that its four-month leak was "25 days longer than the BP oil spill in the Gulf of Mexico" (155). Delivering the information about the gas leak in abstract scientific terminology of parts per million would not have had the same visual and visceral impact as the comparisons he chooses.

Ophthalmic pathologist John Gamel (2009) describes the subject of his essay, "The Elegant Eyeball," with a flurry of sensual language:

> A panorama of crypts and valleys, diaphanous spokes, flecks and spots and strands that dance about with each twitch of the pupil. Dark irises tend toward a tight weave, while light irises fluff up like a shag rug. And then there's the all-important pupil—squeezed into a dot by morphine and bright light; enlarged by fear, darkness, sexual arousal, death."
> (2010, 38)

Figurative details used to clarify the abstract ideas of science and history are necessary and crucial to any nonfiction text. A just-right detail sticks with the reader in a way stacks of dry statistics or facts or definitions never can. Creating details that describe the subject under consideration invites the reader to linger and to truly come to know the information.

When one of my students wrote an informational text about anorexia, for example, she wanted to write it from her own experience, she didn't want it to be a personal narrative or a memoir. She wanted to raise awareness of the disease, not necessarily to focus on her experience. But notice how her experience having lived through the disease and now living as a healthy young woman gives this informational text depth through its details:

> Anorexia has the highest mortality rate of any psychiatric disease. Eventually, severe weight loss causes the heart to atrophy, blood pressure to decrease and heart rate to slow. As the body struggles to maintain functions necessary to life—cognitive function, homeostasis—nonessential bodily systems shut down. Hair falls out, hormone production stops, blood doesn't circulate to the extremities, your fingertips and toes turn blue. There is no glamor in starvation, no beautiful struggle or delicate strength like magazines and movies might have you believe.

A girl I met while in recovery from my eating disorder told me that for her, anorexia was a polite way to die. She thought she could waste away, wither into nothingness. Leave her family with the convenience of only a skeleton to mourn, a bag of bones to bury rather than a fleshy corpse. The endgame of an eating disorder is not skinny. It is not pretty. The endgame of an eating disorder is a quiet, controlled, slow-burning death.

There's information here, for sure, but it's the action of this section—hair falling out, toes turning blue—that pull us toward the last image, the telling and showing detail of "a quiet, controlled, slow-burning death." With these clear descriptive details, the writer has put us on the inside of the subject she's writing about, making us feel and think and care about the information she's revealing in a visceral and active way.

When helping students find details of information, encourage them to look for the kernels of information they find the most interesting. Usually if we find bits of information interesting, our readers will as well. How can the details of information be "shown" instead of told? How can I use a metaphor to share information with the reader in a way that they can visualize?

## Details of Argument

The argument that doesn't touch the reader on a gut level is an argument that won't change the reader on a mental level. Because people remember stories better and feel them more viscerally, the smart rhetorician employs sharp details for her argumentative purposes. Stating the claim is imperative to an argument, but showing us the stakes, the humanity, the flesh of the argument is, arguably, just as important.

Consider a few sentences from David Brooks' 2003 essay "People Like Us":

Maybe somewhere in this country there is a truly diverse neighborhood in which a black Pentecostal minister lives next to a white anti-globalization activist, who lives next to an Asian short-order cook, who lives next to a professional golfer, who lives next to a postmodern-literature professor and a cardiovascular surgeon. But I have never been to or heard of that neighborhood.

Brooks establishes the tension of the essay through his thesis, namely "People want to be around others who are roughly like themselves." His opening paragraph provides a picture of diversity that doesn't really exist in our preferred homogeneous state. This descriptive fantasy juxtaposes with the remainder of the essay, which creates a more realistic classification for the various ways humans group themselves. But the details Brooks uses are clearly wrought pictures—the Pentecostal minister, the short-order cook, the professional golfer, the professor, the surgeon. His abstract argument grows teeth and skin with these specific details, and they move us from an abstract discussion of diversity into a vibrant argument that takes the shape of real people and a real neighborhood.

Details also build the credibility of the writer, reveal logical facts, and touch the reader emotionally. In essence, details can condense the ethos, logos, and pathos of an argument into a sensory experience. When you successfully use narrative details to reveal rhetorical appeals, you allow the reader to move from standing outside the argument to being in the middle of it.

When Regan wanted to write an argument for preventative tests for type 1 diabetes in children, she opened her essay with a powerful story of Arya, whose family thought she was healthy after her annual wellness visit to the hospital.

> But Arya was not healthy. In fact her blood sugar levels had slipped into the low 500s, 5 times that of a healthy person. The stress on her body had caused Arya to go into a coma, and she was unable to fight her way out.
>
> Unfortunately, this is not an uncommon occurrence. Doctors do not typically test for diabetes in children until they are of school age and show signs of the illness. The only exception is if type one diabetes runs in the child's family.

As Regan moves through her argument, to drive home the necessity of preventative testing, she layers in more stories of children who were not diagnosed with type 1 diabetes and who died as a result. She also entertains a counterclaim that the preventative measure would cost too much time and money. She counters with these argumentative details:

> The only things needing purchasing continually are the needles loaded into the lancet, and the test strips. A box of 50 needles costs around 20 dollars. A box of 200 test strips costs around 25 dollars. That rounds

to less than a dollar per finger stick. It will only take one to know if someone has type 1 diabetes or not. I'm sure any parent won't mind digging around in their wallet for a few quarters, especially if it meant knowing if their child's life were in danger.

When students are trying to develop argumentative details, ask them to consider their stories as a way to "prime" their audience (Anderson 2016, 88).

- How would they convince a friend of their claim?
- What story could they tell in their argument that would prime their audience to agree with them?
- What story would show their reader the impact of what they're arguing for?
- What narrative might help explain or illuminate a hard-to-explain concept of their argument?

## Winnowing the Details of a Draft

Selecting details comes with an opportunity cost. Every detail you include comes at the cost of all the details you don't. It's a matter of "winnowing" as Veryln Klinkenborg (2012) suggests, and winnowing is a job that can only be improved with practice. The selection of details is what Leslie Jamison (2017), in the introduction to *Best American Essays 2017*, calls "the mind as curator, plucking what it needed from the world and finding vessels for feelings without shapes" (xvii). She writes "an essay lives in its details, and argues through them."

This winnowing of details is a late process mechanism, not the first thing to accomplish on a student's to-do list. As a writer's awareness of their purpose, their audience, and their frame firms up, the writer usually finds the necessary details to cinch the argument or flesh out the information. Here's a master list of questions students can use to help them make their final decisions about what to leave in and what to leave out when it comes to details:

- Do my details work to help the reader understand the information?
- Do my details illuminate some part of my argument?
- How does this detail work to engage my reader and reveal my purpose?
- Does this detail deliver the image I'm trying to communicate?
- Does this detail illustrate my point more clearly than a fact?
- Are my details both describing and connecting my reader to my central point?

- Are my details both illustrating and reflecting my theme or purpose?
- Do my details of time work both historically and to move my reader through the essay?
- Have I used transitional details that logically or narratively connect the past and present?
- Is there some fact, evidence, quote I've summarized that could be demonstrated more effectively with a sensory detail?
- Are my details specific?
- Are my details concrete?
- Are my details significant?
- Are all my details necessary?

# CHAPTER SEVEN

# LANGUAGE Crafting Words
## and Sentences for Powerful Effect

In the short story "Bullet in the Brain," Tobias Wolff (1995) tells the story of Anders, "a book critic known for the weary, elegant savagery with which he dispatched almost everything he reviewed" who is caught in the middle of a bank robbery. When the robber instructs him to shut up, Anders can't help himself; he bursts out laughing. Then the robber shoots him.

The whole second half of the story chronicles Anders' thoughts as the bullet crashes through his brain. He doesn't think about his parents, his wife, his daughter, or his work as a critic. He thinks about a baseball game played in a long-ago summer. In the memory, a friend's cousin visiting from Mississippi says to Anders, "Shortstop's the best position they is." And the phrase, "they is, they is, they is" in the soft chanting lilt of the boy's voice circles Anders's brain until he dies.

Without the robbery, bullet, and dying parts, many of us have had this experience. A snatch of language embeds itself in our memory. Shimmering and eloquent or quirky and unexpected, the words hang in the air and resonate.

During my tenth year of teaching, I read *The Road*, Cormac McCarthy's (2006) postapocalyptic novel about a father and son, with my English class of fifteen juniors, nine of whom were already parents. Every day we read a couple of pages. When we arrived at the last page, I read the last paragraph out loud:

Once there were brook trout in the streams in the mountains. You could see them standing in the amber current where the white edges of their fins wimpled softly in the flow. They smelled of moss in your hand. Polished and muscular and torsional. On their backs were vermicular patterns that were maps of the world in its becoming. Maps and mazes. Of a thing which could not be put back. Not be made right again. In the deep glens where they lived all things were older than man and they hummed of mystery.

My voice quavered, tears filled my eyes. The passage was so beautiful, the road we'd been on was so long and ashen and gray. When I looked up at the class, my students had their heads down, many of them wiping away tears from their eyes also. In that moment, McCarthy's words, attempting to capture the mystery of the world in its beginning, created a community. That's the power of language. Words and sentences create a reality we all share. I hope my students carry that paragraph with them. Or maybe just the memory of it, if not the actual words.

What I do know is that certain sentences and words stick around long after you've read or heard them. Not because of the epiphany you had while reading, but for the delight of the sound, the savor of the words rolling around on your tongue. At their most basic, words and sentences are vehicles for thought; at their very best, they're pure art.

I want my students to choose strong words that communicate their ideas and arrange strong sentences too, but I also want to introduce the idea that functional writing can be beautiful. A nonfiction text can be poetic, snazzy, whimsical, and at the same time deliver a logical argument and accurate information. Good writing is engaging whether it's for a magazine article, a school research paper, an informational brochure, or an argumentative essay. The aims are clarity and simplicity, yes, but music and beauty are also part of our practice.

# LOOKING CLOSELY AT LANGUAGE: THREE POWERFUL EXAMPLES

In the previous chapter on details I mentioned Nicola Twilley's (2017) "The Billion Year Wave" as an example of how details create a concrete image in the mind of the reader, and examining her first paragraph is also a lesson on powerful language.

With 159 words arranged into eight sentences, Twilley doesn't vary her syntax wildly, but her diction is vivid, clear, and purposeful. She describes the origin of gravitational waves, a phenomenon no one saw or heard or even believed in (even though Einstein theorized they were real) until September 14, 2015, when the waves reached us from space:

> Just over a billion years ago, many millions of galaxies from here, a pair of black holes collided. They had been circling each other for aeons in a sort of mating dance, gathering pace with each orbit, hurtling closer and closer. By the time they were a few hundred miles apart, they were whipping around at nearly the speed of light, releasing great shudders of gravitational energy. Space and time became distorted, like water at a roiling boil. In the fraction of a second that it took for the black holes to finally merge, they radiated a hundred times more energy than all the stars in the universe combined. They formed a new black hole, sixty-two times as heavy as our sun and almost as wide across as the state of Maine. As it smoothed itself out, assuming the shape of a slightly flattened sphere, a few last quivers of energy escaped. Then space and time became silent again.

With thirty-five concrete nouns—all of them specific and significant to the passage—and verbs that explode with the action of *circling, gathering, hurtling, whipping, releasing, distorting, radiating, forming, escaping,* and *colliding,* Twilley convinces us of the veracity of this moment as surely as sci-fi writers might build the fantasy worlds of their novels. Her figurative language, comparing black holes as partners in a mating dance (and later as children running on a trampoline) and the newly formed black hole to the width of the state of Maine, allows us to see and feel and hear something no one saw or felt or heard before.

With vast cosmology in mind, Twilley's language choices are dictated by her subject and the information she wants to explain to her reader. This isn't science writing you might see in an academic journal, but for a broader audience, like readers of *The New Yorker,* who Twilley wishes to inform.

Not all nonfiction texts work this way, of course. Compare this excerpt from Twilley's essay to the rhythms of language used by Wendell Berry (2010) in his essay, "Why I Am Not Going to Buy a Computer." He writes:

> Like almost everybody else, I am hooked to the energy corporations, which I do not admire. I hope to become less hooked to them. In my work, I try to be as little hooked to them as possible. As a farmer, I do almost all of my work with horses. As a writer, I work with a pencil or a pen and a piece of paper.

These sentences are devoid of the details permeating Twilley's boiling, colliding cosmos. Berry's essay is framed by the domestic, the personal. His language is simple and clear with a growing rhythm of the I who is hooked, hopes to become less hooked, and tries to be as little hooked as possible.

In these five sentences, four are constructed exactly the same, using an introductory clause (like *almost everybody else, in my work, as a farmer, as a writer*) followed by the main clause that begins with the pronoun I. The repetitive syntax creates an elegant rhythm instead of lacking for one.

And now compare Berry and Twilley's prose to the single opening sentence of Rebecca Solnit's 2015 essay, "Arrival Gates." Solnit had traveled to Kyoto, Japan, to report on the one-year anniversary of the Japanese earthquake, tsunami, and subsequent destruction of the Fukushima nuclear facility. In a sentence comprised of 454 words and seventeen introductory clauses all beginning with the word *after*, Solnit describes her arrival at the Inari Shrine. Here are just the opening few clauses:

> After the long flight across the Pacific, after the night in the tiny hotel room selected so that I could walk to the world's busiest train station in the morning, after the train north to the area most impacted by the tsunami in the Great Tōhoku earthquake of March 11, 2011 . . . (198)

In a lush, meandering essay about time and the nature of journeys, the rhythm of the *after, after, after, after* in that first long sentence grounds us in Solnit's experience as well as establishes time, place, and scene, but most importantly, serves as a symbol of what the essay is about: arrival.

Later in the essay, she says, "Arrival is the culmination of the sequences of events, the last of the list, the terminal station, the end of the line" (201). Her first sentence is built to support this claim and gives the reader a clue to the essay's purpose.

In these three examples, writers made, either consciously or unconsciously, word and sentence choices that followed only the guidelines the subject and the essay established for itself. There was no recipe—one part figurative language to two parts simple sentence to one part vigorous nouns and verbs—that the writers used. The purpose of an essay determines the kind of words and sentences that best deliver it. The rhythm can be short and staccato with a collection of simple sentences drawn in similar ways, like Berry's, or it can be like Solnit's, perambulatory, weaving in and out of meaning, with sonorous words and languorous sentences.

Like details, the words and sentences a writer selects must do more than one thing: make the idea clear, move the reader closer to the goal of the essay, and make beauty out of the communication. How can I communicate to this person on the other side of the page? What word- and sentence-level decisions can I make that will deliver my point and illustrate it at the same time? And how can I use words and sentences to make this communication as emotionally and intellectually satisfying as possible?

# WORD CHOICE

Writing with concrete nouns and active verbs is the principle rule for poetry, but those same guidelines apply to prose. Successful writers, in both fiction and nonfiction, choose concrete words to communicate both concrete and, perhaps more importantly, *abstract* ideas. But is word choice a *narrative* element? Are there words that have a more narrative or lyrical quality than others? After all, nonfiction has a unique set of parameters because it must square with facts.

Barbara Ehrenreich (2018a) warns in her latest book *Natural Causes* that "a science writer has to guard against overdramatizing and anthropomorphizing the events she is reporting on" (146). So, can we make mountains dance and solar systems grimace? In other words, do nonfiction writers have poetic license?

I believe they do. As we've seen time after time across this book, when writers of nonfiction seek to engage readers, possibly to change their minds or inform them of something, that kind of writing demands concrete language. As with all choices in writing, word choice is a matter of weighing the diction against the purpose of the text. Is this a text that demands a more formal register, or would more casual diction work? For some scientific, technical, or medical journals, grinning solar systems would not be apt. But, as Anne Greene (2013) says in *Writing Science in Plain English*, "small doses of informal register can transmit spirit and enthusiasm" (7). If your purpose is to make a general audience feel and think something by transporting them into a domestic violence shelter, at the bedside of a dying man, or at a birthday party for a three-year-old, then use words that produce pictures.

# Why *This* Word?

I wish there were a few tried-and-true exercises that would teach students how to choose the best words for their writing, but, as is true with so much of what we talk about when we talk about writing, the key is to practice over and over word selection. Writers are faced with hundreds of choices about words every time they set out to write, and each set of choices is a unique problem to solve within the rhetorical situation at hand.

So what can we do? I believe we have to emphasize the importance of word choice crystal clear for our students. As we study mentor texts and we notice interesting language, we need to ask the same question over and over, "Why did the writer choose *this* word?" The conversation that spins out of this question teaches students about the power of word choice and makes them more conscious of their decisions about words in their own writing.

For example, my class was reading Lawrence Jackson's (2017) "The City That Bleeds," about the 2015 riots in Baltimore after the death of Freddie Gray, when I paused to ask this question. In the essay, Jackson writes of Baltimore's first African American mayor whose platform was education: "When he took the job in 1988, he tried to rename Baltimore 'the city that reads,' though the motto curdled into 'the city that bleeds.'"

"Why did he use the word *curdled*?" I asked. "In what context do we normally use the word *curdle*?"

"He's comparing it to milk," McKenna said.

"Why does he do that? Why not just say "the motto *turned* into 'the city that bleeds'?"

"Because it's cool?"

"Because it's his title. It's like the motto soured on the people," said Amelia.

Later in the essay, Jackson walks with a family friend of Gray's after the trial. "As he talked to me about other horrifying cases of wrongful police force, we passed the car wash, and boys raced fat-tired ATVs by us as night came on."

"Why doesn't he just say 'as night fell' or 'as the streetlights came on?'" I asked.

"Maybe that's just the way he talks. He would say that in a regular conversation."

"This reminds me of that essay about the guy who crossed the street," Promise said. "He used the word *warbling*."

Promise was referring to the last two sentences of Brent Staples' (2018) essay "Just Walk on By" where he describes how he whistles Beethoven and Vivaldi when he wants to go on a late-night walk. "Virtually everybody seems to sense that a mugger wouldn't be warbling bright, sunny selections from Vivaldi's *Four Seasons*. It is my equivalent of the cowbell that hikers wear when they know they are in bear country."

Do we know why Jackson chose "the night came on" or why Staples chose the powerful analogy of his last sentence? We may not know the answers to any of these questions. We aren't analyzing these texts for meaning as much as we are mining them for possibilities of imitation, noticing and observing the style and tone produced by the diction and syntax selected by the writer. Speculating about this word or that invites students to hold words up and examine their usefulness, reminding them of this ever-present truism: writing is choice.

## Why *This* Figurative Language?

As we saw in the chapter on details, the comparisons made through figurative language in nonfiction can be effective because they create, as the name implies, *figures* in the mind of the reader who may not be familiar with the topic. The key is to help students understand that figurative language is not employed just to spice things up a bit in non-fiction; it's incredibly purposeful and selected to advance the writer's aim in the work.

Just as we do with words, anytime we see figurative language used in interesting ways in mentor texts, we need to consider the writer's choices. We ask, "Why this image and not another? What does this image help us understand at this point in the text, and also about the author's bigger ideas?"

For example, in "H," Sarah Resnick's (2017) essay about treatment options for heroin users, she describes sitting in the emergency room late one night watching a young addict in a wheelchair suffering withdrawal. He vomits. Resnick writes, "It's viscous, like cake batter" (215). This powerful simile puts the reader in Resnick's reality immediately.

"Raise your hand if you know what *viscous* means," I asked my class. Six students knew the word from science class. "Now raise your hand if you know what cake batter is." Every hand in the room went up.

The reader might not be familiar with the term *viscous*, meaning "a thick, sticky consistency between solid and liquid," but there's no denying that *cake batter* does more as a noun than *viscous* does as an adjective. By pairing the specific adjective with the element of figurative language, Resnick creates a cringeworthy moment for the reader that mimics the emotional experience she must have had. The reader and the writer are on the same page.

In "Wisdom from Psychopaths?" from *Scientific American*, Kevin Dutton (2013), who is a research psychologist at the University of Oxford, creates a convincing argument that psychopaths and surgeons often share many of the same traits such as fearlessness, focus, and mental toughness. In the article, Dutton uses an extended metaphor to describe what a psychopath's brain looks like under an MRI machine when given a moral dilemma. When a normal person is presented the same moral dilemma, Dutton reports:

> I would see your amygdala and related brain circuits . . . light up like a pinball machine. I would witness the moment, in other words, that emotion puts its money in the slot. But in a psychopath, I would see only darkness. The cavernous neural casino would be boarded up and derelict.

The extended metaphor of pinball and slot machines and casinos isn't arbitrary. There are plenty of lit machines Dutton could have chosen to compare to our medial orbito-frontal cortex, but he chose a machine of chance, of gambling, of randomness, which touches on his thesis: it's the unpredictable nature of genetics that makes one person tumble out as a surgeon and another as a serial killer.

I don't burden my students with a checklist of figurative language requirements. Some essays lend themselves to figurative language; some don't. But I do want my students to be familiar with how writers use figurative language for specific expository jobs—to engage the reader, to clarify a concept, to create energy or a visual dynamic, or to connect something familiar to something unknown, such as Twilley's "heavy as our sun and almost as wide across as the state of Maine."

If students want to use figurative language, here are some questions to guide them as they select their images:

- Will this image help the reader to see the subject more clearly?
- Does this image illuminate your theme in any way?
- Are you helping the reader understand the unknown by comparing it to the known?
- Are you trying to embody something inanimate with human qualities? If so, for what purpose?

Asking students to justify their choices helps them see that choice is important and that they are in control of their own decision making. It also asks them to pause and consider the usefulness and the clarity of the language with which they chose to communicate their ideas.

## Understanding Connotation and Denotation

In "The Dark Art of Description," Patricia Hampl (2008) relates an anecdote about J. F. Powers, who was asked by one of his colleagues how his writing was going that day. Powers replied, "I spent the morning trying to decide whether to have my character call his friend *pal* or *chum*" (186).

The words *pal* and *chum* have basically the same dictionary definition—a friend—but there is some connotative difference, in closeness, in intimacy, in rank. Being conscious of the emotional, psychological, or cultural baggage of words will help students make effective word choices. For example, if you're describing puppies, *cute* hits the note more closely than *handsome*, unless, of course, it's a pedigree issue, like hunting show dogs, where handsomeness might indicate strength or virility or breeding.

Developing a gut-level awareness of a word's nuanced meaning helps students harness the power of language. During a summer writing institute in 1995, I picked up two activities I've used in numerous iterations ever since to help students become aware of those nuances. The object is to challenge students not just to understand vocabulary, but to understand language on a deeper emotional or cultural level as well.

### Connotation Corners

In this exercise, I give every student a slip of paper that has one of four synonyms on it. For example, I might use the words: *chilly, frozen, icy,* or *cold.* I ask students not to share what word they have, then I choose four students to stand in the corners of the room making sure each has a different word. In one corner, Jamia has *frozen*; in another corner, Ty has *icy*; Kendra has *chilly*, and Libby has *cold*. I give these four students a dictionary definition of the word they are holding, and Jamia reads the definition for her word *frozen* out loud to the class without using the word itself. The rest of the class must determine if the word they hold in their hand matches Jamia's word.

If Harper believes she holds the same word as Jamia, she moves to Jamia's corner. Then Ty defines his word, *icy*. His definition probably sounds a lot like Jamia's. Harper now believes she might have Ty's word in her hand. She moves over to his corner. Then when Kendra gives a definition for her word *chilly*, Harper is really perplexed.

The problem is, of course, that the dictionary definitions all sound like the same word: being at a relatively low temperature. Students are galloping all over the classroom, unable to figure out which corner to stand in.

In the second round, I ask students to redefine their word using an emotional, psychological, cultural, or social association. They can use this stem to help them, "This is the kind of word you would use if you were describing _____."

"Uh, okay. This is a word you'd use on the first kinda, sorta cold day in the fall. Like when you might bring a sweater to the football game," says Kendra. Kendra is counting on the class to think of *chilly* as more of an autumn word as opposed to *frozen*, which feels more like a winter word. You might not use the word *frozen* to describe merely a cold day, but you would if the temps drop below zero, freezing the lakes and streams. *Frozen* is an intense cold, something you might experience in Alaska or during the polar vortex.

On a scale from least severe to most severe, we might arrange the words *chilly*, *cold*, *icy*, *frozen* based, not on their dictionary definition, but on the sensory associations we have with the words. When students use these associations to define their words connotatively, they immediately go to the correct corner.

This is one of those activities that produces the kind of gut-level word awareness I want students to have about language as they wade into the world of nonfiction texts.

## Connotation Continuums

For this exercise, I usually start by having students carefully consider an author's word choices. I look for a sentence or two with lots of potential, where it seems an author has intentionally selected words for their impact on the reader. For example, when we read Douglas Fox's (2018) "Firestorm" on the behavior of super wildfires, I highlighted this sentence: "There lies the key to understanding the way a wildfire breathes—roaring into a conflagration with bigger gulps of oxygen or sputtering along more slowly on little sips" (101). Students catch on to the personification in a sentence like this, but I also want them to think about the work the words *breathes*, *roaring*, *gulps*, *sputtering*, and *little sips* do to shape their sense of wildfire behavior. I ask questions that help students think about how writers must deliberate about words:

- Why does Fox choose *breathes* instead of *works* or *operates* in the phrase "understanding the way a wildfire breathes"?
- What weight does *roaring* have over *booming*? Both of them are referencing the sound a fire makes, so why do you think he chose *roaring*?
- What advantage do *gulps* and *sips* have to another combination of words like *guzzles* and *drinks*?

- Where does the word *conflagration* land on a positive to negative continuum with other words like *fire*, *blaze*, or *inferno*? Is one more dangerous than the other? Is one more clinical?
- What emotional or psychological effect do you think Fox is hoping for with this sentence?

After a close reading and some discussion, I break students into groups and give them a baggie with a set of related words in it. I then ask them to place these words on a continuum between positive and negative "charge," and then present their rankings to the class and defend their choices (see Figure 7–1).

| Thin | Fat | Sad | Happy | Ugly | Gorgeous |
|------|-----|-----|-------|------|----------|
| Skinny | Obese | Unhappy | Merry | Gross | Cute |
| Lean | Plump | Miserable | Ecstatic | Plain | Lovely |
| Athletic | Chunky | Depressed | Jolly | Appalling | Beautiful |
| Emaciated | Large | Heartbroken | Cheerful | Revolting | Pretty |
| Skeletal | Thick | Morbid | Joyful | Homely | Handsome |

**Figure 7–1** Sample Word Sets for Connotation Continuums

If a group gets *thin, skinny, lean, athletic, emaciated,* and *skeletal*, they will always argue over the social and cultural context in which these words are used. If you're describing an athlete, then obviously, the word *athletic* would be the most positively charged word in the list. If you're describing a racehorse, would you use *lean* or *athletic*? Which is more negative, *skinny* or *thin*? What's the difference between *emaciated* or *skeletal*? Ten or twenty pounds? And which is most or least offensive?

This exercise shows students that culture and context are everything. When we're talking about Old St. Nick, the only word that fits is *jolly. Joy*, my students suggested, had a whiff of the religious to it, like the hymn, "Joy to the World." And *ecstatic* was a word you'd use if you found out you just won the lottery because it has the connotation of a little mania with it, more euphoria than just mere happiness.

Myriad conversations can spin off of this activity—discussions about slang, dog whistle words, political messaging, doublespeak, and propaganda. But the point is to alert students to the idea that even words with the same definition are not created equal. You can't just consult a thesaurus and plug in a synonym; all words have a different positive or negative charge. This activity also fosters an obsession for word-level revision. Does this word really express my meaning or was it just the first word I came up with? How could I tighten up my meaning in this sentence with a sharper word?

# Eliminating Clichés

One of my favorite episodes of *Seinfeld* is the one where Elaine, working for the clothier J. Peterman, promotes Eddie Sherman, a Vietnam vet from the mailroom, because she's afraid to fire him. After a meeting where Eddie offers, "It's tough keeping your feet dry when you're kicking in skulls" as ad copy for Bengalese galoshes, Elaine's copywriting team quits. She's then forced to put out the clothing catalog with only Eddie as her writing partner. The back-and-forth revision scene where Elaine says, "Let's just replace *hail of shrapnel* and *scar tissue* with *string of pearls* and *raspberry scones*" is a scene I identify with on a spiritual level as a teacher.

Every time I conference with a student whose essay is riddled with "A wise man once said" or "Since the beginning of time" or "In America today" or "The reason why is because," I feel like Elaine. Let's just replace these tired, old clichés, shall we? How about a string of pearls and raspberry scones?

The first thing I do to build my students' awareness of worn-out language is share with them a list of 200 journalism clichés often found in print. The list was compiled by journalist Carlos Lozada (2014) and some of his colleagues at *The Washington Post*, and when I share them with my students, we discuss why many of the different phrases are cliché. We might, for example, discuss phrases such as *at first glance* or *at first blush*, *at a crossroads*, *outside the box*, *last-ditch effort*, and *this is not your father's fill-in-the-blank*.

After sharing this list with one class, one student exasperatedly said, "I see those in newspapers and magazines all the time online. If I can't say any of those things, then what can I say?" This question launched a discussion about Twitter trends, catchphrases, online communication, and the viruslike replication of memes and meme culture.

"Being aware of them is half the battle," I said, winking at my students.

Writers often resort to clichés when they're writing about topics they don't really understand or arguments they really don't believe in. When students write about religion and politics, they often parrot the platitudes they've heard from others. When the Pinterest quotes hit the page, my job is to point out these phrases and ask the student what the phrase means in the context of their message: "What does '*turn it on its head*' mean in your sentence? Think more critically. Delve deeper into the ideas you want to communicate. What are you really trying to say here?"

"Does that sentence make sense to you?" I asked Taylor in a conference just yesterday. She exploded in laughter.

"No, but it sounds pretty good, doesn't it?" she said. We both got a good laugh out of that. Even after she had read the sentence out loud, she couldn't explain to me what she meant. When students perceive that writing is merely accumulating truthiness (Colbert 2005) statements and backing them up with more truthiness facts, clichés creep in.

Sometimes I encourage students to use clichés in their first draft if it helps them get their thoughts and ideas on the page, but I remind them to always see a cliché as an opportunity to work on meaning in the second draft. Get the exact right words in the exact order to deliver your point.

## Bigger Is Not Necessarily Better

A final misconception many students have about word choice, especially in nonfiction, is that bigger words are better words. To help disavow them of this notion and to introduce the power of clear, lucid prose, I sometimes offer students two passages of writing from George Orwell's (1946) "Politics and the English Language." Orwell's essay has been anthologized so much students may have read it before, but I still have them compare the King James Version of Ecclesiastes 9:11 and a jargony version of the same text (see Figure 7–2).

| Passage A | Passage B |
| --- | --- |
| Objective consideration of contemporary phenomena compels the conclusion that success or failure in competitive activities exhibits no tendency to be commensurate with innate capacity, but that a considerable element of the unpredictable must invariably be taken into account. | I returned and saw under the sun, that the race is not to the swift, nor the battle to the strong, neither yet bread to the wise, nor yet riches to men of understanding, nor yet favor to men of skill; but time and chance happens to them all. |
| 38 words<br>90 syllables<br>0 vivid images<br>18 words with Latinate roots | 49 words<br>60 syllables<br>6 vivid images<br>16 words with Germanic roots |

**Figure 7–2** Orwell's Text Comparison

Typically, I read these examples out loud to students and then we talk. Which passage do they prefer? Why? Which passage boasts the clearer meaning? Students might nurse the notion that bigger words are better words, but this example disproves that maxim. Fewer syllables, a half dozen images, and solid Germanic words equal a more dynamic passage.

# SENTENCE CRAFT

Just as many of my students come to my class thinking bigger words are better words, many of them also believe longer sentences are somehow more sophisticated. I have no data on why this perception exists. Perhaps somewhere in their writing development, students have been asked to develop sentences from a subject-verb construction like "Donald lied," to a sentence replete with clauses and phrases.

The simple sentence is good. The simple sentence is clear. There is nothing wrong with a serviceable subject-verb-object arrangement: *The sisters flipped the house.* Because we have actors (the sisters) who are acting (flipped) on an object (the house), there's no ambiguity. The sentence is short, tight, and clear.

But I also want students to play around with longer, more complex sentences. I want them to try linking clause upon clause upon clause and ending with a tiny main clause like Rebecca Solnit's "I arrived at the orange gates." If every word should tell, as William Strunk Jr. says in *Elements of Style*, then sentences—those lovely vessels for word mergers—should deliver their meaning *on point*. I preach sentence variety, not for the sake of spice, but for emphasis or contrast or proof or description. Sentences should work; they have jobs to do.

As with every other tool we've considered, mentor texts are the key to helping students understand the power of sentence crafting. Ask students to find sentences in the wild that make their sternum shake and highlight sentences in the texts you study together that do the same. You want students to develop a sentence radar that makes them stop and reread when they encounter a masterful bit of sentence crafting. You want them to stop and ask, "How did the writer do that?"

For example, in "Service with a Smile, and Plenty of Metal," Debra Darvick (2004) examines the body piercings of food servers in restaurants. She writes, "When I can read the latte menu through the hole in my server's ear lobe, something is seriously out of whack" (20). This sentence is not just arranged for clarity, but for impact. Darvick's use of the visual (reading a menu through an earlobe) and her use of common language ("seriously out of whack") is set into a complex sentence charged by an introductory *when* with no concrete subject (something) that pulls us into her essay.

Consider the narrative quality of this single sentence as Hanif Abdurraqib (2018) describes Aretha Franklin's funeral:

> I watched the second half of the funeral from a hotel room in Georgia,
> where I fought back tears when former NBA player Isaiah Thomas told

stories of how Aretha helped raise him into a better man than he'd been, and where I yawned when Clive Davis lovingly droned on about the mechanics of Aretha's singing, and where I cringed during the scolding, 50-minute eulogy by pastor Jasper Williams Jr., a tone-deaf jeremiad that spanned everything from black-on-black crime to the ways single mothers were failing to raise their black sons, delivered while Aretha Franklin—a single mother to four boys—rested right before him.

Abdurraqib's use of parallel structure and repetition ("where I fought," "where I yawned," "where I cringed") creates the frame of a narrative, the beginning, middle, and end of an experience, ergo a mini-narrative. His diction and syntax work together to deliver a snapshot, as intense as if we were standing right next to him. This sentence sings.

Sentences that are long or short, tight or galloping, serve to deliver their ideas in a way the writer intends. The more you draw your students' attention to sentence crafting, the more they will see that a sentence is the delivery mechanism of the idea and ultimately the whole essay.

## Experiment with Models

When students read nonfiction, they will see that writers break all the rules for the purposes of clarity. They begin sentences with conjunctions, they use fragments, they write one-sentence paragraphs, they invent words. They repeat themselves for emphasis and use parallelism to build power.

Syntax dexterity begins with noticing and naming what writers are doing when they craft powerful sentences. Then the next step is to invite students to play around with arrangements that jam along the same vibe as their purpose. Using sentences from mentor texts as models, encourage students to experiment with the syntax in their drafts. Here are some examples my students have tried, along with the models that inspired them.

### Frame a Long Sentence Between Two Short Ones

Model Example: Richard Manning (2010), "Graze Anatomy"

Will Winter and Todd Churchill have a plan. It's simple, it's workable, and if enough people do it, it will shrink our carbon footprint, expand biodiversity and wildlife habitat, promote human health, humanize farming, control rampant flooding, radically decrease the use of pesticides and chemical fertilizers, and—for those of us who still eat the stuff—produce a first-class, guilt-free steak. Their plan: let cows eat grass.

Student Example: McKenna

When children are born, there is a contract. The guardian is understanding that this is a child, a new being, who has not learned anything, who does not know right from wrong, and the guardian has accepted the responsibility to take care of them and teach them. My mother did not sign this contract.

## String a Series of S–V–O Sentences Together

Model Example: Kim Todd (2018), "The Island Wolves"

The map of wolf territories shifted. They fought over borders. They staged coups. Fortunes rose and fell. Packs gathered strength, then disappeared.

Student Example: Griffin

Kojima begins his daily preparations. He jots down ideas in a little notebook. He munches on a rice cracker. He circles "Snatchers—Androids steal human identities?" and "Neo Kobe." He puts the notebook aside and pulls out another, this one more organized and marked officially.

## Try One Long Meandering Sentence

Model Example: Mary Ruefle (2012), *Madness, Rack, and Honey*

I do not think I really have anything to say about poetry other than remarking that it is a wandering little drift of unidentified sound, and trying to say more reminds me of following the sound of a thrush into the woods on a summer's eve—if you persist in following the thrush it will only recede deeper and deeper into the wood; you will never actually see the thrush (the hermit thrush is especially shy), but I suppose listening is a kind of knowledge, or as close as one comes.

Student Example: Kailie

I was sitting in the car, the whole late afternoon world blanketed in January, post my birthday and ripe for seasonal depression, staring at streetlights and listening to *Folie A Deux,* and it was only recently that I'd started buying and listening to whole albums, to whole experiences, and I was able to string together landscapes out of them, little cosmos.

## Use Repetition

Model Example: Hanif Abdurraqib (2017b), "Serena Williams and the Policing of Imagined Arrogance"

And so Serena throws her racket and falls to her knees. And so a little Black girl finds a tennis court on the outskirts of her hood. And so another father finds hope. And so I hit two jump shots in a row in the middle of summer in Oakland. And so I extend my follow through, hold it, and let the breeze blow sweat off my arm. A reminder of how easily things can be taken from us.

Student Example: Autumn

It takes real privilege for a white person to not see the issue with using the N-word. It takes someone who has never faced a day of discrimination in their life. It takes a person oblivious to the world around them. And most importantly, it takes a lack of empathy.

## Use Fragments for Effect

Model Example: Susannah Felts (2017), "Astonish Me: Anticipating an Eclipse in the Age of Information"

In early July, the viewing parties began to twinkle, distant stars on the blank expanse of the calendar, all clustered upon this one August Monday. A city-sponsored gathering at the baseball stadium. Viewing parties at local parks. A brunch at a fancy hotel, with eggs Benedict and waffles.

Student Example: Caden

My mother remembers seeing the Rockettes in a televised parade as a young girl. She remembers wanting nothing more than to join them in the kickline. But do dazzling costumes and elaborate routines make the world a better place? Not really. In her job, though the payoff may be minimal or delayed, she is making a tangible impact in people's lives by bestowing on them the gift of clear communication. But would she trade it all to be a Rockette? In a heartbeat.

## Try Out a Single Sentence Paragraph

Model Example: Jennifer Rich (2018), "A Second Grader Once Pointed a Gun at Me. I'm Glad I Wasn't Armed"

I encourage my students to debate, to learn, to engage whatever strategies work so that each child in their care knows that he or she is valued, and that he or she is safe. I will never, ever advocate that my students arm themselves.

Teachers are not soldiers or police officers.

Schools are not battlegrounds.

Student Example: Regan

Although my blood sugar level had been very high, I had been diagnosed early so my body hadn't begun to shut down yet. I was able to walk out of the pediatrician's office, get in the car, and walk into the hospital on my own. A day later I was able to walk back out.

I didn't die, I didn't slip into a coma, I didn't have DKA.

I was one of the lucky ones.

## Make Good Sentences Great

We write sentences as the words occur to us, as symbols for communicating our ideas. The tumble of phrases and clauses that fall out of our heads are rarely arranged in a way to communicate effectively. Once we get our ideas on the page, our real work is just beginning.

Essentially, I want students to do a cost-benefit analysis on every sentence when they reread their first drafts. I want them to consider how much it will cost readers to make their way through a sentence and grasp its meaning. Could this be sharper? Clearer? If the sentence is poetic but the meaning is obscured, is it worth the reader's effort? It takes a lot of practice and experience to develop an eye for sentences that aren't working, but learning to ask these questions is a start. And, of course, finding a sentence that's not working is only the first step; the next step is to revise it.

To teach my students about sentence-level revision, I typically model the process and show them how I can rewrite a sentence to make it more clear. For example, I once extracted this sentence from an old essay. I wrote it on the board: "Each year before Thanksgiving, my church participates in a whole-day community service where we get into groups and go give Thanksgiving boxes to different houses, apartments, and town-houses where families are in need of food for Thanksgiving."

"OK, this sentence has thirty-eight words and the meaning is pretty clear, but I have to work a bit as a reader to get to the exact meaning. Is there a way we can tighten this up?" I say.

After a few minutes of sentence/word negotiation, we come up with another sentence.

"Each year before Thanksgiving, my church participates in a whole-day community service where we distribute food boxes to families in need."

"OK that's pretty good," I say. "It's twenty-two words long, and have we lost any of the original meaning? No, I think it's all there, but is there a tighter, sharper arrangement?

Two groups in the back offer sentences that are even smaller and tighter: "My church participates in an annual Thanksgiving food drive that collects and distributes food to families in need." This clocks in at eighteen words. Another group offers a twelve-word option: "Every November, my church distributes a Thanksgiving food box to needy families."

"Are we keeping the original thought?" I ask. "Have we lost any of the meaning of this sentence?"

Paired with modeling the process of revision, I sometimes highlight a few sentences when I read student essays that might be good for reimagining as leaner, meaner versions of their original selves. Then, as an exercise in sentence play, students rewrite the sentences in three different ways, attempting to use fewer words and more powerful syntax (see Figure 7–3).

| Original Sentence | Three Rewritten Options |
| --- | --- |
| In both of my parents' lives, the addiction won, taking both of them from me. | 1. The addiction took both of my parents from me.<br>2. The addiction won, taking both of my parents from me.<br>3. Both of my parents died from their addiction. |
| I was removed from my mother's care and separated from all my siblings at two, where I lived with my grandparents. | 1. At two, I was removed from my mother's care, separated from my siblings, and moved into my grandparents' home.<br>2. When I was two, I was removed from my mother's house, and my grandparents took custody of me.<br>3. I was removed from all my siblings and my mother when I was two, and my grandparents took me in. |
| The older I get the further I realize I've seen more dimensions of life than most at my age. | 1. The older I get, the more I realize I've seen dimensions of life that my peers have not seen.<br>2. The older I get, the more I realize I've experienced dimensions of life that my peers have not experienced.<br>3. As I age, I realize I have seen greater dimensions of life than most people my age. |

**Figure 7–3** Examples of One Student's Sentence Rewrites

## Allow Students to Find Their Own Style and Improve Upon It

In the best of circumstances, words spill out of a writer unbidden at the intersection of personality, experience, and beliefs about writing and communication. The writer then styles those words in a way that makes sense to them, hopefully that supports their purpose. They learn to choose Word A over Word B, or the clarity of a simple sentence over the abstraction of a more lengthy one. Like fashion, a student's writing style—voice, tone, point of view, word choice, sentence arrangement—is very personal and often unconscious.

To understand what differences in style look like, consider the feedback that two different students in my class gave to another student, Alec. When Alec wrote an informational text about the economic necessity of small regional airports, he asked for feedback on his tone. He wanted it to be professional.

Students submit their feedback to each other anonymously, so even though their identities weren't known, their different styles were distinct. Student A wrote to Alec: "Your tone is engaging yes, but it is not professional. It reads as if it is an informal piece of writing."

And student B wrote: "Your tone is a very laid-back sort of professional, not overly flippant, but not overly staunch. There were times a much more radically casual Alec slipped in. Sometimes it comes off sounding like something you would put on a personal blog, and other times it comes off sounding like it belongs in an official flying magazine."

These examples show how two students, writing from the same prompt ("Is the tone of my essay professional?") respond in their own individual style. Student A is direct and declarative. Student B is more verbose, offering examples, using language such as "overly flippant" to contrast with "overly staunch."

Some students, like professional writers, will be naturally concise and direct, others more luminous and verbose in their style. Would we correct Berry because he doesn't sound like Solnit? Would we check Solnit because she wasn't writing in the style of Twilley?

Students are no different. How they show up in the world is often how they show up on the page. The savvy teacher helps students to recognize their own style and improve on it, not change it to match a pattern of writing the teacher deems more impressive. This, in fact, is one of the most important steps to creating autonomous, thinking, authentic writers.

# CONCLUSION

## IN THE REAL WORLD

It seems shortsighted, then, in light of the rich and diverse exercise of writing, that students are taught one mode of writing at the exclusion of another or taught modes as isolated or pure forms. Teaching argumentation or narration or information as separate rhetorical approaches with separate tools and sensibilities only leads students to be confused about the writing they produce in school versus the writing they see in the real world.

When students are faced with writing tasks in the real world, as David Coleman (2011) hopes they are prepared for, those tasks don't come assigned by mode. In fact, they don't come assigned at all. They erupt or detonate with no tidy set of directions for how to communicate the answer. Writing in the real world is commanded or demanded by circumstances without a road map for accomplishing the writer's aim, in fact, most of the time, without a clear idea of the writer's aim at all.

Indulge me for a moment while I take you through a single day in the writing life of a professional teacher as an object lesson for how writing tasks emerge uncategorized in the real world. Today I was presented with three writing opportunities:

1. One of my students emailed me requesting a letter of recommendation for her college application.
2. My principal reminded the staff that our professional growth plans as well as our yearly self-reflection needed to be uploaded to the teacher evaluation website.
3. I had received two parent emails. One parent wanted to know if there was anything she could do to help her son become more organized. Another parent was concerned about her daughter's grades.

The three writing tasks required a blend of expository stances and tones: the letter of recommendation was written formally, part reflective argument and part informational text about the student as well as a small narrative about what kind of person she is. The growth plan was also a formal piece of writing. I had to reflect and narrate and argue for my value as a professional plus provide some information about where I would like to be at the end of the year and how I plan to get there. My emails were, of course, letters in form and informative in mode, but they both had mini-arguments embedded in them. In the first email, I made a case for a particular paper management system her son could try out to become more organized. In the second email, I inserted a mini-narrative about her daughter to illustrate a point about why her grades were low and how she could improve them. They were different in purpose and tone.

My successful completion of these writing tasks depended on my ability to ascertain the following things: (1) what I needed to say and (2) how to say it, so I achieved my purpose.

When a student reads a finished text, say Amy Tan's (2011) essay, "Mother Tongue," she is seeing the coalescence of dozens, if not hundreds, of authorial decisions, subtractions, additions, transpositions, adjustments, and maladjustments made and unmade by Tan. We read the finished product of this to analyze Tan's meaning.

However, when we offer students opportunities to write, we are asking them to make those dozens, if not hundreds, of decisions. And they need to have practice at doing that, in addition to reading Tan again with an eye toward how she, as a writer, made them as well.

My point is, writing in the real world doesn't come with a set of instructions; it only comes as an urge to communicate something. The urges we have to communicate something to another person are as rapid-fire and spontaneous as thought. Most of the time our need to communicate will be matched in speed and space with the actual communication. The urge begins and ends in a single text message, taking less than thirty seconds to satisfy.

But many situations demand something larger, more analytical, more concrete, more protracted. And those situations come with many questions: What exactly do I want to say? How will I frame it? Is this an argument? Should I tell a story to illustrate my point or will that muddy things? And, if so, how will I organize it? What words to use? What tone? And how will I determine the answers to all these questions?

"Someday you'll want to tell someone you love them," said my teacher, Wendell Berry, to our class of preservice English teachers on the last dark day of November 1988. The wind had plastered yellow ginkgo leaves against the thick classroom windows. El Greco clouds rolled across the sky. Only twelve of us had hung on through a semester of Composition for Teachers, down from thirty who had signed up in August. He had good-spiritedly rebuked our sentimentalities, rejected our easy thoughts, killed our reliance on bromides. And on that last day, it had all come down to this. Someday we would need to tell someone we loved them. My mind whizzed.

When we teach writing, we are teaching students to, in essence, search for themselves, to make decisions, to forge on when half of those decisions turn out to be the wrong ones. We give them mentors to read and opportunities to practice, and we encourage them to keep asking questions that lead to self-discovery. And we hope that when the time comes for them to tell someone they love them, they'll be ready.

# NARRATIVE NONFICTION: A THREE-TO-SIX-WEEK SAMPLE UNIT PLAN

To help you imagine what a study of narrative nonfiction might look like, here's a sample three- to six-week outline of plans. You could, of course, substitute different texts based on the needs and interests of your students, or spend more or less time with different activities.

| | |
|---|---|
| **Week One, Day One** | <ul><li>Introduce the idea of blended texts by reading three newspaper articles and highlight/annotate for "story."</li><li>Discuss the difference between fiction and nonfiction. The depth of this discussion depends on what kind of texts we've been reading all year and students' awareness of how nonfiction writers use narrative techniques to create immediacy and engagement in their writing.</li><li>Set the expectation that by the end of the week, students will select a personal experience that they could use as a narrative base to write a nonfiction text that will also deliver some information or argue for a claim.</li><li>Complete one of the topic-generating activities from Chapter 2.</li></ul> |
| **Day Two** | <ul><li>Read Becca Cudmore's (2017) essay "The Case for Leaving City Rats Alone" chunked out in a chart that allows students to track information and argument and narrative. Notice/cite/highlight/annotate examples of how she uses the different modes to support her purpose.</li><li>Compare students' analytical findings with your own.</li><li>Ask students to brainstorm three to five strategies that Cudmore uses in her text that they might want to use in their own writing.</li><li>Create a narrative menu on the board that you will add to throughout the unit.</li></ul> |
| **Day Three** | <ul><li>Read Lynda Barry's (1992) "Sanctuary of School" and Jennifer Rich's (2018) "A Second Grader Once Pointed a Gun at Me."</li><li>Brainstorm personal experiences that students might use in the service of arguing for something or delivering information. (You also might do another topic generating activity from Chapter 2, like Universal Timeline or Big Questions.)</li><li>Students generate two or three experiences they might want to explore for a short narrative nonfiction text.</li></ul> |
| **Day Four** | <ul><li>Writing day: students write a draft of a narrative nonfiction piece that is built around their own personal experience, but that also argues for something or delivers some information to the reader that exists outside their experience. Length and form is negotiable. You might suggest students use Barry and Rich's pieces as models.</li></ul> |
| **Day Five** | <ul><li>Writing day: students finish their drafts and turn them in. These will be unpolished, but should show evidence that students have "tried on" some of the strategies. Students will have an opportunity to create a more fully developed blended text later in the unit.</li><li>Share a piece that you've written as well.</li></ul> |

| | |
|---|---|
| **Week Two, Day One** | • Read Tom Philpott's (2016) "How Factory Farms Play Chicken with Antibiotics" and annotate all the ways in which Philpott uses information. Ask students to mark any information that Philpott uses throughout the text and to comment in the margin about the "job" the information does for Philpott's argument. Also, ask students to think about how Philpott moves between story and information. |
| | • Discuss and compare your own and students' annotations. (In my classes, we always have a good discussion on this text because so much of his narrative is also information. You can't cleave the two. That's some good blending.) |
| **Day Two** | • Read Barbara Bradley Hagerty's (2017) "When Your Child Is a Psychopath," and annotate all the ways Hagerty uses narrative. Ask students to mark/highlight any story or anecdote Hagerty uses throughout the text and to comment in the margin about the "job" that this story/anecdote does for her text. |
| | • Discuss and compare your own and students' annotations. Does the story Hagerty uses to frame her text offer an example, create tension, or pose a question? How is Hagerty using story in this nonfiction text to engage us, to deliver information, or to argue her claim? |
| **Day Three** | • Read Alice Walker's (1967) "The Civil Rights Movement: What Good Was It?" and annotate how Walker uses argument. Ask students to mark/highlight any sentence or section where it feels like Walker is trying to convince you of something. |
| | • Discuss and compare your own and students' annotations. What is Walker's central claim? How does she develop her claim? How does she use the story of her mother's life to underscore her claim? |
| **Day Four** | • Break students into small groups and give them a short narrative nonfiction text that has been cut up and laminated. Their job is to reassemble the texts and determine why and how the writer structured the piece. Circulate and ask students to justify why they've assembled the piece in certain ways and what their "clues" were, such as transitional words or an embedded narrative structure. (Ed Yong's [2017] "Tiny Jumping Spiders Can See the Moon" is a good one for this or Joe Bubar's [2018] "Does Facebook Know Too Much?") |
| | • Students present their findings about structure, then switch texts with another group. |
| | • Repeat until all groups have assembled three different texts. |
| | • Hand back students' practice drafts from the week before and make some general comments about the narrative "moves" you saw in them. |
| **Day Five** | • Read David Wallace-Wells' (2017) "The Uninhabitable Earth." Ask students to mark any clues they notice for how Wallace-Wells structures the text. (This is a great essay to read for structure because the essay is divided into clear sections.) Do they see any patterns? Can they identify any organizational bones or architecture of the text? Have them mark any use of lacunas, sections, patterns, outlines, or arrangements that seem to be floating just beneath the surface of Wallace-Wells' text that provide organization for the content. (A shorter text I use with some classes is Chrisanne Grisé's (2019) "Will the Climate Kids Save the Planet?") |
| | • Break students into groups and ask them to draw a visual that represents what they see as the "blueprint" Wallace-Wells uses to "build" this essay. |
| | • Share the different visuals and discuss how each group represented the structure of the text. |
| | • Ask each student to select a celebrity they'd like to read a profile about for Monday's class. (The celebrity profile is a particular kind of narrative nonfiction piece, and students love reading and writing about their heroes. My list this year included celebrities like Kesha, John Mulaney, Taylor Swift, Yara Shahidi, and Grant Hart.) |
| | • Set the expectation that by the following week, students will select a topic they want to write about using a blend of narrative, information, and argumentation. |

| | |
|---|---|
| **Week Three, Day One** | • Read Hanif Abdurraqib's (2017a, 2018) "The Night Prince Walked on Water" and "Too Much and Still Not Enough: Mourning Aretha Franklin" and annotate how Abdurraqib uses narrative to deliver information about these stars while at the same time making an argument for the quality of their stardom.<br>• Distribute individual character profiles and ask students to annotate these looking at the story techniques the writer uses.<br>• Share and discuss these texts, paying particular attention to their organization. Many of them share the same pattern of exposition.<br>• Continue to add craft moves to our list on the board. |
| **Day Two** | Brainstorm day: spend some time in large and small groups, generating ideas or topics students would like to write about. Have students freewrite to find a narrative that might work to blend with the information they want to deliver or the argument they'd like to make. Set the expectation that students will pitch their ideas to the whole class the next day. |
| **Day Three** | Pitching is a skill I intentionally teach across every unit and project cycle. It's not a presentation, but a short two- to five-minute spoken summary of an idea. Typically students explain what they want to write about and why they want to write about it. After each pitch, their peers can ask questions to help them clarify their intentions and purpose for the piece. |
| **Day Four** | Writing day: students can choose to use the time for primary or secondary research, interviewing, drafting, freewriting their narrative, outlining, anything that helps them craft a first draft. Length and form are negotiable. Remind students of the menu of narrative strategies that are on the board. |
| **Day Five** | Depending on your students, your classroom situation, and your calendar, this block of writing days could be as short or long as you need it. It might occur in or outside of the classroom. I'm a firm believer in long stretches of in-class "studio" time for student writers while I am circulating, troubleshooting, conferencing, and assisting with research. |

# A SOURCE LIST OF TEXTS FOR TEACHING NARRATIVE NONFICTION

At some point in my teaching, I've used all these texts to introduce students to some aspect of narrative nonfiction. Some are classics I use every year like Lynda Barry's (1992) "Sanctuary of School," but I try not to rely on the same pieces year after year because they become dated, and I want my enjoyment of the piece to be as fresh and expectant as my students'.

I select (or have my students select) living writers writing about contemporary topics that impact their lives and about which they are interested. If I'm asking them to write into a public conversation, I want them to listen to what others have had to say about these topics first. If I'm using a complex text, like Virginia Hughes' (2013) "23 and You," I pair it with something less complicated that hits the same information and argument, such as Joe Bubar's (2019) "Can Your DNA Solve a Murder?" as an introduction.

Abdurraqib, Hanif. 2017. "The Night Prince Walked on Water." In *They Can't Kill Us Until They Kill Us*. Columbus, OH: Two Dollar Radio.

———. 2018. "Too Much and Still Not Enough: Mourning Aretha Franklin." *Pacific Standard*, September 7. Accessed October 18. https://psmag.com/social-justice/mourning-aretha-franklin.

Adams, Jacqueline. 2018. "Walking on Thin Ice: Will Polar Bears Be Able to Survive a Melting Arctic?" *Scholastic Science World*, December 10.

Barry, Dan. 2012. "At the Corner of Hope and Worry." *The New York Times*, October 13. Accessed January 21, 2018. http://archive.nytimes.com/www.nytimes.com/2012/10/14/us/this-land-corner-of-hope-and-worry-elyria.html.

———. 2017. "The Lost Children of Tuam." *The New York Times*, October 28. Accessed August 11, 2018. https://www.nytimes.com/interactive/2017/10/28/world/europe/tuam-ireland-babies-children.html.

Barry, Lynda. 1992. "The Sanctuary of School." *The New York Times*, January 5.

Barth, Amy. 2017. "The Fight over Fracking." *Upfront Scholastic: The New York Times*, February 20. Accessed June 18, 2018. https://upfront.scholastic.com/issues/2016-17/022017/the-fight-over-fracking.html.

Bliss, Eula. 2007. "The Pain Scale." *The Seneca Review*. http://www.snreview.org/biss.pdf.

Brooks, David. 2003. "People Like Us." *The Atlantic*, September 2003. Accessed January 21, 2018. https://www.theatlantic.com/magazine/archive/2003/09/people-like-us/302774/.

Bubar, Joe. 2018. "Does Facebook Know Too Much?" *The New York Times Upfront*, September 3. Accessed February 11, 2019. https://upfront.scholastic.com /issues/2018-19/090318/does-facebook-know-too-much.html#1350L.

———. 2019. "Could Your DNA Solve a Murder?" *The New York Times Upfront*. February 18. Accessed February 20, 2019. https://upfront.scholastic.com /issues/2018-19/021819/could-your-dna-solve-a-murder.html#1180L.

Bubar, Joe, and Carl Stoffers. 2018. "Friday Night Lights Out?" *The New York Times Upfront*, November 19. Accessed February 20, 2019. https://upfront.scholastic .com/issues/2018-19/111918/friday-night-lights-out.html#1120L.

Carr, Nicholas G. 2013. "All Can Be Lost: The Risk of Putting Our Knowledge in the Hands of Machines." *The Atlantic*, November 2013. Accessed July 18, 2018. https://www.theatlantic.com/magazine/archive/2013/11/the-great -forgetting/309516/.

Costello, Emily. 2018. "Puzzle Solver: Meet the Reigning Rubik's Cube Champ." *Scholastic Science World*, December 10. Accessed February 10, 2019. https:// scienceworld.scholastic.com/issues/2018-19/121018/puzzle-solver.html#910L.

Cudmore, Becca. 2017. "The Case for Leaving City Rats Alone." In *The Best American Science and Nature Writing 2017*, edited by Hope Jahren, series edited by Tim Folger. New York: Houghton Mifflin Harcourt.

Darvick, Debra. 2004. "Service with a Smile, and Plenty of Metal." *Newsweek* 144 (2): 20.

Doyle, Brian. 2004. "Joyous Voladoras." Reprinted in *American Scholar*, July 12, 2012. Accessed July 1, 2018. https://theamericanscholar.org/joyas-volardores /#.W7deli-ZO8U.

Dutton, Kevin. 2013. "Wisdom from Psychopaths?" *Scientific American*, January 1, 2013. Accessed July 1, 2018. https://www.scientificamerican.com/article /wisdom-from-psychopaths/.

Ehrenreich, Barbara. 1999. "Nickel-and-Dimed: On (Not) Getting by in America." *Harper's Magazine*, January 1999. Accessed February 10, 2019. https:// harpers.org/archive/1999/01/nickel-and-dimed/.

———. 2018. "Running to the Grave." *Harper's Magazine*, March 2018. Accessed February 10, 2019. https://harpers.org/archive/2018/03/running-to-the -grave/.

Everts, Sarah. 2017. "The Art of Saving Relics." In *The Best American Science and Nature Writing 2017*, edited by Hope Jahren, series edited by Tim Folger. New York: Houghton Mifflin Harcourt.

Felt, Susannah. 2017. "Astonish Me: Anticipating an Eclipse in the Age of Information." *Catapult*, August 21. Accessed February 9, 2019. https://catapult .co/stories/astonish-me-anticipating-an-eclipse-in-the-age-of-information.

Fox, Douglas. 2018. "Firestorm." In *The Best American Science and Nature Writing 2018*, edited by Sam Kean, series edited by Tim Folger. New York: Houghton Mifflin Harcourt.

Furgurson, Ernest B. 2009. "The Man Who Shot the Man Who Shot Lincoln." *The American Scholar*, March 1, 2009. Accessed May 18, 2017. https://theamericanscholar.org/the-man-who-shot-the-man-who-shot-lincoln/?utm_source=social_media&utm_medium=tumblr#.W9Tipi-ZOgQ.

Gamel, John. 2009. "The Elegant Eyeball." *Alaska Quarterly Review* 26 (1 & 2). Accessed February 9, 2019. https://aqreview.org/the-elegant-eyeball/.

Gawande, Atul. 2006. "The Score: How Childbirth Went Industrial." *The New Yorker*. October 9, 2006. Accessed May 15, 2017. https://www.newyorker.com/magazine/2006/10/09/the-score.

Ghansah, Rachel Kaadzi. 2017. "A Most American Terrorist: The Making of Dylann Roof." *GQ*, August 12. Accessed February 12, 2019. https://www.gq.com/story/dylann-roof-making-of-an-american-terrorist.

Goodall, Jane. 2011. "The Lazarus Effect." In *The Best American Science and Nature Writing 2011*, edited by Freeman Dyson, series edited by Tim Folger. New York: Houghton Mifflin Harcourt.

Grisé, Chrisanne. 2019. "Will the Climate Kids Save the Planet?" *The New York Times Upfront*, February 18. Accessed February 20, 2019. https://upfront.scholastic.com/issues/2018-19/021819/will-the-climate-kids-save-the-planet.html#1300L.

Grunbaum, Mara. 2019. "Fossil Hunter." Scholastic Science, February 11. Accessed February 20, 2019. https://scienceworld.scholastic.com/issues/2018-19/021119/fossil-hunter.html.

Hagerty, Barbara Bradley. 2017. "When Your Child Is a Psychopath." *The Atlantic*, June 2017. Accessed February 10, 2019. https://www.theatlantic.com/magazine/archive/2017/06/when-your-child-is-a-psychopath/524502/.

Halberstam, David. 2004. "Who We Are." *The Best American Essays: Fourth College Edition*, edited by Robert Atwan. New York: Houghton Mifflin.

Hearne, Vicki. 2004. "What's Wrong with Animal Rights?" *The Best American Essays: Fourth College Edition*, edited by Robert Atwan. New York: Houghton Mifflin Company.

Hughes, Virginia. 2013. "23 and You." *Matter*, December 4, 2013. Accessed February 10, 2019. https://medium.com/matter/23-and-you-66e87553d22c.

Jackson, Lawrence. 2017. "The City That Bleeds." In *The Best American Essays 2017*. Editors Leslie Jamison and Robert Atwan. New York: Houghton Mifflin Harcourt.

Jenkins, Gavin. 2016. "The Hidden History of Gas Station Bathrooms, By a Man Who Cleans Them." *Narratively*, November 9. Accessed May 15, 2019. https://narratively.com/the-hidden-history-of-gas-station-bathrooms-by-a-man-who-cleans-them/.

Jones, Chris. 2016. "The Woman Who Might Find Us Another Earth." *The New York Times*, December 7, 2016. Accessed May 15, 2018. https://www.nytimes.com/2016/12/07/magazine/the-world-sees-me-as-the-one-who-will-find-another-earth.html.

Kolbert, Elizabeth. 2009. "The Sixth Extinction?" *The New Yorker*, May 25. Accessed February 10, 2019. https://www.newyorker.com/magazine/2009/05/25/the-sixth-extinction.

Levin, Alan, Marilyn Adams, and Blake Morrison. 2002. "Amid Terror, a Drastic Decision: Clear the Skies." *USA Today*, August 13. Accessed February 10, 2019. https://usatoday30.usatoday.com/travel/news/2002/2002-08-12-clear-skies.htm#more.

Lightman, Alan. 2016. "What Came Before the Big Bang?" *Harper's Magazine*, January 2016. Accessed February 10, 2019. https://harpers.org/archive/2016/01/what-came-before-the-big-bang/.

Lipton, Eric, Steve Eder, and John Branch. 2018. "Dismissing Science." *The New York Times*, December 27. Accessed February 10, 2019. https://www.nytimes.com/interactive/2018/12/26/us/politics/donald-trump-environmental-regulation.html.

Lopate, Philip. 2010. "Brooklyn the Unknowable." In *The Best American Essays 2010*, edited by Christopher Hitchens, series edited by Robert Atwan. New York: Hougton Mifflin Harcourt.

Manning, Richard. 2010. "Graze Anatomy." In *The Best American Science and Nature Writing 2010*, edited by Freeman Dyson, series edited by Tim Folger. New York: Houghton Mifflin Harcourt.

Mozur, Paul. 2018. "Big Brother Comes to China." *The New York Times Upfront*, October 8. https://upfront.scholastic.com/issues/2018-19/100818/big-brother-comes-to-china.html#1190L.

Nijhuis, Michelle. 2012. "Which Species Will Live?" *Scientific American*, August 2011. Accessed July 22, 2018. https://michellenijhuis.com/articles/2012/7/17/which-species-will-live.

Obama, Barack. 2008. "Barack Obama's Speech on Race." *The New York Times*. March 18, 2008. Accessed May 13, 2018. https://www.nytimes.com/2008/03/18/us/politics/18text-obama.html.

O'Conner, M. R. 2017. "The Strange and Gruesome Story of the Greenland Shark, the Longest-Living Vertebrate on Earth." *The New Yorker*, November 25, 2017. Accessed May 25, 2018. https://www.newyorker.com/tech/annals-of-technology/the-strange-and-gruesome-story-of-the-greenland-shark-the-longest-living-vertebrate-on-earth.

Ofri, Danielle. 2011. "Living Will." *The Best American Essays: Sixth College edition*. Boston: Wadsworth Cengage Learning.

Oppel, Richard A., and Jugal K. Patel. 2019. "One Lawyer, 194 Felony Cases, and No Time." *The New York Times*, January 31. Accessed January 31, 2019. https://www.nytimes.com/interactive/2019/01/31/us/public-defender-case -loads.html.

O'Toole, Patricia. 2019. "Theodore Roosevelt Cared Deeply About the Sick. Who Knew?" *The New York Times*, January 6. Accessed February 9, 2019. https:// www.nytimes.com/2019/01/06/opinion/theodore-roosevelt-health-care -progressive.html.

Philpott, Tom. 2016. "How Factory Farms Play Chicken with Antibiotics." *Mother Jones*. Accessed July 11, 2018. https://www.motherjones.com /environment/2016/05/perdue-antibiotic-free-chicken-meat-resistance/.

Potenza, Alessandra. 2019. "Hidden Forest." *Scholastic Science World*, February 11. https://scienceworld.scholastic.com/issues/2018-19/021119/hidden-forest .html#880L.

Preston, Diane. 2018. "Trouble in Paradise." *BBC World History* April/May (9).

Remnick, David. 2012. "We Are Alive." *The New Yorker*, July 30. Accessed February 10, 2019. https://www.newyorker.com/magazine/2012/07/30/we-are-alive.

Resnick, Sarah. 2017. "H." In *The Best American Essays 2017*, edited by Leslie Jamison, series edited by Robert Atwan. New York: Houghton Mifflin Harcourt.

Rich, Jennifer. 2018. "A Second Grader Once Pointed a Gun at Me. I'm Glad I Wasn't Armed." *The Washington Post*, March 15, 2018. Accessed January 5, 2019 https://www.washingtonpost.com/opinions/a-second-grader-once-pointed -a-gun-at-me-im-glad-i-wasnt-armed/2018/03/15/60e4bb86-2230-11e8-badd -7c9f29a55815_story.html?utm_term=.71ce18992312.

Rich, Nathaniel. 2016. "The Invisible Catastrophe." *The New York Times*, March 31. Accessed February 10, 2019. https://www.nytimes.com/2016/04/03 /magazine/the-invisible-catastrophe.html.

Saslow, Eric. 2012. "Life of a Salesman: Selling Success, When the American Dream Is Downsized." *The Washington Post*, October 7. Accessed February 10, 2019. https://www.washingtonpost.com/national/life-of-a-salesman-selling -success-when-the-american-dream-is-downsized/2012/10/07/e2b34aac-1033 -11e2-acc1-e927767f41cd_story.html?utm_term=.e72cdaba3d46.

Simons, Eric. 2018. "At a Snail's Pace: In Which the Distribution of a Common Pacific Coast Sea Snail Explains the Underlying Logic of the Universe." BayNature.org. Accessed July 10, 2018. https://baynature.org/biodiversity /snails/.

Smith, Patricia. 2018. "Coming to America." *The New York Times Upfront*, October 29. https://upfront.scholastic.com/issues/2018-19/102918/coming-to-america .html#1120L.

———. 2018. "Does Nikolas Cruz Deserve to Die?" *The New York Times Upfront*, October 8. https://upfront.scholastic.com/content/dam/classroom-magazines /upfront/issues/2018-19/100818/p14-15-deathpenalty/UPF-100818-Lexile -p14-17.pdf.

———. 2019. "Will Ginger Get to Stay?" *The New York Times Upfront*, January 7. https://upfront.scholastic.com/content/dam/classroom-magazines/upfront /issues/2018-19/010719/p8-11-honduranteen/UPF-010719-Lexile-p08-11.pdf.

Spann, Paula. 2019. "Dementia May Never Improve, But Many Patients Still Can Learn." *The New York Times*, January 4. Accessed February 9, 2019. https://www .nytimes.com/2019/01/04/health/dementia-rehabilitation.html.

Staples, Brent. 2018. "Just Walk on By." In *Uncharted Territory: A High School Reader*, edited by Jim Burke. New York: W.W. Norton.

Starr, S. Frederick. 2009. "Rediscovering Central Asia." *The Wilson Quarterly*, Summer 2009. Accessed December 27, 2018. http://archive.wilsonquarterly .com/essays/rediscovering-central-asia.

Stewart, Sarah. 2014. "O-Rings." In *The Best American Science and Nature Writing 2014*, edited by Deborah Blum, series edited by Tim Folger. New York: Houghton Mifflin Harcourt.

Stillman, Sarah. 2018. "When Deportation Is a Death Sentence." *The New Yorker*, January 15. Accessed August 12, 2018. https://www.newyorker.com /magazine/2018/01/15/when-deportation-is-a-death-sentence.

St. John, Warren. 2013. "Nick Saban: Sympathy for the Devil." *GQ*, August 25, 2013. Accessed October 1, 2017. https://www.gq.com/story/coach-nick-saban -alabama-maniac.

Stover, Dawn. 2009. "Not So Silent Spring." *Conservation*, January 6. Accessed February 10, 2019. https://www.conservationmagazine.org/2009/01/not-so -silent-spring/.

Sullivan, Andrew. 2018. "The Poison We Pick." *New York Magazine*, February. Accessed February 10, 2019. http://nymag.com/intelligencer/2018/02 /americas-opioid-epidemic.html.

Tabuchi, Hiroko. 2019. "A Trump County Confronts the Administration Amid a Rash of Child Cancers." *The New York Times*, January 2. Accessed February 10, 2019. https://www.nytimes.com/2019/01/02/climate/tce-cancer-trump -environment-deregulation.html.

Talese, Gay. 1996. "Ali in Havana." *Esquire*. September. Reprinted in Longforms. Accessed July 16, 2018. http://reprints.longform.org/ali-in-havana-gay-talese.

Todd, Kim. 2018. "The Island Wolves." In *The Best American Science and Nature Writing 2018*, edited by Sam Kean, series edited by Tim Folger. New York: Houghton Mifflin Harcourt.

Twilley, Nicola. 2016. "How the First Gravitational Waves Were Found." *The New Yorker*, November 11. Accessed July 18, 2018. https://www.newyorker.com /tech/annals-of-technology/gravitational-waves-exist-heres-how-scientists -finally-found-them.

Walker, Alice. 1967. "The Civil Rights Movement: What Good Was It?" Reprinted in *The American Scholar*, February 20, 2016. Accessed July 2018. https:// theamericanscholar.org/the-civil-rights-movement-what-good-was-it/# .XETJ5i2ZM_U.

Wallace, David Foster. 1994. "Ticket to the Fair." *Harper's Magazine*, July. Accessed February 10, 2019. https://harpers.org/wp-content/uploads/Harpers Magazine-1994-07-0001729.pdf.

Wallace-Wells, David. 2017. "The Uninhabitable Earth." *New York Magazine*, July 10. Accessed February 10, 2019. http://nymag.com/intelligencer/2017/07/climate -change-earth-too-hot-for-humans.html.

Yong, Ed. 2017. "Tiny Jumping Spiders Can See the Moon." *The Atlantic*, June. Accessed February 10, 2019. https://www.theatlantic.com/science /archive/2017/06/jumping-spiders-can-see-the-moon/529329/.

# REFERENCES

Abdurraqib, Hanif. 2017a. "The Night Prince Walked on Water." In *They Can't Kills Us Until They Kill Us*. Columbus, OH: Two Dollar Radio.

———. 2017b. "Serena Williams and the Policing of Imagined Arrogance." In *They Can't Kills Us Until They Kill Us*. Columbus, OH: Two Dollar Radio.

———. 2018. "Too Much and Still Not Enough: Mourning Aretha Franklin." *Pacific Standard*, September 7. Accessed October 18. https://psmag.com/social-justice/mourning-aretha-franklin.

Adams, Jacqueline. 2018. "Walking on Thin Ice: Will Polar Bears Be Able to Survive a Melting Arctic?" *Scholastic Science World*, December 10.

Allen, Edward. 1998. *The Hands-on Fiction Workbook*. New Jersey: Prentice-Hall.

American Press Institute. 2018. "Good Stories Explore Tensions." American Press Institute. Accessed May 15, 2018. https://www.americanpressinstitute.org/journalism-essentials/makes-good-story/good-stories-explore-tensions/.

Anderson, Chris. 2016. *Ted Talks: The Official TED Guide to Public Speaking*. Boston: Houghton Mifflin Harcourt.

Andersen, Kurt. 2017 *Fantasyland: How America Went Haywire: A 500-Year History*. New York: Random House.

Attkisson, Sharyl. 2017. *The Smear: How Shady Political Operatives and Fake News Control What You See, What You Think, and How You Vote*. New York: Harper Collins.

Austen, Jane. (1995). *Pride and Prejudice*. New York: Dover Thrift Edition.

Barry, Dan. 2012. "At the Corner of Hope and Worry." *The New York Times*, October 13. Accessed January 21, 2018. http://archive.nytimes.com/www.nytimes.com/2012/10/14/us/this-land-corner-of-hope-and-worry-elyria.html.

———. 2017. "The Lost Children of Tuam." *The New York Times*, October 28. Accessed August 11, 2018. https://www.nytimes.com/interactive/2017/10/28/world/europe/tuam-ireland-babies-children.html.

Barry, Lynda. 1992. "The Sanctuary of School." *The New York Times*, January 5.

Barth, Amy. 2017. "The Fight over Fracking." *Upfront Scholastic: The New York Times*, February 20. Accessed June 18, 2018. https://upfront.scholastic.com/issues/2016-17/022017/the-fight-over-fracking.html.

Bascom, Tim. 2013. "Picturing the Personal Essay: A Visual Guide." *Creative Nonfiction*, Summer (49). Accessed January 8, 2019. https://www.creativenonfiction.org/online-reading/picturing-personal-essay-visual-guide

Berry, Wendell. 2010. "Why I Am Not Going to Buy a Computer." In *What Are People For?* Berkeley, CA: Counterpoint.

Biss, Eula. 2007. "The Pain Scale." *The Seneca Review.* Accessed February 9, 2019. http://www.snreview.org/biss.pdf.

Booker, Christopher. 2004. *The Seven Basic Plots: Why We Tell Stories.* New York: Continuum.

Bram, Christopher. 2016. *The Art of History: Unlocking the Past in Fiction and Nonfiction.* Minnesota: Graywolf.

Brooks, David. 2003. "People Like Us." *The Atlantic,* September 2003. Accessed January 21, 2018. https://www.theatlantic.com/magazine/archive/2003/09/people-like-us/302774/.

Bubar, Joe. 2018. "Does Facebook Know Too Much?" *The New York Times Upfront,* September 3. Accessed February 11, 2019. https://upfront.scholastic.com/issues/2018-19/090318/does-facebook-know-too-much.html#1350L.

Bubar, Joe. 2019. "Could Your DNA Solve a Murder?" *The New York Times Upfront,* February 18. Accessed February 11, 2019. https://upfront.scholastic.com/issues/2018-19/021819/could-your-dna-solve-a-murder.html#1180L

Bubar, Joe, and Carl Stoffers. 2018. "Friday Night Lights Out?" *The New York Times Upfront,* November 19. Accessed February 20, 2019. https://upfront.scholastic.com/issues/2018-19/111918/friday-night-lights-out.html#1120L.

Burroway, Janet, with Elizabeth Stuckey French. 2007. *Writing Fiction: A Guide to Narrative Craft,* 7th ed. New York: Pearson-Longman.

Canby, Vincent. 1986. "Film: A Documentary, 'Sherman's March.'" *The New York Times,* September 5, 1986. Accessed July 17, 2018. https://www.nytimes.com/1986/09/05/movies/film-a-documentary-sherman-s-march.html.

Capote, Truman. 2012. *In Cold Blood.* New York: Vintage International Edition.

Carey, John. 1998. *Eyewitness to History.* Cambridge, MA: Harvard University Press.

Carr, Nicholas G. 2013. "All Can Be Lost: The Risk of Putting Our Knowledge in the Hands of Machines." *The Atlantic,* November 2013. Accessed July 18, 2018. https://www.theatlantic.com/magazine/archive/2013/11/the-great-forgetting/309516/.

Castellani, Christopher. 2016. *The Art of Perspective.* Minnesota: Graywolf.

Chan, Sewell. 2017. "Stanislav Petrov, Soviet Officer Who Helped Avert Nuclear War, Is Dead at 77." *The New York Times.* September 18, 2017. Accessed January 20, 2018. https://www.nytimes.com/2017/09/18/world/europe/stanislav-petrov-nuclear-war-dead.html.

Chaudhuri, Amit. 2018. "The Moment of Writing." *The Paris Review,* May 10. Accessed August 8, 2018. https://www.theparisreview.org/blog/2018/05/10/the-moment-of-writing/.

Chernow, Ron. (2005). *Hamilton.* New York: Penguin.

Clark, Roy Peter. 2001. "The Line Between Fact and Fiction." *Creative Nonfiction* (16). Accessed February 10, 2019. https://www.creativenonfiction.org/online-reading/line-between-fact-and-fiction.

———. 2012. "Why Nonfiction Writers Should Take a 'Vow of Chastity.'" *Poytner*, July 23. Accessed February 20, 2019. https://www.poynter.org/newsletters/2012/why-nonfiction-writers-should-take-a-vow-of-chastity/.

Clinton, Hillary Rodham. 2017. *What Happened*. New York: Simon and Schuster.

Cohn, Jonathan. 2017. *The Paradigm: The Ancient Blueprint That Holds the Mystery of Our Times*. Lake Mary, Florida: Frontline.

Colbert, Stephen. 2005. Episode 1. *The Colbert Report*. October 17, 2005. Comedy Central. http://www.cc.com/video-clips/63ite2/the-colbert-report-the-word---truthiness

Coleman, David. 2011. "Bringing the Common Core to Life." NYSED.gov. April 28, 2011. Accessed July 2, 2018. http://usny.nysed.gov/rttt/docsbringingthecommon coretolife/fulltranscript.pdf.

Costello, Emily. 2018. "Puzzle Solver: Meet the Reigning Rubik's Cube Champ." *Scholastic Science World*, December 10. Accessed February 10, 2019. https://scienceworld.scholastic.com/issues/2018-19/121018/puzzle-solver.html#910L.

Cudmore, Becca. 2016. "The Case for Leaving City Rats Alone." In *The Best American Science and Nature Writing 2017*, edited by Hope Jahren, series edited by Tim Folger. New York: Houghton Mifflin Harcourt.

Darvick, Debra. 2004. "Service with a Smile, and Plenty of Metal." *Newsweek* 144 (2): 20.

Diamond, Jared. 1997. *Guns, Germs, and Steel*. New York: W.W. Norton.

Doty, Mark. 2010. *Art of Description*. Minneapolis, MN: Graywolf.

Doyle, Brian. 2004. "Joyous Voladoras." Reprinted in *American Scholar*, July 12, 2012. Accessed July 1, 2018. https://theamericanscholar.org/joyas-volardores/#.W7deli-ZO8U.

Dutton, Kevin. 2013. "Wisdom from Psychopaths?" *Scientific American*, January 1, 2013. Accessed July 1, 2018. https://www.scientificamerican.com/article/wisdom-from-psychopaths/.

Egri, Lajos. 2004. *The Art of Dramatic Writing*. New York: Touchstone.

Ehrenreich, Barbara. 1999. "Nickel-and-Dimed: On (Not) Getting by in America." *Harper's Magazine*, January 1999. Accessed February 10, 2019. https://harpers.org/archive/1999/01/nickel-and-dimed/.

———. 2018a. *Natural Causes: An Epidemic of Wellness, the Certainty of Dying, and Killing Ourselves to Live Longer*. New York: Hachette Book Group.

———. 2018b. "Running to the Grave." *Harper's Magazine*, March 2018. Accessed February 10, 2019. https://harpers.org/archive/2018/03/running-to-the-grave/.

Everts, Sarah. 2017. "The Art of Saving Relics." In *The Best American Science and Nature Writing 2017*, edited by Hope Jahren, series edited by Tim Folger. New York: Houghton Mifflin Harcourt.

Felts, Susannah. 2017. "Astonish Me: Anticipating an Eclipse in the Age of Information." *Catapult*, August 21. Accessed February 9, 2019. https://catapult.co/stories/astonish-me-anticipating-an-eclipse-in-the-age-of-information.

Flood, Charles Bracelen. 2005. *Grant and Sherman: The Friendship That Won the Civil War*. New York: Farrar, Straus, and Giroux.

Florey, Kitty Burns. 2006. *Sister Bernadette's Barking Dog: The Quirky History and Lost Art of Diagramming Sentences*. New York: Harcourt.

Folger, Tim, ed. 2017. *The Best American Science and Nature Writing 2017*. New York: Houghton Mifflin Harcourt.

Fox, Douglas. 2018. "Firestorm." In *The Best American Science and Nature Writing 2018*, edited by Sam Kean, series edited by Tim Folger. New York: Houghton Mifflin Harcourt.

Franzen, Jonathon. 2018. "The Essay in Dark Times." *The End of the End of the Earth*. New York: Farrar, Straus, and Giroux.

Furgurson, Ernest B. 2009. "The Man Who Shot the Man Who Shot Lincoln." *The American Scholar*, March 1, 2009. Accessed May 18, 2017. https://theamericanscholar .org/the-man-who-shot-the-man-who-shot-lincoln/?utm_source=social_media &utm_medium=tumblr#.W9Tipi-ZOgQ.

Gallo, Carmine. 2016. *The Storyteller's Secret: How TED Speakers and Inspirational Leaders Turn Their Passion into Performance*. London: St. Martin's Press.

Gamel, John. 2009. "The Elegant Eyeball." *Alaska Quarterly Review* 26 (1 & 2). Accessed February 9, 2019. https://aqreview.org/the-elegant-eyeball/.

Gardner, John. 1983. *The Art of Fiction: Notes on Craft for Young Writers*. New York: Random House.

Gawande, Atul. 2006. "The Score: How Childbirth Went Industrial." *The New Yorker*. October 9, 2006. Accessed May 15, 2017. https://www.newyorker.com/magazine /2006/10/09/the-score.

———. 2014. *Being Mortal: Medicine and What Matters in the End*. New York: Metropolitan Books/Henry Holt.

Ghansah, Rachel Kaadzi. 2017. "A Most American Terrorist: The Making of Dylann Roof." *GQ*, August 12. Accessed February 12, 2019. https://www.gq.com/story /dylann-roof-making-of-an-american-terrorist.

Gladwell, Malcolm. 2008. *Outliers: The Story of Success*. New York: Little, Brown and Company.

Goldberg, Natalie. 1986. *Writing Down the Bones: Freeing the Writer Within*. Boston: Shambhala Publications.

Gonchar, Michael. 2014. "200 Prompts for Argumentative Writing." *The New York Times Learning Network*, February 3, 2014. Accessed June 12, 2018. https://learning.blogs .nytimes.com/2014/02/04/200-prompts-for-argumentative-writing/.

———. 2016. "650 Prompts for Narrative and Personal Writing." *The New York Times Learning Network*, October 20, 2016. Accessed June 12, 2018. https://www.nytimes .com/2016/10/20/learning/lesson-plans/650-prompts-for-narrative-and-personal -writing.html?module=inline.

———. 2017. "401 Prompts for Argumentative Writing." *The New York Times Learning Network*, March 1, 2017. Accessed June 12, 2018. https://www.nytimes.com/2017/03/01/learning/lesson-plans/401-prompts-for-argumentative-writing.html?module=inline.

———. 2018. "Over 1000 Writing Prompts for Students." *The New York Times Learning Network*, April 12, 2018. Accessed June 12, 2018. https://www.nytimes.com/2018/04/12/learning/over-1000-writing-prompts-for-students.html.

Goodall, Jane. 2011. "The Lazarus Effect." In *The Best American Science and Nature Writing 2011*, edited by Freeman Dyson, series edited by Tim Folger. New York: Houghton Mifflin Harcourt.

Goodwin, Doris Kearns. 2005. *Team of Rivals: The Political Genius of Abraham Lincoln*. New York: Simon and Schuster.

Gottschall, Jonathon. 2012. *The Storytelling Animal: How Stories Make Us Human*. New York: Mariner Books.

Grann, David. 2017. *Killers of the Flower Moon: The Osage Murders and the Birth of the FBI*. New York: Vintage Books.

Greene, Anne. 2013. *Writing Science in Plain English*. Chicago: University of Chicago Press.

Grisé, Chrisanne. 2019. "Will the Climate Kids Save the Planet?" *The New York Times Upfront*, February 18. Accessed February 20, 2019. https://upfront.scholastic.com/issues/2018-19/021819/will-the-climate-kids-save-the-planet.html#1300L.

Gross, Terry. *Fresh Air*. National Public Radio. Retrieved from https://www.npr.org/templates/story/story.php?storyId=5013

Grunbaum, Mara. 2019. "Fossil Hunter." *Scholastic Science*, February 11. Accessed February 20, 2019. https://scienceworld.scholastic.com/issues/2018-19/021119/fossil-hunter.html.

Gutkind, Lee. 1996. *Creative Nonfiction: How to Live It and Write It*. Chicago: Chicago Review Press.

———. 1997. *The Art of Creative Nonfiction: Writing and Selling the Literature of Reality*. New York: John Wiley & Sons, Inc.

———, editor. 2005. *In Fact: The Best of Creative Nonfiction*. New York: W.W. Norton.

———. 2012. *You Can't Make This Stuff Up: The Complete Guide to Writing Creative Nonfiction from Memoir to Literary Journalism and Everything In Between*. Philadelphia: Da Capo.

Hagerty, Barbara Bradley. 2017. "When Your Child Is a Psychopath." *The Atlantic*, June 2017. Accessed February 10, 2019. https://www.theatlantic.com/magazine/archive/2017/06/when-your-child-is-a-psychopath/524502/.

Hakim, Joy. 2005. *A History of US: The First Americans, Prehistory to 1600, Revised Third Edition*. New York: Oxford University Press.

———. 1997. Acceptance speech upon receipt of the 1997 James A. Michener Prize in Writing. Accessed July 16, 2018. http://gos.sbc.edu/h/hakim.html.

Halberstam, David. 2004. "Who We Are." *Best American Essays: Fourth College Edition*, edited by Robert Atwan. New York: Houghton Mifflin.

Hampl, Patricia. 2008. "The Dark Art of Description." *The Iowa Review* 38 (1). Accessed July 4, 2018. https://ir.uiowa.edu/cgi/viewcontent.cgi?article=6413&context=iowareview.

Hart, Jack. 2011. *Storycraft. The Complete Guide to Writing Narrative Nonfiction*. Chicago: University of Chicago Press.

Hearne, Vicki. 2004. "What's Wrong with Animal Rights?" *The Best American Essays: Fourth College Edition*, edited by Robert Atwan. New York: Houghton Mifflin Company.

Hemingway, Ernest. 1996. *Death in the Afternoon*. New York: Scribner.

Hollis, Rachel. 2018. *Girl, Wash Your Face: Stop Believing the Lies About Who You Are so You Can Become Who You Were Meant to Be*. Nashville: Nelson Books.

Hughes, Virginia. 2013. "23 and You." *Matter*, December 4, 2013. Accessed February 10, 2019. https://medium.com/matter/23-and-you-66e87553d22c.

Irving, John. 2001. "Getting Started." *Writers on Writing: Collected Essays from The New York Times*. New York: Henry Holt.

Isays, Dave. (Founder and producer.) *Storycorps*. [Audio podcast.] Retrieved from https://storycorps.org/about/.

Jackson, Lawrence. 2017. "The City That Bleeds." In *The Best American Essays 2017*, edited by Leslie Jamison and Robert Atwan. New York: Houghton Mifflin Harcourt.

Jamison, Leslie. 2017. "Introduction." In *The Best American Essays 2017*. New York: Hougton Mifflin Harcourt.

Jenkins, Gavin. 2016. "The Hidden History of Gas Station Bathrooms, By a Man Who Cleans Them." *Narratively*, November 9. Accessed May 15, 2019. https://narratively.com/the-hidden-history-of-gas-station-bathrooms-by-a-man-who-cleans-them/.

Johnson, Charles. (1998). *Middle Passage*. New York: Scribner.

Jones, Chris. 2016. "The Woman Who Might Find Us Another Earth." *The New York Times*, December 7, 2016. Accessed May 15, 2018. https://www.nytimescom/2016/12/07/magazine/the-world-sees-me-as-the-one-who-will-find-another-earth.html.

Kamara, Mariatu, and Susan McClelland. (2008). *The Bite of the Mango*. London: Bloomsbury.

Kidder, Tracy. 2013. *Good Prose: The Art of Nonfiction*. New York: Random House Trade Paperbacks.

Kiernan, Denise. 2017. *The Last Castle: The Epic Story of Love, Loss, and American Royalty in the Nation's Largest Home*. New York: Touchstone.

Kitchen, Judith. 2005. *Short Takes: Brief Encounters with Contemporary Nonfiction*. New York: W.W. Norton.

Klinkenborg, Veryln. 2012. *Several Short Sentences About Writing*. New York: Vintage Books.

Kolbert, Elizabeth. 2009. "The Sixth Extinction?" *The New Yorker*, May 25. Accessed February 10, 2019. https://www.newyorker.com/magazine/2009/05/25/the-sixth-extinction.

Krakauer, Jon. 1996. *Into the Wild*. New York: Anchor Books.

Lea, Richard. 2016. "Fiction v. Nonfiction—English Literature's Made Up Divide." *The Guardian*, March 24. Accessed February 10, 2019. https://www.theguardian.com/books/2016/mar/24/fiction-nonfiction-english-literature-culture-writers-other-languages-stories.

Levin, Alan, Marilyn Adams, and Blake Morrison. 2002. "Amid Terror, a Drastic Decision: Clear the Skies." *USA Today*, August 13. Accessed February 10, 2019. https://usatoday30.usatoday.com/travel/news/2002/2002-08-12-clear-skies.htm#more.

Levy, Ariel. 2015. "Introduction." In *The Best American Essays 2015: The Best American Series*. Houghton Mifflin Harcourt.

Lightman, Alan. 2016. "What Came Before the Big Bang?" *Harper's Magazine*, January 2016. Accessed February 10, 2019. https://harpers.org/archive/2016/01/what-came-before-the-big-bang/

Lipton, Eric, Steve Eder, and John Branch. 2018. "President Trump's Retreat on the Environment Is Affecting Communities Across America." *The New York Times*, December 27. Accessed February 10, 2019. https://www.nytimes.com/interactive/2018/12/26/us/politics/donald-trump-environmental-regulation.html.

Livesay, Margot. 2004. "The Character Is Action." *The Atlantic*, December 2004. Accessed July 9, 2018. https://www.theatlantic.com/magazine/archive/2004/12/character-is-action/303652/.

Lopate, Philip. 2010. "Brooklyn the Unknowable." In *The Best American Essays 2010*, edited by Christopher Hitchens, series edited by Robert Atwan. New York: Hougton Mifflin Harcourt.

———. 2013. *To Show and to Tell: The Craft of Literary Nonfiction*. New York: Simon & Schuster.

Lozada, Carlos. 2014. "200 Journalism Cliches and Counting." *The Washington Post*, February 20. Accessed February 9, 2019. https://www.washingtonpost.com/news/opinions/wp/2014/02/27/the-outlook-list-of-things-we-do-not-say/?utm_term=.705c8c97327b

Mamet, David. 2010. "David Mamet Memo." *Scribd*. Accessed May 25, 2018. https://www.scribd.com/document/100244214/David-Mamet-Memo.

Manning, Richard. 2010. "Graze Anatomy." *The Best American Science and Nature Writing 2010*, edited by Freeman Dyson, series edited by Tim Folger. New York: Houghton Mifflin Harcourt.

McCarthy, Cormac. 2006. *The Road*. New York: Alfred A. Knopf.

McCullough, David. 2003. *Truman*. New York: Simon and Schuster.

McPhee, John. 2013. "The Writing Life: Structure." *The New Yorker*. January 14, 2013. Accessed July 15, 2018. https://www.newyorker.com/magazine/2013/01/14 /structure.

———. 2015. "The Writing Life: The Art of Omission." *The New Yorker*, September 14, 2015. Accessed July 6, 2018. https://www.newyorker.com/magazine/2015/09/14 /omission.

Miller, Brenda, and Suzanne Paola. 2012. *Tell It Slant: Creating, Refining and Publishing Creative Nonfiction*. New York: McGraw-Hill.

Miranda, Lin-Manuel and Jeremy McCarter. (2016). *Hamilton: The Revolution*. New York: Grand Central Publishing.

Morrison, Toni. 1997. *Paradise*. New York: Vintage Books.

Mozur, Paul. 2018. "Big Brother Comes to China." *The New York Times Upfront*, October 8. https://upfront.scholastic.com/issues/2018-19/100818/big-brother-comes-to -china.html#1190L.

Newkirk, Tom. 2014. *Minds Made for Stories: How We Really Read and Write Informational and Persuasive Texts*. Portsmouth: Heinemann.

Nijhuis, Michelle. 2012. "Which Species Will Live?" *Scientific American*, August 2011. Accessed July 22, 2018. https://michellenijhuis.com/articles/2012/7/17/which -species-will-live.

Obama, Barack. 2008. "Barack Obama's Speech on Race." *The New York Times*. March 18, 2008. Accessed May 13, 2018. https://www.nytimes.com/2008/03/18/us/politics /18text-obama.html.

O'Conner, M. R. 2017. "The Strange and Gruesome Story of the Greenland Shark, the Longest-Living Vertebrate on Earth." *The New Yorker*, November 25, 2017. Accessed May 25, 2018. https://www.newyorker.com/tech/annals-of-technology/the -strange-and-gruesome-story-of-the-greenland-shark-the-longest-living-vertebrate -on-earth.

Ofri, Danielle. 2011. "Living Will." *The Best American Essays: Sixth College Edition*. Boston: Wadsworth Cengage Learning.

Oppel, Richard A., and Jugal K. Patel. 2019. "One Lawyer, 194 Felony Cases, and No Time." *The New York Times*, January 31. Accessed January 31, 2019. https://www .nytimes.com/interactive/2019/01/31/us/public-defender-case-loads.html.

O'Reilly, Bill, and Martin Dugard. 2017. *Killing England: The Brutal Struggle for American Independence*. New York: Henry Holt.

O'Toole, Patricia. 2019. "Theodore Roosevelt Cared Deeply About the Sick. Who Knew?" *The New York Times*, January 6. Accessed February 9, 2019. https://www.nytimes .com/2019/01/06/opinion/theodore-roosevelt-health-care-progressive.html.

Orwell, George. 2011. "Politics and the English Language." *One Hundred Great Essays*. Edited by Robert DiYanni. NewYork: Pearson Education, Inc.

Philpott, Tom. 2016. "How Factory Farms Play Chicken with Antibiotics." *Mother Jones*. Accessed July 11, 2018. https://www.motherjones.com/environment/2016/05 /perdue-antibiotic-free-chicken-meat-resistance/.

Pinker, Steven. 1997. *How the Mind Works*. New York: W.W. Norton.

Plimpton, George. 1966. "The Story Behind a Nonfiction Novel." *The New York Times Book Review*, January 16, 1966. Accessed July 1, 2018. https://archive.nytimes.com/www .nytimes.com/books/97/12/28/home/capote-interview.html?mcubz=3.

Polito, Robert. 1996. *Savage Art: A Biography of Jim Thompson*. New York: Vintage Books.

Potenza, Alessandra. 2019. "Hidden Forest." *Scholastic Science World*, February 11. https:// scienceworld.scholastic.com/issues/2018-19/021119/hidden-forest.html#880L.

Power, Arthur. 1949. *From the Old Waterford House*. Dublin, Ireland: Mellifont Library, Carthage Press.

Prather, Liz. 2017. *Project-Based Writing: Teaching Writers to Manage Time and Clarify Purpose*. Portsmouth, NH: Heinemann.

Preston, Diana. 2018. "Trouble in Paradise: How the Arrival of Europeans Rocked the Native Cultures of Tahiti and Australia." *BBC World History*, April/May (9).

Remnick, David. 2012. "We Are Alive." *The New Yorker*, July 30. Accessed February 10, 2019. https://www.newyorker.com/magazine/2012/07/30/we-are-alive.

Resnick, Sarah. 2017. "H." In *The Best American Essays 2017*. Edited by Leslie Jamison, series edited by Robert Atwan. New York: Houghton Mifflin Harcourt.

Rich, Jennifer. 2018. "A Second Grader Once Pointed a Gun at Me. I'm Glad I Wasn't Armed." *The Washington Post*, March 15, 2018. Accessed January 5, 2019. https:// www.washingtonpost.com/opinions/a-second-grader-once-pointed-a-gun-at-me -im-glad-i-wasnt-armed/2018/03/15/60e4bb86-2230-11e8-badd-7c9f29a55815 _story.html?utm_term=.71ce18992312.

Rich, Nathaniel. 2016. "The Invisible Catastrophe." *The New York Times*, March 31. Accessed February 10, 2019. https://www.nytimes.com/2016/04/03/magazine /the-invisible-catastrophe.html.

Ruefle, Mary. 2012. *Madness, Rack, and Honey: Collected Lectures*. Seattle: Wave Books.

Sarton, May. 1984. *At Seventy: A Journal*. New York: W.W. Norton.

Saslow, Eric. 2012. "Life of a Salesman: Selling Success, When the American Dream Is Downsized." *The Washington Post*, October 7. Accessed February 10, 2019. https:// www.washingtonpost.com/national/life-of-a-salesman-selling-success-when -the-american-dream-is-downsized/2012/10/07/e2b34aac-1033-11e2-acc1-e927 767f41cd_story.html?utm_term=.e72cdaba3d46.

Schwartz, Alexandra. 2016. "Click Here to Visit Hell: An Interactive 'Garden of Earthly Delights.'" *The New Yorker*, April 12. Accessed January 19, 2019. https://www.new yorker.com/culture/rabbit-holes/click-here-to-visit-hell-an-interactive-garden-of -earthly-delights.

*Sherman's March*. 1985. Directed and produced by Ross McElwee. First Run Features. 2 hours, 37 minutes.

Shetterly, Margot Lee. 2016. *Hidden Figures: The American Dream and the Untold Story of the Black Women Mathematicians Who Helped Win the Space Race.* New York: Harper Collins Publishers.

Simons, Eric. 2018. "At a Snail's Pace: In Which the Distribution of a Common Pacific Coast Sea Snail Explains the Underlying Logic of the Universe." BayNature.org. Accessed July 10, 2018. https://baynature.org/biodiversity/snails/.

Skloot, Rebecca. 2011. *The Immortal Life of Heinretta Lacks.* New York: Random House.

Smith, Patricia. 2018a. "Coming to America." *The New York Times Upfront*, October 29.

———. 2018b. "Does Nikolas Cruz Deserve to Die?" *The New York Times Upfront*, October 8. https://upfront.scholastic.com/content/dam/classroom-magazines/upfront /issues/2018-19/100818/p14-15-deathpenalty/UPF-100818-Lexile-p14-17.pdf.

———. 2019. "Will Ginger Get to Stay?" *The New York Times Upfront*, January 7. https:// upfront.scholastic.com/content/dam/classroom-magazines/upfront/issues/2018 -19/010719/p8-11-honduranteen/UPF-010719-Lexile-p08-11.pdf.

Smith, Zadie. 2007. "Fail Better." *The Guardian*, January 13, 2017. Accessed May 15, 2018. https://www.scribd.com/doc/73273033/Zadie-Smith-s-Fail-Better-Read-Better.

Solnit, Rebecca. 2015. "Arrival Gates." In *2015 Best American Essay*, edited by Ariel Levy, series edited by Robert Atwan. New York: Houghton Mifflin Harcourt.

Span, Paula. 2019. "Dementia May Never Improve, But Many Patients Still Can Learn." *The New York Times*, January 4. Accessed February 9, 2019. https://www.nytimes .com/2019/01/04/health/dementia-rehabilitation.html.

Staples, Brent. 2018. "Just Walk on By." In *Uncharted Territory: A High School Reader*, edited by Jim Burke. New York: W.W. Norton.

Starr, S. Frederick. 2009. "Rediscovering Central Asia." *The Wilson Quarterly*. Summer 2009. Accessed December 27, 2018. http://archive.wilsonquarterly.com/essays /rediscovering-central-asia.

Staton, Brandon. *Humans of New York*. [Blog]. Retrieved from https://www.humansof newyork.com.

Stern, Jerome. 1991. *Making Shapely Fiction*. New York: W.W. Norton & Company.

Stewart, Sarah. 2014. "O-Rings." In *The Best American Science and Nature Writing* 2014, edited by Deborah Blum, series edited by Tim Folger. New York: Houghon Mifflin Harcourt.

Stillman, Sarah. 2018. "When Deportation Is a Death Sentence." *The New Yorker*, January 15. Accessed August 12, 2018. https://www.newyorker.com/magazine/2018/01/15 /when-deportation-is-a-death-sentence.

St. John, Warren. 2013. "Nick Saban: Sympathy for the Devil." GQ, August 25, 2013. Accessed October 1, 2017. https://www.gq.com/story/coach-nick-saban-alabama -maniac.

Stover, Dawn. 2009. "Not So Silent Spring." *Conservation*, January 6. Accessed February 10, 2019. https://www.conservationmagazine.org/2009/01/not-so-silent-spring/.

*Stranger with a Camera*. 1999. Produced and directed by Elizabeth Barrett. Appalshop Films. Whitesburg, Kentucky. 1 hour, 1 minute.

Sullivan, Andrew. 2018. "The Poison We Pick." *New York Magazine*, February. Accessed February 10, 2019. http://nymag.com/intelligencer/2018/02/americas-opioid -epidemic.html.

Tabuchi, Hiroko. 2019. "A Trump County Confronts the Administration Amid a Rash of Child Cancers." *The New York Times*, January 2. Accessed February 10, 2019. https://www.nytimes.com/2019/01/02/climate/tce-cancer-trump-environment -deregulation.html.

Talese, Gay. 1996. "Ali in Havana." *Esquire*. September. Reprinted in Longforms. Accessed July 16, 2018. http://reprints.longform.org/ali-in-havana-gay-talese.

Tan, Amy. 2011. "Mother Tongue." *One Hundred Great Essays*. Edited by Robert DiYanni. New York: Pearson Education, Inc.

Todd, Kim. 2018. "The Island Wolves." In *The Best American Science and Nature Writing 2018*, edited by Sam Kean, series edited by Tim Folger. New York: Houghton Mifflin Harcourt.

Thomas, Frank P. 1984. *How to Write the Story of Your Life*. Cincinnati, OH: Writer's Digest Books.

Tolstoy, Leo. (2004). *Anna Karenina*. New York: Penguin Classics.

Twilley, Nicola. 2017. "The Billion Year Wave." In *The Best American Science and Nature Writing 2017*, edited by Hope Jahren, series edited by Tim Folger. New York: Houghton Mifflin Harcourt.

Tyson, Neil deGrasse. 2017. *Astrophysics for People in a Hurry*. New York: W.W. Norton.

Vanderbilt, Tom. 2008. *Traffic: Why We Drive the Way We Do (and What It Says About Us)*. New York: Alfred J. Knopf.

Vogler, Christopher. 2007. *The Writer's Journey*. Studio City, CA: Michael Wiese Productions.

Walker, Alice. 1967. "The Civil Rights Movement: What Good Was It?" Reprinted in *The American Scholar*, February 20, 2016. Accessed July 2018. https://theamericanscholar.org/the-civil-rights-movement-what-good-was-it/# .XETJ5i2ZM_U.

Wallace, David Foster. 1994. "Ticket to the Fair." *Harper's Magazine*, July. Accessed February 10, 2019. https://harpers.org/wp-content/uploads/HarpersMagazine -1994-07-0001729.pdf.

Wallace-Wells, David. 2017. "The Uninhabitable Earth." *New York Magazine*, July 10. Accessed February 10, 2019. http://nymag.com/intelligencer/2017/07/climate -change-earth-too-hot-for-humans.html.

Ward, Geoffrey C. and Ken Burns. 2017. *The Vietnam War: An Intimate History*. New York: Knopf.

Williford, Lex, and Michael Martone, eds. 2007. *Touchstone Anthology of Contemporary Creative Nonfiction: Work from 1970 to the Present, First Edition*. New York: Touchstone.

Whitehead, Colson. 2016. *The Underground Railroad*. New York: Anchor Books.

Wikipedia. 2019. "Boston Corbett." *Wikipedia, The Free Encyclopedia*. Accessed February 4, 2019. https://en.wikipedia.org/wiki/Boston_Corbett.

Wikipedia. 2019. "Chemical weapons in World War I." *Wikipedia, The Free Encyclopedia*. https://en.wikipedia.org/wiki/Chemical_weapons_in_World_War_I.

Will, George. 2001. "Reality Television: Oxymoron." *Townhall*. June 20, 2001. Accessed February 14, 2019. https://townhall.com/columnists/georgewill/2001/06/20/reality-television-oxymoron-n1328547.

Williams, Joy. 2003. *The Florida Keys: A History and Guide, Tenth Edition*. New York: Random House.

Wolff, Tobias. 1995. "Bullet in the Brain." *The New Yorker*, September 25: 82. Accessed July 7, 2018. https://www.newyorker.com/magazine/1995/09/25/bullet-in-the-brain.

Yong, Ed. 2017. "Tiny Jumping Spiders Can See the Moon." *The Atlantic*, June. Accessed February 10, 2019. https://www.theatlantic.com/science/archive/2017/06/jumping-spiders-can-see-the-moon/529329/.